D0504837

I hope you enjoy this book.
Best Regards

2016

TOMCAT

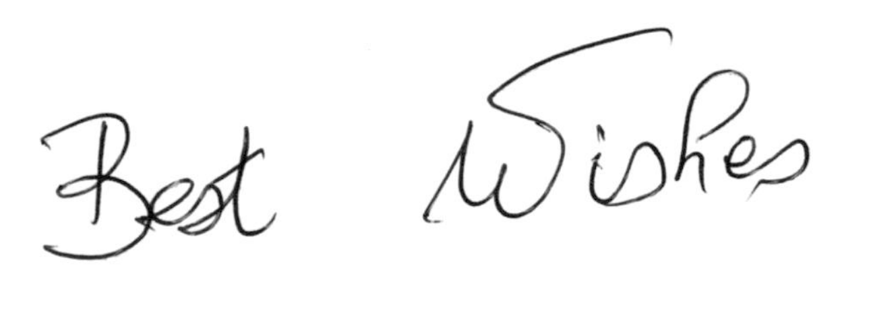

TOMCAT

CPI Group (UK)

First published in Great Britain by
Black Cat Publishing (UK)

A CIP catalogue record for this book is available
from the British Library.

ISBN: 978-1-874339-21-2

First Edition

Typesetting and Formatting by Luke Feenan

Printed and Finished in Great Britain by
CPI Group (UK), Croydon CR0 4YY

This book is dedicated to Sarah Elizabeth (Lizzy), my wonderful Nan,
who set me on my long journey into a military career. God bless you.

- TOMCAT.

&

To Ken who always believed in my writing.

- Shirley Domb.

ACKNOWLEDGMENTS

The majority of the images in this book are the personal property of TOMCAT.
Without the guidance and contributions of the following friends, relations and experts, it would not have been possible to produce this book.

Sincere thanks go to the members of the Royal Marines Association, Deal, Annette Kidd in particular.

Nick Kidd, son of Basil Kidd, Deal, who has been responsible for many of the earlier black and white images.

The following are comrades and good friends of TOMCAT:
Patrick Donovan RN, Sub Mariner (Ret.), for technical advice,
Hannah Eastwood for front cover design,
Mne Dennis Roberts RM (Ret.),
Cpl Nobby Sargent RM (Ret.),
Alistair Martin RM (Ret.),
Cpl Derby Allan RM (Ret.),
Mne 'Spike' Milligan RM (Ret.),
Sgt Dave Pattison RM (Ret.),
Andrew Roberts, Military Historian, Author and Journalist,
Sgt Pete Brown RM (Ret.),
Simon Anderson,
Andy Lane, Author.

Whilst every effort has been taken to identify the source of some images in this book, which were in the public domain, copyright free.

If anyone recognizes images that belong to them, please contact the publisher.

CONTENTS

For obvious reasons, some of the names, places and operations have deliberately been changed in order to protect operatives and maintain the high secrecy and security within the SBS. In addition, the time frames have been changed.

The facts are true but it was found necessary to protect the security of operatives and their families by a positive veil of secrecy as to the precise details.

The Royal Marines Commando Insignia

The SBS Emblem

Left: General Service Medal. The two bars are for Northern Ireland and Radfan, South Yemen. The Bronze Oak Leaf represents a Mention in Dispatches.
Middle: United Nations Peacekeeping Medal, Cyprus 1974
Right: Pingat Jasa Malaysia, Malaysian Emergency 1966-67

Sargent Insignia, Swimmer Canoeist Badge and Parachute Wings, Royal Navy Badge (SBS, RM)

INTRODUCTION

TOMCAT is the code-name for this member of the UK Special Forces, who although retired from the Corps, is still active in the world of Security and Anti-terrorism, in view of this he has to remain anonymous for the time being.

His story is completely true, as told to his biographer and starts with his early years as a young boy to set the scene and progresses through various career moves, until he becomes one of Her Majesty's Royal Marine Commandos.

His postings have seen him travelling to many war-torn countries, from the Far East to three tours of Northern Ireland, plus a wide variety of other countries, some missions very covert.

He has the gift of laughter and has had many humorous adventures, eventually passing selection for the SBS (Special Boat Service), which is the more discreet relative of the SAS and taking part in heroic and dangerous operations. His life story contains a wealth of accurate detail regarding his specialized on-going training, without divulging any intimate secrets of tactics, procedures or techniques used. Other books on the subject do not cover these details.

The training itself is arduous and designed to produce extremely fit fighting men, with the most important asset of all, PMA (Positive Mental Attitude). There are many anecdotes throughout the narrative, to amuse the reader, in the seventeen chapters, plus photographs and illustrations for everyone.

TOMCAT is an inspirational man and has achieved in his lifetime, what many wish that they had been able to have the nerve to do. 'ARMCHAIR COMMANDOS'.

The Early Years

The submarine HMS Otus dove twenty feet down into the clear, blue waters of the Mediterranean Sea. It looked like a sleek, sinister, black "Messenger of Death". Inside one of the torpedo tubes, Tomcat was tightly wedged, head-first into the steel compartment, unable to move a muscle. It was pitch black and he could not see anything. All he could hear was the violent thumping of his heart. He knew that there would be no way he could contact anyone, should there be a last minute malfunction in the system. He was completely sealed in and within a matter of seconds, the water would come flooding in, totally engulfing him. The outer door would open and he would be swiftly shot out into the open sea. Those few seconds felt like a lifetime and he almost regretted volunteering for this highly dangerous task.

The SBS (Special Boat Service), of which he was a member, were testing the escape route, which if successful, might be used for emergency evacuation of a stricken vessel and also may enable operatives from each of the six tubes to be deployed at the same time. This action could allow a clandestine water insertion by divers on a mission.

Tomcat fought to control his breathing. The Raba, (Rechargeable Air Breathing Apparatus) gripped tightly in his mouth was very uncomfortable. It only had life-support for ten minutes, so he had to prevent a panic situation and keep his breathing slow and even. It was like being entombed in a metal coffin, deep underground.

The sweat was pouring off him and anxiety started to set in. At this point, a hydraulic valve operated and the tube started to fill rapidly with sea-water. The outer door then opened, showing a pin-prick of light at the far end. Tomcat relaxed. Suddenly there was a great gush of water under pressure. He was sliding along the tube and with a flourish, shot out into the open sea. His goggles had been ripped from his face by the pressure of the water and as he exited the tube, he caught his left shoulder on the outer casing of the submarine, tearing a large hole in his wet-suit. Blood was pouring from a deep gash in his shoulder, leaving a scarlet trail behind him. The Raba had now been torn from his mouth and the pain from his shoulder was so intense, that he thought he was about to pass out. With two or three very sharp and powerful kicks, he managed to fin up to the surface where the safety boat was waiting for him.

He was hauled on board by two of his colleagues and his wound was dressed from the Medikit and at great speed, transferred back on to HMS Otus, where he was taken straight to the sick bay. After receiving a tetanus jab and eleven stitches, he lay there reflecting about the journey his life had taken him on.

This is the story of an extraordinary man. A hero, a man of steel, one of Her Majesty's Royal Marines Commandos. He doesn't think of himself as a hero or a man of steel, just a man doing his job in the service of his country, for which he had been continuously highly-trained to the peak of physical fitness and human endeavour.

Starting in 1966, his first posting was to 40 Commando based in Singapore. He has travelled to numerous war torn countries and been involved in many conflicts, known as Britain's brush fire wars, from the far and Middle East to Mediterranean areas, including three tours of Northern Ireland, plus many more. He was always aware that his next operation could be his last. The smell of fear was familiar to him but he had trained himself to focus on the mission in hand and to exclude all negative thoughts, for him this was the only way to stay alive.

Due to the secret and sensitive nature of the work he was involved in, he has to be known by his code-name of 'TOMCAT', or TC to his close mates.

You can be sure that this is a man you can trust with your life, as many people have done, while all the time there is an abundance of wit (mariner's wit is down to earth). Laughter relieves tension, which is very necessary and the many thrilling stories he has to tell are packed with his off-beat humour. His life reads like adventure stories from a Boys Own comic and has been full of incidents and events that most people are totally unaware of and could never ever imagine.

Tomcat was born at the end of WW2 in South East England. Even as a new-born, he was like a cat with many lives. He escaped death three times, surviving twice from pneumonia and once from a V1 flying bomb, known as a doodle-bug or buzz bomb. On that occasion, he was saved by his aunt Vi, who threw her body across his pram, when the bomb exploded just yards away, causing deep cuts in both her legs and showering the pair of them with dust and debris.

He can trace his military history a long way back, as his father and both grandfathers were in the Army. Five of his uncles, a cousin and numerous other relatives served in the UK forces. His mother was also active in the war effort, working in a munitions factory at night, which was highly dangerous because it was a prime target on Hitler and Goering's Luftwaffe hit list. Being born into a world at war, where shortages of everything were quite normal, his playgrounds were the many bombed-out buildings and bomb sites of the town. He was the only son of four children and always took the brunt of every scrape, whether he was involved or not. His father,

HMS Otus tied up at the dockside. Notice the blue canopy over the forward torpedo loading hatch. The large blister on top of the bow is the sonar housing.

Cramped forward torpedo room, six forward tubes and two aft. Two centre tubes open.

Top: Divers carrying out submerged entry/exit procedures through the forward hatch.
Above: A forward torpedo tube. Crew member repairing a strip known as landings, these prevent the torpedo from coming into contact with the sidewalls of the tubes. Very confined space to work in.
Right: Sub in dry dock. The outer torpedo tube doors are open and the cover panels retracted inwards as shown.

Diver using the Raba emergency air, this will give life support for about ten minutes or 54 breaths.

Rubber inflatable boat (Rib), Gemini or Zodiac general service and safety boat.

an army sergeant and a strong disciplinarian ran his family with a strict regime and thought nothing of a heavy smack round the head or a hard kick up the 'arse' for any real or imagined misdemeanour. The treatment he meted out was cruel and abusive and it produced a harsh bitterness and simmering aggression in the young boy. At first he does not strike one as a man who would take kindly to authority, particularly if the authority in question is flagrantly wrong but he has a very strong sense of duty.

His maternal grandparents were central in his life and his grandmother, 'Nan' would sit and tell him stories about the war. He was totally fascinated and asked her endless questions. He loved her stories and she became his very best friend. When he was thirteen, his beloved Nan died suddenly, leaving him quite distraught. The day before the funeral, he went to see her for the last time. The door to the front room (which was only used on special occasions) was open, he went in. She was lying in her coffin looking as he had never seen her. She had not ever worn make-up nor had her hair styled previously but the embalmer who had attended to her had been very skilful and her appearance was very well done. To TC she looked absolutely beautiful.

After the funeral, he went into 'hate mode' and became very difficult to get on with. He always seemed to be in trouble at school but nobody tried to understand that he was in deep mourning for the loss of his Nan. On one occasion, the school bully came up against TC and got the worst of it from a punch, full in the face. TC got twelve strokes of the cane for that and had to make a public apology to the boy and his parents. Surprisingly, they ended up the best of friends. TC left school at fifteen, glad to be free of all academic restrictions.

Unfortunately being the only boy, with three sisters (the oldest very much favoured), he came last in the pecking order for affection of any kind from his parents and this cold fact, after a series of jobs from apprentice engineer to qualified welder, pointed him on the pathway towards a military career. Luckily he found his way to HM Royal Marine Commandos.

Upon leaving school, his first job was at Vickers Armstrong in Crayford (not far from home), working as an apprentice engineer in the 'Barrel Mill'. This company restored and renovated gun barrels (not made wooden ones as TC had imagined) and this fitted in with his boyhood enthusiasm for weapons of war. As a trainee engineer, he was sent on many unusual errands, for example, the foreman asked him to go to the stores and get a long weight. It was a fifteen minute walk to the stores on this huge site and at the stores, he was asked how long a weight he wanted but as he did not know, he had to go all the way back to find out.

He was then told "as long as possible". On his return he was told to sit down and the store man would come back soon. Thirty minutes later he returned and asked TC if he'd had a long enough 'wait'. The penny finally dropped at last for the now embarrassed trainee.

Other requests involved a gross of large skyhooks, a gallon of black and white chequered paint, a left-handed screwdriver and as many pins and needles as he could get. This last requisite had him squatting in a corner for twenty minutes, before a grinning store man asked whether he had enough pins and needles. TC was again red-faced and in the future, he was very suspicious of any errand to the stores.

As a beginner in the 'Barrel Mill', he was set to work on a Capstan lathe turning out thousands of anything required, very boring, reminding him of the Albert Finney film, 'Saturday night and Sunday Morning'. The whole work system was run like a prison camp. Sirens to start work, sirens to break and sirens to finish. To TC it felt like sirens to breathe.

During one lunch break, he wandered down to the basement, where he was amazed to see gun barrels of all different sizes resting on trestles. He could not resist touching these objects, with awe and reverence and imagined himself firing his favourite, twin 40mm Bofors (that he had only seen before in war films) at aircraft. Of course he would never miss!

At lunch one day, he discovered that the company also designed and made radar equipment. One lunchtime he felt very privileged to observe a test on radar-operated gun sights. He was enthralled by the radar testing, which involved a Gloster Meteor aircraft on flypast, to which the 40mm Bofors locked on and tracked it through the sky, the guns moving on their own. He also found out that they made the famous Maxim gun of which he had heard and realised that guns were going to be one of the great passions of his life.

With regret TC left his first job after seven months, to join his friend Bob, who was working as a lorry drivers mate. The money was four times better and for a while he followed the money from job to job, each one paying more than the last.

One day he met a young man called Ron in the local coffee bar and while chatting, he discovered that they shared the same interest in guns. He found that Ron had his own twelve bore shot gun and he invited TC to go shooting with him. TC jumped at the chance and the next day, they went to the local marshes, which led down to the river Thames.

As soon as a pigeon flew overhead, Ron fired the gun. The noise was deafening but unfortunately, he missed. Ron then handed the gun to TC, who loaded it and watched carefully as another pigeon approached. Ron told TC that the bird was too high for the gun but TC fired anyway. His ears rang and his shoulder felt like it had been hit by a brick but the pigeon fell from the sky, a perfectly clean shot. By the end of the day, he had fired the gun many times. His shoulder was black and blue and very sore. To quote TC, "It hurt like bloody hell". Sometime later, he bought that gun from Ron for five pounds and eventually bought a second one. The licences, at that time, only cost ten shillings from the Post Office. Since then TC has always had shotguns and still has a few today.

When he was seventeen, the atmosphere at home was unbearable and after a particularly strong disagreement with his family, TC moved out and into lodgings. At this time he was working at the London Paper Mills as a dryer man, having worked and trained up for this position over the course of a year.

During this period, TC married for the first time. He had arranged for a work friend to collect his mother by car to take her to the ceremony but the day before the wedding, he met his eldest sister in the town and she coldly informed him that his mother would not be attending. TC was very upset. This turned out to be completely untrue, as he discovered the next day. His mother had planned to come and had bought a new outfit, a present and some beautiful flowers. She was all dressed up and waiting for the car to come for her, which of course it never did. She was extremely upset thinking that TC did not want her at the wedding. The reception was held at his aunt Vi's house and his mother was greatly missed by all, (Vi was his mother's younger sister and she was very upset and disappointed too).

At nineteen, he got a job with a local engineering and prefabrication company, helping welders to make all sorts of large containers. Welding fascinated him and subsequently, the company sent him to night school twice a week. He had really loved this at his school and positively excelled at metalwork. First he became a welder's mate and then a qualified welder.

The company gave him plenty of work, which kept him happy but his primary love was still guns and the Army in particular. Sadly, TC's marriage only lasted four years but produced a much loved son Vincent, before ending in divorce. Seeing the youth of the young couple this was not surprising.

One day, while having dinner in the canteen, he was told some exciting stories by a workmate, who had served in the army in Italy during the Second World War. He mentioned that he had come across a contingent of Royal Marine Commandos. Until that moment, TC had never even heard of these Commandos. The story his mate told was that (during the war) his troop were crossing a road that ran through a forest, deep into German occupied territory in Turin. They managed to get safely across, one by one, except his mate, being the last one and carrying a wooden stretcher diagonally across his back and shoulder. As he got ready to make his dash, the stretcher, which kept catching on the branches of trees and bushes, suddenly snagged on a branch once again. At this moment, a German tank appeared round a corner. The man was impaled by this branch. He shut his eyes and prepared to die but the tank just rolled on by, completely ignoring him. He said at the time, he felt like 'Jesus on the Cross' and said to himself, "Fuck the stretcher". He undid the buckle, managed to wriggle free and legged it, leaving the stretcher stuck in the tree. By the time he caught up with the rest of his troop, they had given him up for dead. Nevertheless, his sergeant was none too pleased that he had left the stretcher behind and threatened to send him back for it.

The infamous V1 flying bomb, doodlebug or Buzz Bomb, as it was known. The nose cone was packed with a ton of high explosive. They were launched by a steam generator from ramps in Peenemunde on the Baltic Coast.

V1 Bomb damage that just missed TC. His Aunt Vi was injured and both covered in dust and debris from the fallout.

TC was very intrigued by this and other stories of Royal Marines and on another occasion, asked about them again. "Who are they, what do they do?" He was told that they were 'Commandos' and were known as the 'elite' of all the fighting forces in the world. His workmate told him of the time he was on patrol with his troop, when they actually met a company of Royal Marines, who had been in a terrible fire-fight. These marines were involved in the rescue of some Americans, whose exit had been cut off when encircled by Germans. They had no water or food and were almost out of ammunition. The Marine Commandos secured an escape route and went in to relieve them. The Americans were supposed to send in reinforcements afterwards but they never arrived and the commandos had to fight their way out. Although they took out a lot of Germans, sadly, they sustained heavy casualties themselves. The man telling the story was actually there and saw the commandos walking down the road towards his troop. The whole of his troop stood to one side to allow them through. Not a word was spoken as they walked straight past, without even a sideways glance. His workmate told TC that these men were the most fearsome and hardest that he had ever seen.

TC could not think of anything else. He simply had to find out about the Marines and not long after, he saw an advertisement in a newspaper recruiting for Marine Commandos. He sent off for a brochure to Chatham in Kent, (which at the time was a fully operational naval base). The brochure arrived very quickly. It explained in detail what the Royal Marines were all about and how to became one. TC was excited and immediately sent the form back asking to enlist. He received notification that he would have to go to Chatham for an interview and a medical. TC could hardly wait and kept saying to himself, over and over again, "God, I'm going to be a Royal Marine Commando".

Two weeks later, he arrived at Chatham with his paperwork. He had a brief interview with a naval officer, then was told to sit in the waiting-room until he was called for his medical. There were several other lads in the waiting-room but TC was the only one for the Royal Marines, the rest were all there to join the navy.

At this point, a door opened and in walked an officer of truly magnificent appearance. He was wearing a well-tailored uniform of lovat green with a Sam Brown belt and crosspiece, highly polished shoes and of course, a much-prized 'Green Beret'. He stopped in front of them and said in a voice (that seemed to TC) of superior command, "Morning lads". They answered him in unison, he then strode away down the corridor. TC's heart was thumping with excitement; he thought to himself, "Wow, is that what I will be wearing? Is that what I will look like? Where do I collect my machine gun and bullets?"

At that moment, a naval rating appeared in the doorway and called out TC's name. He jumped to his feet, "That's me", he said. The rating looked at the card in his hand and said, "Are your here to join the marines"? TC said that he was, with pride, knowing he was going to join the 'elite'. The rating then said with great emphasis, "You must be a fucking idiot". TC felt his

Early machine gun assembly shop, Vickers Crayford, circa 1951.

Vickers munitions factory Dartford 1944.

TC's famous 40mm Bofors AA Guns.

The Meteor used at Vickers for radar testing that TC watched.

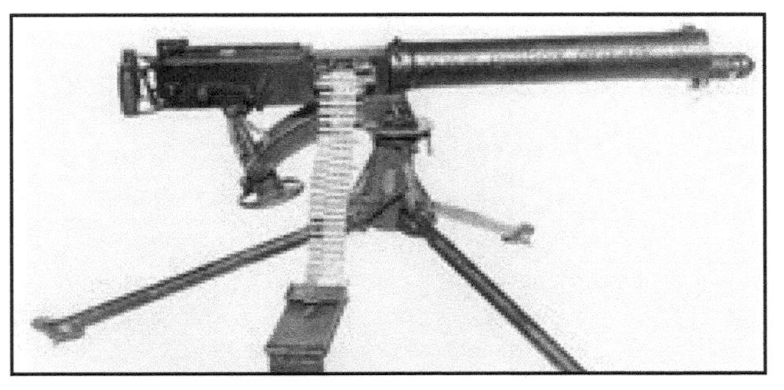

The famous Maxim gun built at Vickers.

Vickers barrel mill where TC first worked and became enthralled with weaponry.

Vickers old gun assembly shop, circa 1940's.

pride and ego totally deflate. He suffered a few more insults during his medical too, from the examiner. He was told to strip off and stand in front of the doctor, then told to turn to his left. He turned. The doctor then said, "No, your other left". TC realised that he had turned the wrong way. He was then told to turn his back and touch his toes. After the examination, the doctor turned to the rating and said, "Why does this lad want to join the marines? He has two of everything and looks pretty normal to me". The rating replied, "We will soon find out sir, when we remove his brain and examine it. If we don't put it back, he will make a first class 'Bootneck'. (Slang for marines)

TC did not know what they were talking about but it all ended in laughter, when they both shook hands with him and said, "You're in and good luck mate, you're a brave lad". The doctor remarked that they had only been joking and that they had the highest respect for the Royal Marines and that they were the finest fighting force in the World.

All the way home, TC was floating on air. He was thinking, "I've made it, I'm really going to be a Commando". He had no idea of what was to come during the forty-three weeks of his training. He knew it was going to be really tough in fact it would be a long period of sheer, exhausting punishment. It would be a lot of fun but in general, very gruelling work. He had to complete all this before he could call himself a real Royal Marine Commando and receive the ultimate prize, the coveted 'Green Beret'.

Three weeks later, TC still had not received the call to start his training and wondered why they were taking so long. He considered telephoning them to say, "Hey, I'm still here and waiting to get into a fight somewhere in the World". One day at work, a mate asked him, "You're the one going into the marines, aren't you?" TC puffed out his chest and said, "No mate, I'm going into the Royal Marine Commandos". The other man smiled at that, then showed him an article in a newspaper, about the Royal Marines in a street fire-fight, complete with very graphic pictures, taking place somewhere in Indonesia.

TC became quite anxious now and was starting to think that perhaps they had changed their minds. Another two weeks passed before the papers arrived, calling him to start his training, with a list of what to bring and a train travel warrant to Deal in Kent. TC's first thought was, where the hell is that? He found it on the map. It was five miles up the coast from Dover.

He had to wear a suit and tie, well-polished shoes and catch the train on the day and time he had been given. He was to change trains at Chatham and was so excited by the prospect of his new life, it was all he could think about. He was sure that once he arrived at Deal, things would gain momentum and before too long, he would be able to call himself a real Commando. Without doubt, he would be collecting his very own machine-gun and bullets.

Depot Deal

At last he was on his way and TC was really excited. He kept saying to himself, "I'm actually going to be a Royal Marine Commando." He did not have a clue at this point about what he would be facing. He later described it as forty-three weeks of sheer torture, a bit of fun but extremely gruelling. He reflected that if he had previously seen a film of the training through which he would have to undergo, it possibly would have put him off. The truth was, torture or not, he thoroughly enjoyed every minute of it.

He caught the train as he was told and after changing trains at Chatham, he watched as the countryside sped past. As the train was nearing Deal station, it slowed, he was looking out of the window, when he spotted a large field with a lot of men dressed in dark green combat clothing, scrambling over an assault course and some running around in small groups carrying telegraph poles between them.

There were others, who he guessed must be the instructors, they looked very fit, wearing dark blue tracksuit trousers, white sleeveless tee shirts with red borders round the armholes and a red logo on the breast. These men really had to be physical training instructors. They were awesome, ferocious and in control. For a moment, they scared him a little. He started to think, oh my god, what am I doing here? Am I going to like this or maybe it's not for me? Should I just get on the next train back and get the hell out of here?

Reason set in and he thought, of course not get a grip and go for it. It was now too late to change his mind. The train had entered Deal station. He got out and noticed several other young lads, all in suits and carrying cases, like himself. Outside the station, two Royal Marines were waiting to greet them and ushered them into a 4-ton lorry. It was only a ten minute ride to North Barracks in Canada Road.

There were about ten lads in the back of the lorry and the mood was of excitement, if a little nervous. The barracks were a huge complex of tall buildings and a large parade ground bustling with groups of soldiers marching around, while instructors shouted and bellowed at them.

It was an all inspiring scene and in his gut, TC felt great. He was longing to start his training and thought that soon he could collect his machine gun and bullets.

They were taken to a large building of two floors. TC was on the upper floor and shared the room with forty-four other recruits, some of whom were already unpacking. He chose his bed space and everyone was chatting together comparing notes. A few moments later, a Royal Marine walked in, smartly dressed, uniform immaculate and wearing the Green Beret, (the ultimate goal of forty-three weeks of training and sheer torture) and said in a very commanding voice, "Stop what you're doing and gather round." He introduced himself as Marine Grey and informed them that he was their personal instructor for the next two weeks and that he was called Marine because he had no rank. They were told to call him Staff.

The block they were occupying was known as the New Intake Block and after two weeks, they would be moved over to the main buildings, which faced the parade ground. He also told them that they would not be allowed ashore (meaning out of barracks), nor be able to go home on leave for these first two weeks and during this time, he would come round every evening to show them how to shower, wash, dry and press their uniform.

The following morning, they were all marched over to the barber's shop (actually it wasn't a march more of a shamble and they were stopped several times to get them all back into step). To the lads, it was more like a butcher's shop, not a barber's shop, as they all ended up scalped, for hygienic purposes.

The old barber had a cigarette burning between his lips all the time, he was a wiry man with a thick moustache and yellowy nicotine stain from heavy smoking, this was evident from his fingers as well. The ash tray was piled high with dog-ends and he smelled strongly of tobacco. TC was surprised that his father told him to get his hair cut short the day before he went to enlist, this he did and for the first time he had a short back and sides which in those days was the norm for any military personnel.

TC was quietly confident that when it was his turn for a hair cut there would not be much to remove but the amusing part that whenever a recruit sat in the chair, the barber would ask, "How would you like it sir?" Whatever the recruit asked for, the electric clippers would just shear the whole lot off, everyone fell about laughing, so a few just asked for it all to be taken off, "Certainly Sir", would come the reply from the old barber.

By now the floor was just a carpet of human hair. One cheeky chap said, "Can I have a Tony Curtis style?" The barber looking at him through the mirror said, "Is that Tony Curtis the famous American actor, who has a quiff at the front?" "That's him", replied the recruit. With this the barber took the whole lot off, saying, "How's that, is it ok?" The recruit's face was one of horror saying, "Shit, that's not how Tony Curtis has his hair done". The barber swiftly said,

'Lambs to the slaughter' new recruits at Deal BR Station being collected by a Royal Marine driver to whisk them away to their new life at The Depot Royal Marines.

Recruit pass out day after 17 weeks, PT display parents and girlfriends attending. Then the big move to CTCRM Lympstone Devon.

"He fucking would if he came in here". Everyone was now in hysterics, needless to say TC joined the rest, bald.

Afterwards they were marched over to the galley (ship's terminology for the dining room). It was becoming clear to TC that he needed to learn a completely new language. On the second day, just before lunch, all the recruits were mustered in a classroom and shown how to sit to attention when called for. This was done when an officer entered the room. They rehearsed this several times, in front of a man with a large, polished black stick under his left arm. This man was a WO2 (Warrant Officer) and was called First Drill. He was in charge of the drill instructors, also present was the Provost Sergeant (Military police) and he looked very mean. He had ginger hair and moustache and a flat nose that looked as though it had been broken several times.

The recruits were all handed forms with their names and addresses on, which were actually their attestation papers (the Official Secrets Act) for being sworn in. At that moment, a door at the back of the classroom opened and the First Drill shouted, "Room, attention". An officer walked down the middle of the isle and was saluted by First Drill and the Provost Sergeant. The officer was a Captain and Adjutant of the depot. His uniform was immaculate. He had a highly polished Sam Brown belt and cross-strap on, which carried a bright silver sword and scabbard on his left hip. His riding boots were so shiny you could see reflections in them and he was wearing silver spurs. TC thought how magnificent he looked. The Adjutant was the only one to ride a horse.

After two weeks TC was allowed home on leave and his mother was very pleased to see him, however there was no reaction from his father, who appeared to be disinterested in his son's achievements so far. That was not unusual. He met up with a friend in town who had joined the Army a bit earlier. As Royal Marine recruits are not allowed to go home in uniform at this stage, his pal was strutting around in his, (according to TC) 'crappy' army uniform and peaked cap, boasting that he was only required to do six weeks training and that forty-three was a waste of time. TC told him if he only knew what skills they had to master he wouldn't be saying that.

TC found that the marines called the army personnel crap hats and pongos (their personal hygiene left a lot to be desired). Although the Royal Marines are classed as the elite, they are referred to as bootnecks, Royals, green slime or gravel bellies. The Paras are cherry berets, the RAF, crab fats and naval ratings, matelots, deck apes or dab dabs. TC could not wait to get back to his training.

He knew it was going to be a bitch but what the hell. He just wanted his machine gun and bullets now, so he got back on board (the barracks) early. First thing on Monday morning, they were all moved over to the main recruit block at one side of the parade ground. The rooms were smaller there, off long corridors and housed eight to a room. TC made sure that he had the bed by the window and noticed how clean the rooms were, the floors were highly polished woodblock or parquet. He thought great respect to the cleaners. Little did he know that the recruits would be the cleaners. The main block faced the parade ground and there was a large drill shed at one end, designed for shelter in bad weather. Outside was a huge silver bell which hung below a small housing in front of a very high flagpole.

The recruits were handed over from Marine Grey to a corporal, who was in fact a drill instructor. TC thought, oh lovely! They were handed a large photograph of how to lay their kit out on their beds for inspection, including their lockers. All this had to be perfect every time. After four weeks, the duty corporal decided to do a crash room inspection to see how they were getting on but when he got to one particular recruit, he could not find any clothes or underwear. He said to the lad, "Where are all your clean clothes?", the lad mumbled, "I don't know sir, I think they're being washed." The corporal shouted at him telling him that he was not a sir but a corporal.

He was very angry now. He pulled the recruit's tunic off the rail and shook it. Out fell dirty, smelly underwear, the corporal was livid. He grabbed the lad's greatcoat and found that the sleeves and pockets were stuffed with more dirty clothes and socks, with this the corporal upturned his bed all over the floor, then pulled out his personal drawer and threw this on the floor also, followed by wrenching all the contents out of his locker and throwing them down the corridor, to the shock and horror of everyone else in the other rooms, who were standing by their beds waiting to be inspected.

The corporal inspected the rest of the room and upon leaving to go to the next room he turned and said, "You have a crabby bastard in your room who is going to infect you all, deal with it". All the other lads were furious, they frog-marched the crab down to the heads, (showers and toilets), dumped him in an empty bath with all his dirty clothes, covered him in detergent and held him down while they scrubbed him with a yard-broom. Subsequently, they were all punished because the whole room was held responsible for his lack of hygiene. They had to parade in their rooms at 2200hrs that evening in their No.1 Blues (their best uniform) for another inspection and all leave was cancelled. Not long after that the recruit left.

A few days later, in the afternoon, they were marched (they could all do it in step now) over to the QM's stores, where they collected a very large amount of kit from uniforms, fighting order, boots, shoes, and steel helmets to gas masks and water bottles. They were also given a large holdall to carry everything back to their rooms. TC was a bit disappointed because the QM was not handing out weapons at this stage so sadly, no machine gun and bullets.

They took all this kit back to their grots (rooms), they would call their beds pits. The recruits had to get up at 0600hrs to the sound of the bugle playing reveille outside, followed five minutes later by the duty corporal strutting down the corridor, flinging doors open and banging

Aerial view of The Depot Deal showing the drill shed top end of the parade ground with the galley, white roof in the foreground and to the right, the new intake block, white roof where 11 Bandsmen lost their lives by an IRA bomb in 1989.

The Adjutant leading the march through Deal town, exercising the right bestowed on them in 1945 by the town, to march with colours flying, drums beating and bayonets fixed.

(switching) on the lights. The first morning, TC found that the heads were very busy and he had to wait quite a while to get a shave and shower. After this, he decided to set his alarm watch for 0545hrs. He also spent two hours each night, cleaning and preparing his kit, ready for the next day. He would get up before everyone else and go quietly to the heads, to find that he was the only one in there. TC realised that his new routine was foolproof.

He arrived at the galley for breakfast and discovered that there were only two people waiting ahead of him. The smell of bacon frying wafted on the frosty morning January air. This tantalised his nostrils and palate, so he had a massive plateful of everything on offer (a very large English breakfast). To quote TC, "When in hard training, it's vital to eat like a horse, you really do need that extra energy and protein."

On returning to his grot one morning, he carried a full cup of tea with him as usual, only to see the duty corporal who, on his way to the galley for breakfast, stopping recruits, who like TC, had cups of tea with them and making them tip it out on the ground. TC seeing this quickly held his cup tight to the right side of his hip and passed the corporal on his left, he was not spotted and from then on he would check outside the galley for the all clear.

Back in his grot TC glanced out of the window and saw recruits jogging round the perimeter of the parade ground, still in their pyjamas and some in bare feet, carrying their bedding, including a rolled up mattress across their shoulders. There were two carrying a cast-iron frame bed between them, complete with the mattresses jogging on the early morning, icy ground. These recruits were the ones who were found still in bed when the duty corporal came round for the second time. This was their punishment. The rest of the lads were rushing to shower and some were even cleaning their shoes and the brass fittings for their white belts. It was quite common in order to save time in the mornings, some never bothered to shave but then on parade were picked up for this and made to stand on the flank (one side of the parade away from everyone else) and shave in ice cold water from their water bottles and mess tins. This was in the middle of the Deal winter. Needless to say, many of these didn't make it, they just couldn't cope with being organized and getting to grips with basic discipline.

The Monday after moving to the main block, they had their first parade with the whole contingent from Deal. Four hundred marines on parade most of whom were recruits in varying uniforms. These were at different stages of training. Some carried weapons. There were Junior Marines and Junior Bandsmen plus the training teams, marines, sergeants and corporals all wearing the awesome Green Beret. TC found it a stunning sight and the Green Beret, a symbol of all the hard, gruelling, teeth-gritting and painful training yet to come. Am I going to be up to this? Kept going through his mind as they were told that the failure rate was very high, sometimes from injuries. Only one recruit in four was expected to get through.

"Yes of course I will, bring it on and lets dispel these negative thoughts", he muttered to himself.

Just before 0800hrs, there were three officers pacing back and forth, (he found out that this was called perambulating). He wondered what everyone was waiting for, when suddenly he heard the echo of horses hooves, as the sound bounced off the labyrinth of high buildings in the still morning air. This was quite eerie as 400 men were all standing still, with not a sound from anyone.

Suddenly the Adjutant appeared from around the corner on his horse. This was a beautiful tall horse, called a Military Charger. It was chestnut brown and absolutely stunning dressed in its highly polished livery. At this point the sun flashed off the horse's silver snaffle and bit, also the Adjutant's spurs and sword. The RSM (Regimental Sergeant Major) called the whole parade to attention, his voice booming out so stridently, that the birds all flew from the trees and building tops in fright. A minute later, a black car drew up and out stepped the Commanding Officer, who then climbed onto the dais. It was then that TC noticed a bugler standing by the bell. The Adjutant took over the parade and shouted, "Bugler, strike the bell and sound the fall-in." With this, the bugler struck the bell four times, each with a double strike. It was 0800hrs precisely. As he played the first note, a Provost Corporal, standing at the base of the flagpole, pulled on the halyard and the Union Jack, (flag) broke open, fluttering proudly in the morning breeze. This ceremony took place on parade, nearly every day.

The band struck up and they all marched round the parade ground, giving eyes right as they passed by the Colonel on the dais. He returned the salute. TC loved marching to the band, he found it very easy and it helped everyone to keep in step.

Every Tuesday morning, after parade, they would leave the confines of the barracks and march out through the main gate into the road and along the seafront, round the town and back to barracks, with the band leading. This took about an hour with the police stationed at different junctions, having stopped the traffic for them. This was done in order to exercise their rights because the Marines had been given the Freedom of the Town and were allowed to march through with bayonets fixed and bands playing. This was tradition.

Intensive training went on every day and now they were allowed ashore, to go out of camp in the evenings and weekends but not before they reported to the Guardroom and requested permission from the duty Provost Corporal (known as the Gestapo). There was always a queue as the procedure to get permission was, quoting TC, "A nauseating waste of time and a real pain in the arse".

The procedure was that when called forward by the Provost Corporal they would march in smartly, halt and say, 'Corporal I am recruit RM 25124L Johnson, request permission to go ashore Corporal'. The corporal would be casting his eyes up and down the very nervous recruit to make sure he was smart enough to go ashore and represent the Royal Marines in the eyes of the public. If they defaulted on any of the regulations, they were sent away to rectify this, then

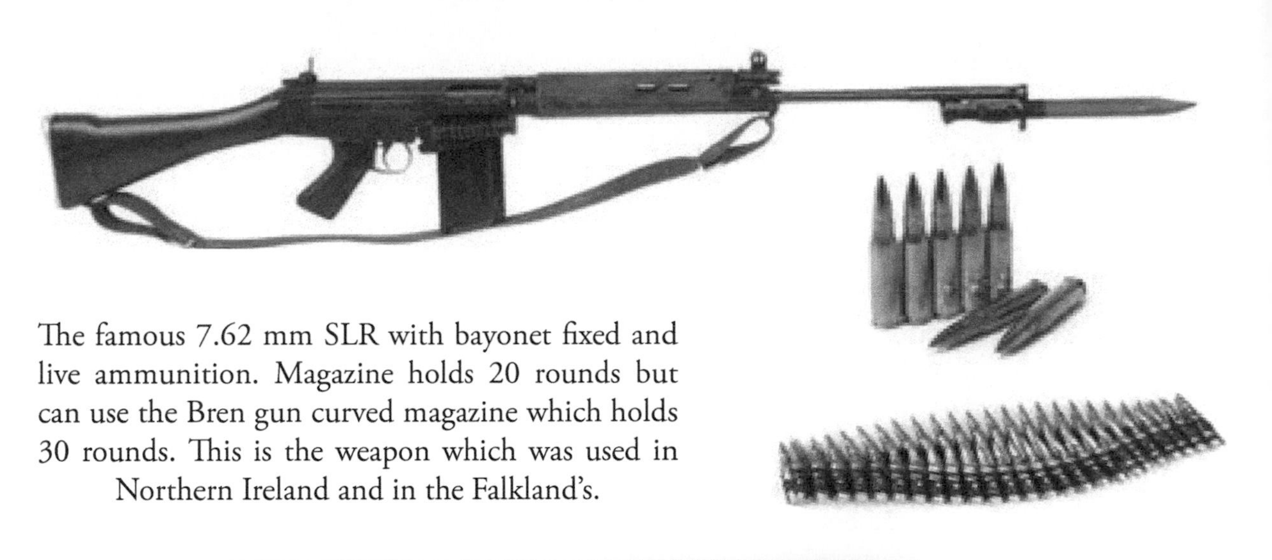

The famous 7.62 mm SLR with bayonet fixed and live ammunition. Magazine holds 20 rounds but can use the Bren gun curved magazine which holds 30 rounds. This is the weapon which was used in Northern Ireland and in the Falkland's.

TC's favourite weapon, the awesome 7.62 mm GPMG belt fed with link ammo above.

The art of camouflage and concealment, see but not be seen.

join the back of the queue again. Things that would get a refusal would be, not marching in properly, forgetting or stammering with your number and name, in need of a haircut, shoes not polished properly, trousers not pressed with a sharp crease, hands not clean or fingernails.

Then you had to be in possession of a clean handkerchief, four pennies for the phone and recite the number for the guardroom, fail any of this and you could be sent back to your room with shore leave revoked. Having passed the test to get out for the evening, you had to be back on board by 2200hrs and go through all this again. If you turned up inebriated, you were likely to be placed in the cells and the Duty Officer called for. You could be up on a charge the next day. This never happened to TC, as he made sure he was not going to blot his record at this early stage.

By week four, they were all marched over to the armoury. TC was very excited, as he had a feeling finally, he was going to get his beloved machine gun and bullets. This was still not the case, they were all issued with a rifle instead. This was an SLR (Self-loading Rifle), it fired 7.62mm bullets and had a twenty round magazine. They also received a very nice bayonet. This made TC think that he would not have much use for the bayonet, because he would not be getting that close to the enemy and anyway they would die from a very serious gunshot wound long before that. TC was happy with this rifle but disappointed that they did not give him any bullets to go with it.

Now, instead of spending hours on the parade ground just marching up and down and round and round, they had to be taught how to do rifle drills, including fixing and unfixing bayonets on the march. This turned out to be very funny and awkward at first because some of the lads could not master it straight away and as they marched around the parade ground, there would be a loud clatter as half a dozen bayonets fell off, not having been secured. The Drill Corporal, very angry would mutter, "Oh shit" but would not stop to let them be picked up and would wait until they were halted over the other side of the parade ground, then make the lads run across to collect the dropped bayonets.

TC got on very well with his weapon handling and range work, this was very important to him and he enjoyed every moment, he would be quite happy to spend all day, every day on the ranges. He was totally dedicated and was not about to accept anything less than a marksman for any test. He just wanted to be the best of the best, this was his drive throughout all his training.

One exercise they had to do, was to strip down their rifles and lay the component parts in order, on the ground, and then reassemble them accurately, speedily, repeatedly against the clock, even wearing a blindfold. The first parade with rifles was an unexpected test of how well the recruits were doing, with regards to weapon handling and rifle drills. At the end of the parade one morning, just as everyone was dismissed, TC and his squad were told to stand easy and remain at attention.

At this point the Adjutant approached them and TC heard the Drill Corporal mutter, "Oh fuck." The Adjutant wanted to inspect them. They were told to strip down their rifles and lay the parts on the ground in front of them. The rifle had to be broken in half, like a shotgun and they had to wait as the Adjutant went down the line, followed by the corporal with his notebook, taking names where appearance or the rifle was not acceptable.

Appearance had to be nothing less than immaculate (a word that TC was hearing more and more) and the rifle had to be pristine, with no brass filings from spent cartridge cases or cylinders left inside. He passed by TC with no comment but farther down the line, he came to one of the lads, who had a reputation for joking and messing about, (he was one of the fools caught in bed by the duty corporal and ended up running round the parade ground with bare feet and in his pyjamas, carrying his bedding that morning) and his name was taken for looking like a 'scran bag' (naval speak for a complete mess). The Adjutant held the lad's rifle up to the light and looked down the barrel, he then handed it back to the recruit in disgust and said, "Look up that barrel man and tell me what you can see?" The lad held up the rifle and looking down the barrel said calmly, "I can see the galley, sir." With that, the Adjutant exploded in a rage, snatching the rifle, he threw it about forty yards across the parade ground. The wooden forestock came off and shattered into pieces. The rest of the squad were now trying desperately not to laugh but also shitting themselves at the same time.

The Adjutant ordered the corporal to have the recruit marched at 'double-time' down to the guard room and the rest of the squad were dismissed. The unfortunate recruit ended up with fourteen days detention in the cells and then kicked out of the Corps. Every day they would have drill, double periods, weapon training, double periods and physical training, oh yes, double periods. They were now being trained in field craft, out in the woods and wilds, faces blackened, camouflaged, crawling through the undergrowth in the wet, rain and covered in mud. They had to learn the art of total concealment.

Their physical training changed now, they had to run round the assault course with their rifles and sometimes with telegraph poles. They had races, four to a pole where the pole was not allowed to touch the ground. TC thought that this was great fun. There was one occasion when five PTIs got together to demonstrate an exercise, adding humour into the training. This took place on the main parade ground in front of the whole depot. These five PTIs came out carrying a telegraph pole in front of them. There were two at each end and one in the middle. The one in the middle was a huge Welsh man, twice the size of the other four, his name was Ted Kelland. Ted was a legend in the Corps and little did TC know at this stage, he would become very good friends later on in his career.

They stood in line side by side facing the parade, holding the pole waist high. Then another PTI standing to one side, gave the order, "On the count of one, you will raise the pole up to your chest, on the count of two, you will lower it. Stand by – one." They lifted the pole to their

Above: TC's recollection of the PTIs demo on the parade ground referred to on page 30. Sketch by TC.

Left: TC with his beloved GPMG on Kingsdown ranges Deal.

TC receiving his section commanders diamond from the commanding officer, RM Depot Deal.

Ceremonial line up, bayonets fixed to SLR's and white pith helmets, left arms up to correct their dressing, (spacing)

Part of the assault course at Deal. The swing bridge.

The Queens Hotel Deal seafront, closed in 1977 and destroyed by fire April 1981set by local vandals.

chests but because Ted was such a man-mountain, when he raised the pole, it was so high that the feet of the other four left the ground and they were hanging on the pole, with their legs kicking desperately in the air. At the count of two, Ted lowered the pole and the whole parade were amazed at this routine. More so, when the PTIs repeated this five times. The whole parade was now in hysterics at this performance, it was awesome; Ted was awesome. *Whilst this book was being written TC was informed that big Ted had passed away. RIP Ted, never forgotten.*

TC had to spend many hours at the swimming pool, learning life-saving, how to tread water for long periods without becoming exhausted and swimming in full kit. There was a swimming test at the end, which had to be completed by all. This comprised of jumping into the deep end of the pool from the highest diving-board, wearing full battledress, webbing pouches, rifle slung diagonally across the back and even wearing a steel helmet. Swim two lengths, tread water for two minutes, remove the helmet, webbing, and rifle and let them drop to the bottom, then at a signal from the PTI, dive down and recover their kit, piece by piece but at no time touching the sides of the pool or holding on. Once this was completed, they would be called out of the water, test complete. This test was called battle-swimming test.

The recruits spent much of their time now on the ranges, shooting from 900 yards down to 25 yards. One of TC's favourite disciplines was the Walk Down, from 100 yards to about 10 yards, walking in extended line. Every time the targets appeared, he had to stop, fire two rounds and be ready to move on when ordered to do so by the range officer. He was taught different stances each time, standing, squatting, kneeling, and laying. TC loved it all.

At this point, he was introduced to other weapons, the SMG 9mm (Sub Machine Gun) and eventually, his much longed for GPMG (General Purpose Machine Gun). To quote TC, "Oh yes my son, this is one motherfucker of a machine gun. This one's mine." He said that when you're firing at the enemy, you would shout, "Get some, get some, ave some of that". The GPMG is a belt fed weapon, firing 7.62 mm bullets on a 200 round belt. TC was now in his element. He had waited so long for his beloved machine gun and bullets. He had no idea it was so big and powerful, all he could think of was, 'Yiha'.

TC wrote a letter back home to his mother every week telling her all the things he was doing and learning but when she wrote back she always enclosed a ten shilling note. To TC this was a lifesaver knowing how hard she had to struggle financially, he blessed her. It helped him a lot, as the recruits were not paid very much.

There was a large hotel in the town called Queens Hotel; this had a basement dance club called The Dive Bar. Many of the recruits frequented this as it was the only place in town where there was any excitement and a good chance of chatting up the local girls, sometimes to the annoyance of the local lads, so many punch ups took place inside and outside. One evening, two members of TC's squad, were set upon by about 8 local so called tough guys, with a certain reputation to uphold. These had formed a gang and attacked the recruits with bicycle chains and tyre levers, causing some serious injuries.

Two nights later all the squad went ashore and grouped together on the seafront, they had been instructed not to use the dive bar but two decided to enter the club and cause an argument with a few of the previous attackers. They then allowed the locals to chase them out and along the seafront. These tough guys had quite a nasty shock, when about 10 Royal Marine recruits emerged from behind some of the fishing boats beached there and taught them the error of their ways, with a large helping of 'summary justice'.

Unfortunately, the next morning the Provost Staff paraded them in front of the local police, who severely reprimanded them and as such all shore leave was cancelled for the next two weeks. TC's thoughts were, oh well it was worth it.

The weeks went by quite quickly now and they were coming to the end of their seventeen weeks at the Depot. By now out of the original forty-six recruits that TC had joined with, they were now down to just fourteen. This was partly due to injuries, forced or voluntary dismissal. One particular recruit only stayed for a very short time because he said that he had been serving in the French Foreign Legion and he found the Royal Marines training was not tough enough for him. More likely, he thought that he could not cope with the intensity and discipline and was trying to save face by spinning this yarn. He was treated as a joke. They were put through what TC thought was hell at the time but he realised that it was all a necessary evil to get them in shape and mentally attuned to handle the infamous Commando Course, which was ahead of them at Lympstone, Devon. This is known as CTCRM (Commando Training Centre Royal Marines).

Once every two weeks, a squad would pass out from Deal, having completed their seventeen weeks basic training then transferred to Lympstone CTCRM. Before they left Deal, their families would be invited for the day and given various demonstrations on what their little Jimmy had been taught so far, followed by lunch with them in the galley.

The squad would be in battle order and would have to run along the seafront up to Kingsdown ranges two miles away, while their families would pass by them in a coach and thus reach the ranges before them. Upon arrival, the recruits were given live ammo; this included two hundred rounds for the spectacular GPMG, which was in the hands of TC. He was one happy bobby. They would then carry out a demo, showing their expertise in weapon handling and shooting for their families to see.

After everybody returned to the Depot, the recruits got changed into their No.1 Blues (best ceremonial uniform) and gave a drill demo, with the band, on the parade ground. This was with rifles and fixed bayonets, then after lunch, the families took their photographs of little

Jimmy in his very smart uniform and then they left.

Later, the squad would go ashore (the only time they did not have to report to the guardroom), with their training team for a farewell drink but when they returned, slightly inebriated, their noise and high jinks would disturb the other recruits by running up and down the corridors, kicking all the doors open, banging on the lights and eventually waking the duty corporal, who was not best pleased. The following morning, complete with hangovers, they had to be marched down to Deal railway station and be escorted all the way down to Devon and CTCRM.

The next time this would happen would be two weeks later but this time, having had the experience, TC and his squad put broom and mop handles through the big brass door handles of their room, so they would not get disturbed. It worked very well but wait until it was their turn! Their last day at Deal finally came and TC's family (including his father) arrived to see the demo. They did exactly the same as the preceding squads, except that some of their drill was done without any orders, this they had practised repeatedly during the past few weeks, as their drill instructor had worked them very hard putting them through their paces.

They carried out several manoeuvres in complete silence, just by timing, and no orders. This went very well and they received a standing ovation from the watching families. At the end of the day, TC and his squad went ashore with their training team as usual. On their return, they were warned off from any boisterous or noisy behaviour, it would not be tolerated, as the next morning; they would be on their way to the West Country and CTCRM. The big one.

Now, these recruits were a lot brighter than the previous lot and they decided to raid the rooms very quietly. They belly-crawled into every room and removed one shoe, one boot and one plimsoll (which they called pumps) from under every bed. They then stockpiled all their booty down on the main landing. The next morning all hell broke loose, as the other recruits had to sort through sixty or seventy items of footwear to find their own. The duty corporal thought this was extremely funny and positively brilliant, as they did not make any noise or wake anyone up, particularly him.

After breakfast, they were marched with their kit bags, to Deal railway station and on to Lympstone, where they would be met at the other end by their new training team. After many hours on the train they eventually arrived at Exeter station. As the train slowed and entered the station, there standing in a line, were a bunch of mean looking Royal Marines dressed in combats and wearing Para smocks. Oh yes and of course, their green berets.

They were sergeants and corporals. They looked absolutely ferocious and meaning business. TC's first thought was, oh Christ look at this lot of mean bastards, as were the rest of his squad, some saying, "What the fuck have we walked into now?"

CTC Lympstone

The squad from Depot Deal assembled in three ranks on the platform at Exeter and the new training team, really scary, mean-looking Royal Marines, officially took over from the escort team. They gave the order for the squad to embark on the train waiting on the opposite platform. TC saw that this was a small diesel train. Off they went, next stop it seemed to TC, in the middle of nowhere, although he had noticed that the train appeared to be running parallel to a large river. As the train started to slow down, a sergeant stood up and said, "Look at that river, it is the river Exe, you will be familiar with it later and I kid you not, you will never forget it."

TC thought, wow, we will be boating and canoeing on it. The train finally came to a halt at a very small station called Exton. It was completely devoid of any life until the squad were told to disembark from the train and form up in a single line with their backs to the train. TC was looking for the coach or lorry to take them to the camp but there was nothing except a very small station building.

They were given the order to turn right and then marched along to the end of the platform, which was quite short. TC thought, where on earth are they taking us? The station entrance was behind them as they marched off the end of the platform and along a narrow grassy pathway that followed the rail track. The path seemed to run for miles and disappeared into infinity. TC thought, where the hell are we going now? Oh bugger this is typical, a bloody route march carrying full kit and dressed in my best suit and my nice polished shoes, shit and once again shit. After about ten minutes, they came to a large field and although it was fenced off, there was a small gap through which they were led, leaving behind the beautiful view of the River Exe.

They could hear a lot of shouting and activity going on and as soon as they cleared the hedgerow into the field, TC saw PTIs taking recruits round an enormous assault course, which just seemed to go on forever.

There were twenty-foot walls, climbing bars, rope swings across water, cargo/scramble nets and lads hanging off rope works and falling into large tanks of filthy water, when they were exhausted and could no longer hang on. They had on full fighting order with their rifles across their backs as well. TC's first thought was "Oh crap." Some of his squad were actually saying this out loud and other expletives. At this point, one of the training team shouted out, "Don't worry lads, you'll be doing this on Monday morning and I can promise you, 'we won't feel pain". TC remarked to himself, "Oh yeah, thanks a bunch sarge" but suddenly TC had this overwhelming feeling of awe and he felt he could hardly wait for Monday to come. He thought, bring it on. This is what it's all about.

They were taken to a tower block, which would become their home until their training was complete and they were dismissed and posted to their respective duties. TC's room was on the ground floor, again sharing with seven other lads from his squad and after dumping their gear, they were marched across to collect their bedding and shown where the galley was. They were then left to their own devices and TC was very keen to check out the notice board, as all their movements for the rest of the week were listed on it. It began with the assault course, PT, Tarzan course, PT, weapon training, PT, speed march – three miles, PT, endurance course on Woodbury Common. TC remarked, "Where the hell is that?" (He soon found out that it was four miles from camp and four miles back speed marching, with forty five to fifty minutes of the most awesome assault course that TC had ever seen). Part of the PT was something else. It made TC realise why he would never forget the river Exe, for when the tide went out, it left miles and miles of thick stinking mud. The squad had to run in it, crawl in it and roll over and over in it. Afterwards they had to stand in line and get hosed down, front and back with a full-sized fire hose and freezing cold water.

The first few weeks were really hard compared to The Depot Deal but it was only then that TC realised the extreme necessity for those seventeen weeks of gruelling training. Without it, nobody would be fit enough, strong enough or with the right mental attitude to cope with the now-advanced commando training at Lympstone. You needed upper-body strength, strong legs to carry all the weight and most important of all, PMA (Positive Mental Attitude).

The assault course at the bottom field consisted of a thirty-foot vertical rope climb, up to the top, touch the cross bar and descend slowly hand over hand, without using your feet. You had to be wearing full fighting order and your SLR Rifle slung diagonally across your back. After a short run to the start of the course, it was up and over the scramble/cargo nets, up several steps and a run across single scaffold boards. These were eight inches wide and eight feet off the ground, in sections and placed in a zigzag pattern, (this was for balance and courage), with no hand holds at all, jump off the end and onto the ground, hand over hand across monkey bars, then onto the next obstacle called the 'Regain'. This was a climb up some scaffolding and onto a tightrope stretched across a large tank full of dirty, smelly water. Lying on your stomach, pulling yourself across and when about halfway, hang off by your hands, then by swinging your legs up and over the rope, continue across to the other end. Should you fall off into the tank, climb out soaking wet and heavier than before and start all over again.

Next there was the swing bridge, it was a wooden plank eighteen inches wide and twenty feet long, supported by four cables – one at each corner, hence the swing. You had to run over it as fast as you could. Balance is essential here and courage, because if you lost your balance, you landed in a pit of barbed wire. On and up the hill to a twenty foot wall, up and over then carry on further up the hill to a long tunnel, two foot in diameter. Down on your belly and crawl through the tunnel (there were three like this). The first two were about twenty feet long but the third was double, forty feet. You had to do all this in order to pass the test, which would come in several weeks. All the obstacles had to be cleared to a set time limit and failure was not an option.

TC absolutely revelled in all this action. The Tarzan course was just as difficult, starting with a climb up a rope ladder to a small platform, perched forty feet up in a tree. You had a short piece of rope called a sling, which was kept in a bucket of water on the ground, to keep it cool and a loop spliced in each end. When you reached to the top of the platform, there was a long rope secured to the tree, just above your head. You put one hand through the loop in your sling and threw it over the top, then put your other wrist in the other end. You then stepped off the platform and slid down the line towards the ground. The line was secured a hundred feet away at the bottom of another tree. This was called the 'Death Slide' and it was only the start of the course. Climb the ladder up to another tree, jump to a single rope hanging twenty feet up and swing into a cargo net, climb up to the top and make your way across an array of rope obstacles, high up from tree to tree, eventually landing back on terra firma.

The next part was to run and crawl through the same tunnels that were at the end of the assault course. The Tarzan course was also timed and had to be completed, in order to pass one of the feats of 'Commando' skills'. TC was absolutely in his element and loved every moment of it. They had to do these two courses every week but the toughest was yet to come, the endurance course. This took place outside the camp on Woodbury Common, which was four miles from camp, reached through long, narrow, winding lanes. The common was also used for Royal Marine exercises, field craft and survival training. TC loved the outdoors, learning how to survive on the countryside and in particular, making the best use of the surroundings for concealment and movement, to see but not be seen.

The endurance course started with a short run on the common and a crawl through a small tunnel thirty feet long, then a run on down the hill, where at the bottom lay a pond full of muddy, stinking, water known to all as Peter's Pool, (every Commando will know that name), which you had to wade through, holding your rifle above your head. This was because even though TC was six foot, the water would come up to his chin. The shorter lads in the squad had to hold their breath and go under the water. The object was to ford the pond without getting your rifle wet. By the time you came out, you were twice as heavy with water pouring out of

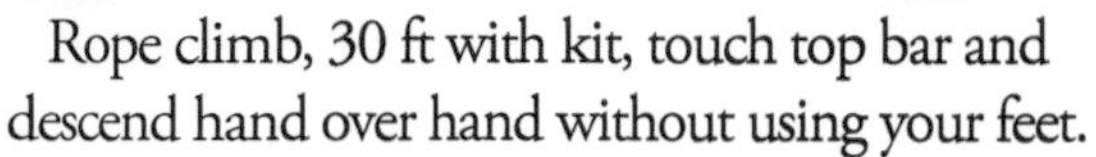

Rope climb, 30 ft with kit, touch top bar and descend hand over hand without using your feet.

Firemen's carry, length of football pitch in 90 seconds.

The monkey bars, miss one and you're in the drink only to go back and start again.

The rope crawl and regain, 10 ft drop into muddy water, get it wrong and start over.

Cat crawling in the stinking mud of the river Exe, TC said, "No canoeing here".

all your clothes, boots and ammo pouches but you had to run up hill to the next obstacle, lots of swinging across ropes and climbing over structures of various sizes and difficulty. Next came the small tunnel or pipe – eighteen inches in diameter and about six feet long. This was totally submerged under water. The principle was that on this course, they went round in syndicates of three and helped each other. On arrival at this pipe, all the rifles would be laid on the ground to one side, one person jumped into the water at each end of the pipe. The third took a deep breath and submerged under the water and with arms stretched out in front, entered the pipe, being pushed in by one lad with the other one reaching in from the other end, grasping his hands and pulling him out. They then changed round and repeated this procedure until all three had gone through the pipe. After that, they all jumped out, grabbed their rifles and ran to the next obstacle. This had you crawling on your belly through three more concrete pipes, three feet in diameter but these were buried under ground and sixty feet long. By the time that TC had exited the last one, he was totally drained and exhausted but the 'punishment' was not over yet.

Now they had to run four miles back to camp, down the narrow, winding lanes, the last of which was notoriously known as Heartbreak Lane, entering the main gates of the camp in threes, down the driveway, seven hundred yards and onto the bottom field to the twenty five metre firing range. Once there, you would be given ten live rounds of ammo and in prone position (lying down) you fired ten rounds onto your respective targets and every shot had to count. All this was against the clock. You were only allowed eighty minutes in all. Once again, they had to practice these courses many times before they would be ready to complete the final one.

Speed marching now became a regular occurrence. The idea was to jog and power walk in a group to cover long distances but to arrive together and be able to fight at the other end, the marines call this Yomping. They travel as fast as the slowest man, as it was imperative not to leave any one behind. They marched at a fast pace up hills and gradients but jogged in time along the flat and down hills. The distances would be three, six and nine miles, which always ended in Heartbreak Lane leading toward the camp, where over the years there have been casualties and one or two fatalities due to heart attacks or total exhaustion. This can happen even to young, fit men. "It happens!"

Later came a twenty-mile endurance load-carry (this was with full loaded pack). The finale was the thirty mile cross-country over Dartmoor, map and compass work in threes again and had to be completed in eight hours or less.

While all this activity and tests were going on (which TC absolutely loved) they spent hours and days weapon training, map and compass work on Dartmoor, night marches and ambush techniques, which meant lying in wet, muddy grass and bracken all night without moving a muscle. They would be cold, wet and hungry but this was very necessary, as TC would discover later in his career. The first two weeks at CTCRM, TC and his squad were the 'new boys on the block', getting used to the camp, which was huge, knowing where everything was – the classrooms, clothing and bedding stores, the armoury, the guardroom and many other training areas. Once they had settled in, they were then known as X-Troop.

TC found that he thoroughly enjoyed the part of the commando training that was detached from CTCRM, for two weeks on board HMS Belfast, anchored up in Portsmouth docks, called HMS Bellerophon. This name derives from four previous Royal Navy ships dating back to the late 1700s. HMS Bellerophon was known as a stone frigate and this description relates to all Royal Navy shore-based establishments. All Royal Marines had to live on the ship and learn how to find their way around the ships, by use of the codes depicted on the bulkheads, hatchways, ladders and gangways. Once this is understood, it is simple to establish where one is and find the way to the galley and the heads. (This is all a marine needs to know).

During these two weeks on board, there are various classes and lectures on ships discipline which is very strict. If a marine or any crew member makes the slightest misdemeanour, he would be up in front of the old man (Captain) and get weighed off (punished). Ship's routine is very different from anywhere else, for instance, turning out (getting up) in the morning and making sure all your bedding and belongings are safely stowed away. This routine is serious because in case of fire or flooding, any loose items like clothing or a single towel could easily be sucked into the pumps.

At 1900hrs every night, the Captain would do his rounds. All areas of the ship and all the mess decks have to be spotlessly clean and nobody is allowed on the mess deck, while it is being inspected. After this, the lads can chill out, go up on deck for exercise, go walk about, sit in the Galley playing cards, reading or watch TV.

Part of this course was being taught how to splice various ropes and tie knots of many kinds. All have their own specific tasks and reasons. They also had a day's instruction on 'Pulling'. TC thought it was about chatting up the ladies but alas it meant rowing boats. These are referred to as ship's boats or whalers, which are 27 feet long and are quite heavy to pull, so it is vital that all the crew pulled together and in unison. Once TC and his crew were quite proficient, they would have a race around the ships in the dockyard and this added great fun and a challenge, as it is very hard work therefore one needs to be very fit. Later on, it was announced by one of the chirpy instructors, that everyone would have to row much harder and faster, because the Captain had decided he wants to go water skiing, very amusing, TC thought.

After a few days on board, they were allowed some well earned shore leave this was very welcome, as TC found it to be a little bit claustrophobic, all living in close proximity. Sometimes, tempers can get a bit frayed. In order to get ashore, as the ship was anchored about 100 yards off shore out in the basin, it was necessary to walk across a series of floating pontoons, chained together

The Cat Crawl, rope obstacle, high up in the trees.

The start of the Tarzan Course and the Death Slide.

Tarzan course, swing from a rope into the cargo net, up and over the top.

The water tunnels. Freezing dirty water, hold your breath, think of England and trust in your buddy!

Now you're wet, heavy and exhausted, there is a four mile run back to camp and put 10 rounds on a 25m target, all in 80 minutes.

with a gap between each one. This was not a problem when the water was flat but when it was a little choppy, the pontoons would bob and sway quite violently and it would take a bit of a balancing act to cross to the shore and of course to get back on board after a few sherbets. TC found that the strange thing about this, was that after being ashore and visiting the many ale-houses, such as they have in Pompey (Portsmouth), staggering back and crossing the pontoons seemed to be a 'piece of cake'.

One night TC had decided not to bother going ashore and when some of the lads returned, one in particular, a 'scouser', who did not like TC and vice versa, thought he would take a broken broom handle to attack TC, while he was in his hammock, (all slept in hammocks during this two week period, as part of the training). TC was not asleep and jumped out of his hammock. He told this lad that they should go out in the gangway and settle this once and forever. Outside, TC asked the lad if he was incapable of fighting without a weapon in his hand. This made him angry and dropping the piece of wood, went for TC grabbing him by the lapels on his shirt and attempting to head-butt him. TC knew that this was the lad's favourite and only means of attack. TC quickly moved his head to one side, so the head-butt landed on his shoulder. The other lad let go, at this stage, thinking he had connected but was completely shocked, when TC landed a perfect punch on scouser's chin. He went down, to quote TC "Like a sack of shit".

This is considered very dangerous on board ship, as everything around is made of steel and the punishment for fighting on board is extremely severe. Fortunately for TC there was nobody around at the time, just two or three members of TC's squad, to make sure that the broom handle stayed on the floor. TC never had any more 'crap' from this lad after that but admitted that he did feel bad at having to go down this route to settle differences.

The following six weeks involved learning more about weapons, like the Anti-Tank Weapon and much more of live firing on various ranges, TC once again was in his element. Another part of their training at Lympstone, encompassed two days at RNAS Culdrose, in Cornwall. This was to spend some valuable time with the helicopters, being taught embus and debus drills. It also involved different types of landings and take-offs under different conditions. These helicopters were Wessex Mk5 and would be one of their most important means of getting to and from quickly, on short and sometimes covert journeys, in essence, their taxi service.

Apart from jumping in and out of choppers, it was essential for the Commandos to be able to accomplish rapid rope down techniques, in the event that the aircraft was unable to land. This could be due to a variety of reasons, for instance, in the jungle, where the tree canopy is often 90 feet high. In this scenario, the only way to deploy is by rope, while the aircraft is in hover. Another example of this is where there may be a clearing of some sort but because of low ground obstacles or soft ground, bushes, walls or tree stumps, the aircraft will hover at about 5 feet and the Marines would jump to the ground. Added to this, another quick deployment is on a track or short road, the aircraft can land like a small plane, travelling along the track

HMS Belfast ,TC's training ship at Portsmouth.

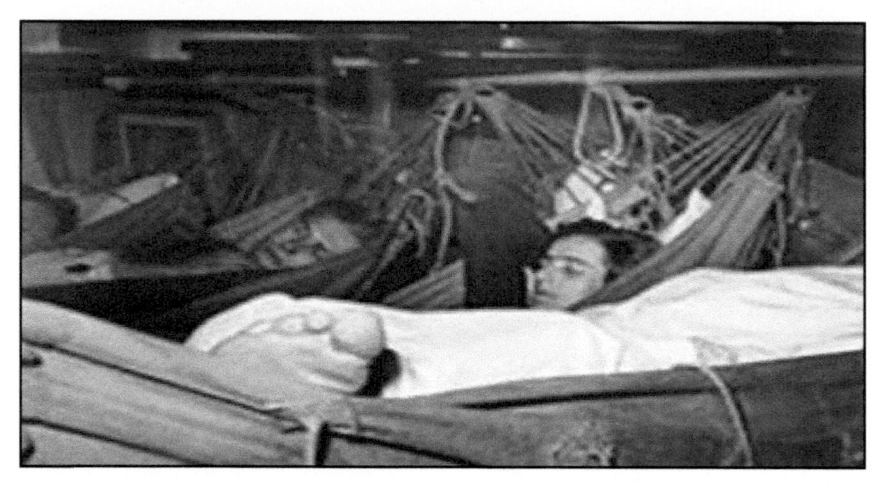

Snug as a bug in a rug sleeping quarters and mess deck, HMS Belfast.

Portsmouth docks. Floating pontoons can be seen, as arrowed.

or road at 10 to 15 MPH, and the marines would jump out and roll away. The moment the last man exits the aircraft, the crewman would tell the pilots via his intercom and the aircraft would take-off. This is done mainly when there are several aircraft in flight together and one after another would fly in and deploy the teams rapidly, so as not to leave the rest queuing or being held static in the sky, where they could become a sitting target.

Once these drills have been practiced several times, the finale would be a ditching drill showing what to do in the event of engine failure. The aircraft would fly up to 2000 feet, then the pilot would disengage the main rotors, a loud bleeper would sound and the aircraft would drop dramatically towards the ground. At the sound of the Emergency Bleeper, the Marines would put their rifles on the deck and put their feet on them to stop them flying about. Just before impact, the pilot would pull the aircraft up and would land heavily with a thump. The second it hit the ground, the crewman would signal to all on board and they would get out as quickly as possible. The pilot is able to control the aircraft during its rapid descent. This is called 'Auto Rotation'.

In addition, TC was taught many other skills, like deploying by RIB (Rigid Inflatable Boat), used for speedy beach assaults plus working with landing craft and helicopters, which included lots of rope work. All this rope work is so essential to Commando Training, particularly as hours were spent abseiling and cliff-climbing (mostly at Land's End).

During the two days they spent at 'Royal Naval Air Station' Culdrose, TC and his squad had one full day at Land's End, training in cliff assault techniques. This entailed ascending and descending in different styles, the first being the 'Abseil', which is descending down the cliff face on a rope, fed through a karabiner.

As this is quite complicated and technical, it is necessary to quote TC's instructions and comments, at the cliff top you stand with your back to the edge leaning back, then pushing off with your legs against the face of the cliff, swinging you out and by controlling the rope, you allow yourself to descend about 20 feet. By the time your bodyweight has swung you back to the cliff face and bending your knees, pushing off again, repeating this over and over again until you reach the base. The further you push out and allowing yourself to descend quicker, before swinging back in, the further you descend on each repeat, with a bit of confidence you can descend 40 to 50 feet each time, thus ending up at the base much quicker, which is the idea.

There is an exception to this called the 'free abseil'. This is when you go over the edge of a precipice or overhang so that you do not have any contact with the cliff face at all and you can descend as fast as you like. This method is also used for descending off a bridge, railway arches and especially where The Royal Marines are concerned, a rapid rope down from a hovering helicopter at 30 or 100 feet.

Another technique he explained is the run down. This is a very fast descent and requires total confidence, skill, training and a degree of guts. On this one, you leave the top of the cliff, facing downwards and at 90 degrees to the cliff face, as you step off, you can literally run down, controlling the rope as it passes through your hands, again you are in control of the speed of your descent but with this one in particular, there is a safety man at the base keeping the loose end of the rope fairly taught, so that if the climber slips or loses control, the safety man pulls hard on the rope and this acts as a brake. The climber stops abruptly, allowing him to reset and continue.

The cliffs they were using were 300 feet high and although this did not bother TC, there were a few of his squad who were a little apprehensive. One lad in particular was extremely scared of heights, this being totally alien to them all. TC wondered what this chap was expecting from the Royal Marines when he joined. The lad was of Egyptian origin and although this made no difference, however, there were several other issues that became apparent later and unfortunately he did not make the grade.

Lunch time arrived and the squad were handed their packed lunches, made up for them by the cooks at RNAS Culdrose. These consisted of brown paper bags with a meat and potato pie, commonly known as an oggy (more pastry than meat), a chocolate Penguin biscuit, some fruit and a carton of fruit juice.

As it was such a lovely day, the squad sat around on the cliff top, chatting and laughing about the morning's experience. The air was full of noisy seagulls, obviously realising that there might be some tasty morsels going spare. These oggies are not very popular, unless you were extremely hungry, so it was not very long before some of the lads threw some pieces of pie crust onto the grass. They thought it was very amusing watching the gulls, come down fighting for the scraps. A few moments later there was an onslaught of gulls, as their gull-network clicked in, letting them all know that there was food being supplied by Royal & Co. The sky was full of the screaming birds but this was certainly not ideal, due to the possible bombing of bird poo.

More lads started throwing pieces of crust into the air again, good entertainment, watching the gulls catching the food and fighting each other for it in mid air. TC had no intention of eating his oggy and not wishing to break it up into small pieces for the birds, (typical of TC), he stood up and threw the whole oggy up high and out over the edge of the cliff. One dumb seagull swooped in, grabbed the oggy out of the sky, not realising that it was heavier than itself and refusing to let go, went down like a lead balloon, vertically towards the salty oggin, (water).

Now all the lads were on their feet with TC, watching over the cliff, as this stupid bird went down and down into the water and disappeared from sight, with the oggy still in its beak. To their amazement, it suddenly rose up with the pastry and decided to sit on the surface and eat it, before long the seagull was joined by all the others. Big seagull 'punch-up' high in the sky!

After lunch and all the excitement, they all had to abseil again to the bottom of the cliff, apart from four, who were held back to act as horsepower. Having completed the run down, they now had to do the run up. The idea was to tie the loose end of the rope round their waist, using a bowline knot, with the other end going up the cliff and over the top through a pulley. At a given signal, the group at the top would run from the cliff edge inland, thus pulling you up quite fast. You had to lay back at 90 degrees to the face and run up. TC found this exhilarating and great fun.

The last part of the day, was spent doing basic cliff climbing. Hands, fingers and foot holds this is what TC was waiting for, as this would be the ultimate challenge. During the climb, he had caught up with the lad from Egypt, who had frozen and could not move, despite the instructors yelling at him and threatening to do nasty things to him.

He was now a threat, as TC came up behind him and could not get past. TC spent 10 minutes talking to him and managed to calm him down but he would still not let go. The lad was terrified and he was only 40 feet from the base, TC hooked him to himself via his karabiner and was able to climb back down with him, coaxing all the way. Once at the base, he was unhooked from TC by one of the instructors and TC went off up again. The lad was forced to do a run up again, he did not like this either.

On his return to Culdrose at the end of the day, TC passed on the flying compliments to the cooks for their tasty pies. The seagulls dined well that day.

After the six weeks in X- Troop, finally they were fit and skilful enough now, to enter the final stage, which was another six weeks on the commando course. Now they were down to the 'nitty-gritty'. All the gruelling work was so that they could get through the final main course and now they were taught many more advanced fighting techniques (which TC was not at liberty to divulge), although he was free to recall the many different military personnel from various other countries to attempt the commando course. These people were officers from the American Marines, Parachute Regiment and in particular four senior Naval Officers from Iran who actually were placed on TC's squad. Unfortunately many of these fell by the wayside including all four Iranians, this was not necessarily because they were not fit enough, it was more than they did not have PMA and thought that the course would not be as difficult as it was. One particular case remained in his memory because it became quite high profile. An American Marine Captain (who the squad nick-named Captain Fart, for obvious reasons) failed the course twice but because he could not remain in the UK any longer, he insisted that he should be awarded the 'Green Beret', as he would lose face back home in his unit. The CO refused because the beret was earned, not given away.

The American complained to the British Government and the whole debacle turned political. Nevertheless, the Commandant General upheld the refusal and the beret was not awarded. TC

Royal Naval Air Station Culdrose, formally HMS Seahawk. Cornwall.

The Wessex Mk V, TC's favourite taxi, superseded by the Sea King AKA The Jungli.

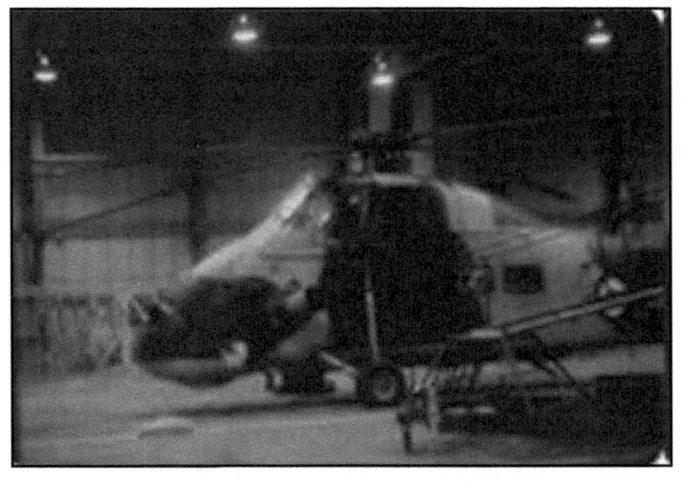

Wessex Mk V in hangar HMS Bulwark (known as the rusty B).

Helicopter flight from Culdrose.

Rapid rope insertion onto ship.

Rapid rope down from the Lynx.

The Abseil descending at speed.

Two marines on the rapid descent.

One of the cliff faces popular with all climbers, civilian and military alike.

Right: Random shots of various cliff ranges on the Cornish coastline used for cliff assault training and exercises.

thought "Quite right too".

During the last two weeks the squad would have to cover all the tests against the clock. The assault course, the Tarzan course, and the endurance course – three, six and nine mile speed marching (which they called 'Yomping' – the Army refer to it as 'tabbing'), the twenty mile load-carry, followed by the dreaded thirty miler. Thankfully, this last one was only done once, unless of course, you got injured or could not complete it in the eight hours required. TC and all his squad got through it the first time in syndicates of three. The very last moments of this yomp are when you come off the moors onto a single track, of course it was uphill to the finish. They jogged all the way, using the last of their energy. TC recalled that about half an hour before this, he had saved himself a nice juicy orange (stowed in his ammo pouch) but had no energy to peel it and could not stop or use his left hand because it was securing his rifle to his body, to stop the barrel thumping the back of his head as he jogged, so he ate the orange like an apple, peel, pips, the lot. The acid from the peel stung the corners of his mouth but the orange was just what he needed. This last track just seemed to go on forever, until they could see the very top, where the training team were standing and clapping and shouting encouragement to them to keep going. "Push it, push it", they shouted, a PTI was looking at his watch, at last, through the line with the team jumping up in the air with glee, they must have had bets on us. There was a four-ton truck and a couple of Land Rovers parked up, TC said they were not allowed to stand still or sit down but to keep moving about for a while.

He was amazed to discover that he and his syndicate were the first back and their timing was 6 hrs and 21 minutes. The Colonel was there and shook their hands, plus there was a lovely big mug of tea and an oggy, oh no not these again. They had set out at 0415 hrs that morning and they had completed everything that was thrown at them and now it was all over but no – wait until TC gets posted to his first Commando Unit.

The last two weeks until they officially passed, they were called the 'Kings Squad', now they were the senior squad on camp and allowed to wear their well-earned 'Green Berets'. TC commented "Oh boy, I can't tell you how good it feels to wear it". He said that he feels the same today, all these years on, when he goes to Remembrance parades and other official functions. On the very last day at CTCRM, once again mums, dads and families came for the day to see the pass out parade on the parade ground (God's Half Acre). After the drill display, the final order they were given was from the Adjutant, when he bellows out "Royal Marines to your duties, fall out". Most of the squad went home with their families to have a few days leave before they had to report to their respective postings or units.

TC was posted to 40 Commando which was based in Singapore, where he was scheduled to be for the next two and a half years. On the way home, driving back to Kent, TC reflected on his military journey so far, through all those weeks at Deal and Lympstone CTCRM. He wondered if he would ever run into any of his squad-mates again during his career and thought about some of the funny incidents he had enjoyed at Lympstone.

There was an occasion during a tactical exercise on Woodbury Common, where they were dug in on a forward-facing hillside for four days and nights. Living and sleeping in five foot trenches and going out on night reconnaissance patrols, where they would be ambushed by members of the training team, taking the correct action, as taught and eventually arriving back in their trenches. These tactics vary from country to country but the ones that TC learned have been tried, tested and proved to be highly successful (TC was not at liberty to reveal these fighting tactics and techniques).

The next day they were all handed lengths of black cable, twin flex used for the field telephones. It was called D10 cable and had a multitude of uses, as TC would discover in times to come. The squad were told to link this cable between the trenches as means of communication and that whoever was on watch in each trench, should have the end of the cable tied around his wrist, as at 0400 hrs they would be carrying out a tactical withdrawal from the location. The signal would be two sharp tugs on the cable and two back in reply. As TC occupied the trench at the top of the hill, all the cables from every trench were attached to his trench. When 0400 hrs came, he was approached by a member of the Training Team to signal the withdrawal. TC signalled to all the trenches in order and received confirmation, until he came to the last one but when giving the two sharp tugs, the cable felt solid, with no response. Once again he gave two more tugs and again there was no response. TC then thought that the cable must be snagged on something, so he gave a really massive tug and kept pulling on it. At this point TC became aware that the rest of the squad were quietly walking past in single file towards the forming-up point at the top of the hill, by this time, TC and his trench buddies, three in number, were all hauling on the cable and wondered if perhaps it had been tied to a tree but suddenly it started to give a little and they heard someone yelling out to stop, which they did. They found out shortly after, that it was scouse again and whilst on watch had tied the cable round his neck and fallen into a deep sleep. He had actually been pulled out of his trench and was in danger of choking to death. Although the whole squad fell about laughing, the training team were furious with this silly fool for giving our position away and we were all punished by having to run six miles back to camp with full kit and back packs instead of riding in a truck.

Another occasion he recalled occurred during an exercise on Dartmoor. They had bivvied up for the night in two-man tents. It was really foggy and visibility was about 20yds but something woke TC in the early hours of the morning. He could hear something outside the tent. It was sniffing at the canvas and pushing it, right by TC's head. Whatever it was, TC punched it and it went away. He thought it might have been a sheep. In the morning, when TC emerged from the tent into the foggy Dartmoor air, he noticed something lying about six feet away from the side of their bivvy. On closer inspection, he realised it was a cow and dead as a Dodo. He wondered if it was the punch that had done it but nothing was said or done, except a few days later, when they were live firing, TC noticed a poor old sheep with a broken leg, it was about

200yds away at the time and in obvious pain, so he shot it, to put it out of its misery, only to have his sergeant jump all over him and saying, " What is it with you? Every time you see an animal you kill it. You'll make a 'first class marine' lad."

These memories would not be complete without TC mentioning what happened on his last exercise on Dartmoor. They were given a task to go to a dam which would be guarded by the training team acting as enemy. On the way to the target they came across an irrigation ditch running at right angles across their front and half way up a hillside. They needed to cross this, as it was eight feet across and two feet down to the surface of the water. It was very dark and they could not assess how deep the water was, so they sent one lad to the left and one to the right about 50yds to see if there would be a crossing place further down but they both returned saying there wasn't. At this point, Taff said, "I can run and jump that, all we need to do is take off all our kit. I'll jump across you throw all the kit over then you can all jump across".

This seemed logical, so Taff went back about 20 to 30 feet, they couldn't actually see him as it was so dark, then they heard him running up toward them. He loomed out of the darkness then stopped. TC asked, "What's up mate?", to which Taff said, "I can't see the edge of the trench in order to launch off". They decided that two of them would stand right at the edge, five feet apart, so that Taff would know when to take off – brilliant! Off went Taff again into the darkness, then once again he could be heard running up and again loomed out of the darkness like a frightened beast of the Moors. As he launched off with gusto, his foot slipped and he belly flopped, straight into the water, huge splash and immediately he started swimming. Suddenly he jumped up and standing in a foot of water, shouted, "For fucks sake".

At this point, Training Team on the warpath or not, they couldn't help falling about laughing in hysterics. Eventually they all put their kit on and walked across. TC could not stop laughing at this recollection and said, "Memories like this stay with you forever". Little did he know that there would be many more funny incidents in the years to come?

Heartbreak lane, the finish of all speed marches, 3, 6 and 9-milers. These were done more than once throughout commando training. The object of this was that the whole troop travelled together and be able to fight at the other end. No one gets left behind. Timings for these are 30 minutes, 60 minutes and 90 minutes.

The Pièce de Résistance. The end of the 30-mile cross-country over Dartmoor in less than 8 hours and the end of recruit training. The award of the Coveted Green Beret follows this immediately and recruits now become 'Kings Squad' before being posted to commando units. Training never ever stops. Every Royal Marine Commando will never forget this emotional final test.

Singapore - 40 Commando

After two weeks of well-earned rest and getting married for the second time, TC found himself en route to RAF Brize Norton, along with his new wife and a small mountain of luggage, on a two year honeymoon to one of the most beautiful jewels in the Far East - Singapore.

Before long, they all boarded an RAF VC10 plane, which TC thought was very plush. They were told that the flight would take around twenty six hours and being an RAF flight, sadly, no alcohol was allowed. "Damn," thought TC, "this is going to be one hell of a boring flight", (no music, TV, or movies in those days).

After some time in flight and a snooze, they were told that they were landing in Bahrain, which lies on the East Coast of Saudi Arabia, in the Gulf. The time was 0130hrs and as they stepped off the plane, the heat and dryness smothered them, it was completely overpowering.

TC had never before left the coast of the UK and he was quite enthralled that here he was, in an Arab State, on his way to the Far East. They were ushered into a waiting-room, where they stayed for nearly three hours, while re-fuelling took place but they were not given any refreshments, although TC recalled being offered tea and coffee.

So off they went again and a few boring hours later, they started to descend. TC thought, "At last, this must be Singapore" but once again, he said that he had been really 'peed off' to discover that this time they were landing at RAF Gan, which is a very small Island of the Maldives Group, in the Indian Ocean, south west of Sri Lanka.

As they came in to land, TC could see how beautiful the island was, surrounded by bright, clear, blue sea and white coral reefs. The only thing that disturbed him was that the island did not look big enough to land a plane on. By this time, it was mid-day and of course, the plane landed perfectly safely. (TC has said that unfortunately the island airbase was closed in 1975) and once again, they sat around in blistering heat for three hours, then off they went once more.

VC10 on take off at RAF GAN, the smallest of the Maldives' in the Indian Ocean.

RAF Gan runway on final approach to the postage stamp size of this coral island.

Slightly bigger Airport RAF Changi Singapore.

VC 10 at RAF Gan being unloaded and refuelled. Closed in 1976 as part of government cutbacks also RAF Changi fell victim to the cutbacks when the British pulled out in 1971.

Eventually, they landed at RAF Changi in Singapore and were met by their respective reps. from various units, RAF, Navy, Army and of course TC's was a Royal Marine sergeant. There were nine of them for the Marines and once outside, in the hot, humid atmosphere, they were shown onto a bus, which delivered TC and his wife to their accommodation. This was a two-bed semi-detached house in a cul-de-sac called Jalan Kuak, on the Thompson Garden Estate.

TC and his wife were very pleasantly surprised to find that they had been given a box of basic supplies, which were waiting for them in the house but truthfully, all that was needed was some tea and a good bed. The next morning, a note was put through the door with orders for TC to report to Dieppe Camp in two days time. The Camp was situated on the Simbang Road, a few miles away.

On investigation, they discovered that their local provision store was just down the road, run by a friendly chap called Sun (Soon) and TC was surprised to see other western people in there. Sun would offer you a chair, while getting your order ready and a cool can or bottle of Coca Cola or Seven Up. Once your order was ready, it was packed in a box and he would offer one of his staff to carry it to your house for you. TC thought, "These people certainly know how to do business."

Later, they found out that there were several Western married couples in the same road, also marines and they all made TC and his wife (newly-weds) very welcome. So while TC was on duty; his wife had many coffee mornings with the wives' club, run by the wife of the Commanding Officer. They frequently went on trips and visited beaches all over the Island.

Within a couple of weeks, they also acquired an 'amah', a pleasant, friendly Chinese lady, who came every other day, to clean their house and do the dhobi, (washing and ironing), she would also cook for them and actually considered it an honour to do so. She called TC's wife 'Madame' and TC, she called 'Master.' The first morning that TC had to report to camp, he caught a taxicab called a 'flyer.' These cabs were black and yellow and were mainly old Mercedes or Austin Cambridge's. They would drive up and down the road and would stop when one flagged them down. They would often have other passengers on board, so one would be sharing the taxi. One just told the driver when one wanted to get out. It was a very cheap way of getting around, just costing twenty cents from house to camp, which was about four miles. TC recalled that at this time, the Singapore Dollar was eleven to the pound.

On arrival at the camp, TC had to carry out what was known as the 'Joining Routine,' where he was given a card, which listed all the different departments he had to visit and register with them. This took all morning because some of the departments were not open so early. He also found out that the Main Unit was away on exercise in Malaya and all that was left was a small rear party. TC palled up with another new chap called Denis and together they toured the camp to acquaint themselves with the general layout.

They worked Tropical Routine in the Far East, which is 0730 – 1300hours, as the temperature reaches scorching at mid-day. After registering with all the names on the card, TC came away with a ton of clothing and equipment, he thought, "I've got more than enough already" but nevertheless, there were green towels, green underwear, shirts, fatigue trousers, shorts, long socks, jungle boots, fighting order, on and on and on, oh yes, he was also given a pale blue lanyard (40 Commando colours).

The following day, he had to report at 0730 hours in PT kit and was taken with a group on a long run around the camp and across an old WWII airstrip. This was the start of the acclimatisation course, to get them used to working in the heat and high humidity. Two days later, the unit returned and TC was posted to 'B' company. He had to muck in and help clean the equipment and put it away in the company stores. Due to the heat, they just wore shorts to work, with no tops.

Now he was issued with his guns. This time, there was an M15 Rifle or Colt Armalite, as it was known, which was used in Vietnam by the Americans. It had a 30 round magazine of 5.56 calibre and could fire single or automatic. It was very light and easy to handle, ideal for close combat, for example, in the jungle. He was also given the SLR 7.62 and his very favourite GPMG 7.62. In addition to those, he had Browning pistols and Browning pump-action shotguns, these were used by lead scouts if being ambushed, (as TC would find out, when he himself became one after a few weeks course).

He quickly settled in and enjoyed it, especially after another two weeks, when TC found himself with the rest of the new guys, on a 'Jungle Warfare Course' in Johor Bahru, which is over the causeway from Singapore into South Malaya. Royal Marines run the Cadre, who also trained other units from different regiments. They were taught how to survive in the jungle – or by now, it was known as the Ulu - what to eat and what not to eat, where to obtain water from vines and which vines to obtain water from, how to lay traps for animals and also 'booby' traps.

TC thoroughly enjoyed every minute of this course and could not wait to get into the real thing. He did not have to wait too long. All fired up, TC rejoined his unit and every morning at 0730 parade, off he went, PT and long runs carrying all his kit and weapons. After 1300, it was home and down to the beach or one of the military clubs, around the swimming pool. TC's favourite was Tanglin and the best beach was RAF Changi, passing the crocodile farm, which was a popular sightseeing place, as they reared crocodiles in different pens, from babies to fully-grown adults. One could lean over the wall and poke them with a wooden stick and watch them snap at the stick. When the adults were killed, one could watch them being skinned and the tanning of the hides and then go into the shop and buy the goods, shoes, boots, wallets, purses, and handbags.

One day at RAF Changi, TC and his wife were on the beach with four other married couples.

GPMG belt fed 7.62mm medium machine Gun.

9mm Browning Self loading Pistol.

M16 colt 5.56mm semi or fully automatic assault rifle.

84mm Carl Gustav Anti Tank recoilless launcher.

Two of the many rounds available for the 84mm. **Left:** HEAT, High Explosive Anti Tank. **Right:** HE/FRAG, High Explosive Fragmentation.

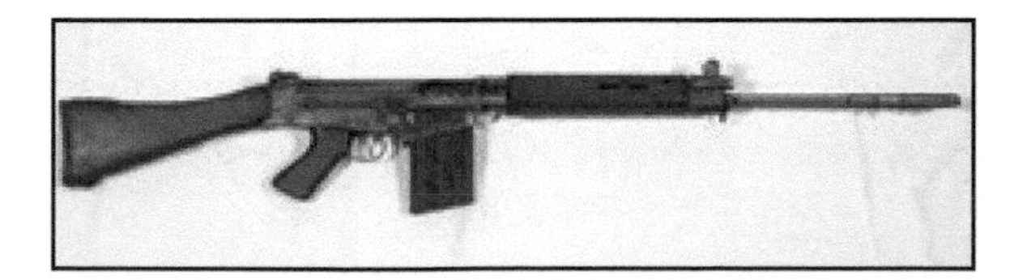

SLR (Self Loading) 7.62mm Rifle 1960's to early 80's.

They were able to get about quite a lot, as by now, they had their own car, a Vauxhall Victor, (there were many British cars out there at that time, all in good condition). A few of the crowd were in the water, when it was decided that they would swim out and around some boats that were at anchor about 200 yards off shore. On the way back, TC was around 50 yards from the beach, when something wrapped itself round his right leg and to quote TC, "Stung the hell out of him." He gave a loud shout and quickly told some kids playing nearby, to get out of the water.

His leg appeared to be paralysed and he could not use it. He made it to the beach, where his mates were waiting. They thought he had cramp but as he was helped out of the water, they could see a string of stings from the top of his leg, wrapping round and ending at the top of his foot. The most painful one was behind his knee. His leg was so swollen, he could not walk properly. His friends bundled him into a car and took him straight to the RAF sick-bay. TC's leg was covered in a thick, white cream and lightly bandaged. The cream did relieve the pain, which only lasted two days. He was told later, that a shoal of Portuguese Man O' War jellyfish had been washed up the Singapore Straits and they were the culprits.

Nights out in Singapore City were great and TC and his friends often ended up in Bugis Street (commonly called Boogie Street), which was an all-night market for food and beer after midnight. One of the sights to be seen was the appearance of some beautiful Chinese ladies of the night. They would emerge, with expensive hairdos and exquisite low-cut dresses, showing a reasonable amount of cleavage, the only problem here, was that these gorgeous creatures were actually men, known locally as 'Kities' and if you watched them long enough, you would eventually see the 'midnight shadow' coming through the make-up. Some of them spent thousands of dollars on various operations.

One place that TC liked to visit during the day was 'Thieves Market'. You could buy almost anything from there, mostly stolen or illegal – or both and he soon discovered that there was another way of getting around Singapore – using the trishaws. Great fun, if you did not mind hair-raising rides, as there were cars coming at you from all directions. They did not stop at junctions at all, just weaved in and out of the traffic. A few times, TC and his friends paid the trishaw owners to sit in the passenger seat, while they rode the bicycles, having races around the city.

There was a part of the city called Chinatown, which was out of bounds to all service Personnel – of course, this was the first place that TC and his mates headed for. They had a lot of fun, because you could walk from junk (a Chinese boat) to junk across boards and some of the boat owners would cook food on board. Very few spoke English but they always managed to communicate – money had its own language.

Pretty soon, TC and his section were on their way by helicopter, from camp to the commando

Bugis Street night market Singapore 1967 frequented by public and service personnel from all over the world.

Lady boy/Kitie strutting their stuff in Bugis Street Singapore.

Kities posing for the camera in Bugis Street Singapore.

Croc pen on the farm near RAF Changi.

Typical Trishaw old Singapore City.

carrier HMS Bulwark, docked at Sembawang Naval Base, HMS Terror. They then set sail into the South China Seas and up the East Coast of Malaya. The ship anchored about twenty five miles off the coast and they transferred back to the helicopter. They flew to a small airstrip called Gemas.

They were split up and sent in different directions, on various patrols into the deep jungle. TC was amazed at the sight of the foliage, some of which were massive. Elephant grass and plants were growing off trees, a strange, exotic world.

It was not long before it got very dark but only inside the Ulu, outside it was bright sunshine. The trees were extremely tall, with foliage only at the top, about eighty or ninety feet high. The top was called the canopy. They were all soaking wet by now from sweat, while cutting their way through secondary jungle. Lots of fallen dead trees made extra obstacles to cross, small streams and stagnant ponds, up to their armpits in smelly, stinking water that had probably not been disturbed for many years.

After a while, they received the signal to stop for five minutes to take a drink. All communication in the jungle is by hand-signal only. Some of the lads sat on the jungle floor, leaning against a tree or sat on a log. TC was lucky, he stopped beside a large brown boulder or rock. He sat on that, took out his water bottle, and drank, not too much. He suddenly felt the rock move slightly, which he thought was a bit odd, then it moved again. This time it raised up a bit. TC jumped up wondering what the hell it was and to his astonishment (and everyone around him), the rock sprouted legs and started walking – it was a giant tortoise.

The tortoise must have been about one hundred years old. Its shell was covered in brown moss. Out came the cameras and all their silent tactics were forgotten. The whole patrol, including their Officer and the Navy photographer were interested in this large brown 'rock', with four legs, a tail, and a head. Off it went into the blackness of the foliage.

Darkness fell at 1530hrs and they all had to make camp and put out sentries. Some of the lads prepared meals; others erected bivvies (tents). They worked in twos at this time and the sergeant came round with the duty rosters to let them know what time they would be on sentry duty and how long for. By now, it was very dark and the jungle came alive with all sorts of noises. Gibbons, bullfrogs, tree beetles, crickets and of course, hundreds of fireflies. The fireflies looked like people coming through the jungle with torches and TC was totally fascinated.

Just before dawn, they all had to 'stand to'. This was because it would be the best time for an attack. It was also done in the evening, just before the light faded. In this part of the world, there is no dusk, as in the Western world. In the Far East it goes from daylight to pitch black in thirty minutes and the same in reverse in the morning, about 0400hrs. After the order to 'stand down'; they had to clean up their camp area, leaving nothing behind, TC found his clothing was still soaking wet and freezing cold but this only lasted a short time because once they were on their way again, they soon warmed up.

Several Gurkhas from 32 Regiment now joined them. These men were experts in the jungle and TC was very glad that they were on his side. They always carried a bottle of rum, dried fish and lots of rice with them. By now, the patrol was about thirty in all and when they came to a river, they decided that it was easier to follow this, rather than cutting their way through the jungle. They all ended up walking in the river, as the banks on either side got higher and higher. They were now wading knee high and even waist high in places, the flow being relatively gentle but as they started to ascend very gradually, they were going against the flow. TC was near the rear and began taking photographs, as they stretched out over a hundred yards or more. His camera was a 16mm Minolta, small enough to fit into his shirt pocket and the sight of his patrol in the river was awesome to him and he got some really good shots.

It was about lunchtime and into the monsoon season, when the skies opened up on them with very warm rain. TC said that it felt lovely, although it stopped an hour later, just as fast as it had started. The river was getting deeper and faster flowing, they were now up to their waists and it became obvious that the rain was the cause. At this point, they were signalled to go up the bank. It made a nice change to get out of the water.

Now they walked along the side of the bank, about twenty feet from the river, which had become even faster flowing and quite noisy. The noise was useful tactically, as this hid any sound the patrol made. TC could see a small waterfall up ahead, about one hundred yards on, where the water was flowing extremely fast, coming down from the high ground. Suddenly, Sam, who was just in front of TC, lost his footing and fell. He slid down the bank, rolled over and dropped into the river. He was in trouble. Quick as a flash, TC dropped his rifle, pack and fighting order and slid down the bank after him. He saw an arm coming out of the water and grabbed it, pulling Sam to the surface but he was going under now as well, because Sam still had all his kit on and was very heavy. TC managed to pull it off him, including his rifle. They were struggling in eight foot of water but eventually TC managed to get Sam to the bank and into shallower water. By now Sam was semi-conscious and three lads from the patrol helped to get him out.

Their patrol officer also came to the rescue, stopping the patrol. He gave TC a 'well done' but wanted to know where the rifle was. He then asked TC to try to find it. By then they had travelled some yards downstream from where Sam actually fell in, so TC went back to the approximate spot and dived down, groping around on the bottom of the river, which was now in full flow. Sam's pack had floated away but had been recovered by the 'tail-end Charlies' at the rear. Suddenly TC's hand caught something soft. He could not see anything but as he pulled, he realised it was the sling, which was attached to the rifle. TC came to the surface holding up the rifle and was astonished to see all of the patrol waving, shouting and cheering on the bank.

TC thought, "This is a bit over the top for just finding the rifle," then out of the corner of his eye, he spotted just upstream, a huge tree trunk that was being washed over the small waterfall, heading straight at him. This is what they were all shouting at him for, to warn him. He made it to the bank, just in time, as the tree trunk went sailing past down the river. They estimated that it must have weighed at least three tons. Quite a close shave!

This patrol lasted three days and they were eventually picked up by helicopter and flown back to 'Mother' (their ship), which was waiting for them off the East Malay coast. Hot showers, clean clothes and real, hot food were all very welcome after the rigours of the jungle. They landed on the flight deck and disembarked from the helicopters, where Naval Ratings were waiting to usher them down the ladders to their mess decks. TC wondered why they kept away from them; he thought that perhaps they were scared of them, until he was told how bad they smelled.

Back in Singapore, they all went to their company lines to clean their kit and weapons, before they were allowed to secure for the day. TC was brought before the Commanding Officer and given a Commendation, not only for saving Sam's life but in particular for saving the rifle! Unfortunately, during the rescue, TC lost his camera from his shirt pocket. He thought, "All those great photo shots gone, Bugger!"

Training went on day after day now. It never stopped but for TC it became even more enjoyable. On the ranges all day, at least three or four times a week, sometimes in Malaya. Lots of work up country, honing and sharpening their skills for FFR (Fitness for Role). They still had to parade in full kit on the Parade Ground in the mornings but not every day.

TC had to do the occasional guard duty in the camp, which meant spending twenty-four hours in the guard room and patrolling the camp all night, sometimes at weekends, although they did try to keep the 'inliers' for weekend duty, as they lived in the camp, as opposed to the 'outliers' like TC, who lived outside with his wife (some married couples had children).

TC soon discovered that the camp had two speed boats, which could be used for water skiing. They had to be booked in advance via a book kept in the guardroom, so when TC or his mate Peter wanted to use a boat for a Saturday or Sunday, they put their names in the book. The only problem they had, was that a couple of duty officers, when visiting the guardroom used to take the book away, down to the officer's mess and would book for days and weeks ahead, as they considered that water skiing was not for ordinary ranks. TC and Peter complained and had this stopped.

They used to go with their wives, to small islands at the weekend and spend the day skiing. There was always a 'goffa wallah' on these islands, so one could get tea, coffee and hot food. It soon became clear that of the two boats, one was much better than the other, so they made sure of always getting the best one. TC's sergeant major had his own boat, which he had built himself and he took them out a few times and taught them how to water ski and how to handle the boat. Both TC and Peter became very proficient skiers and boat handlers.

They had booked the boat for the coming weekend and together with their wives, TC and Peter set off for the day with their picnics and full fuel cans for the boat. It took half an hour to reach their favourite island, which was never over-crowded, as the only way to get there was by private boat – no ferry.

They had been on the beach about two hours, skiing and having taught the wives how to handle the boat, while TC and Peter were eating, the wives took a trip on the boat round the perimeter of the island. This would take thirty minutes but just before they returned, the other boat arrived and parked on the beach, close by. It was one of their officers from the camp and his wife, (the officers were known to the men as Nigels or Ruperts and their wives were called Fionas). This particular officer was a pompous ass and not well liked. Now the two wives had returned and parked alongside the other boat. At this point, the officer approached the wives but TC and Peter quickly intervened and asked what the problem was. The officer stated that he had signed for the boat that TC had taken, so he had the wrong one. Obviously, this was denied but the officer was not happy and said that he would double-check in the guardroom on Monday morning.

After this, the officer went out on his skis, with his wife driving the boat. He was demonstrating how good he was, (probably for TC's benefit). When he decided to finish and come ashore, he had his wife drive straight at the shoreline, and then made a hard turn to the left, catapulting him onto the shore, at which time, he would let go of the toe-line and land on the beach, so as just to step out of the skis, as they came to rest.

This was a technique that TC and Peter had practised many times. Of course, one needs to judge the speed and distance or one would stop short and sink or go too fast and the skis would stop dead on the beach but the skier would carry on. This idiot came in much too fast, his skis hit the beach, he lost his footing, rolled head-over-heels twice, crashed through his picnic area and flew past TC's group like a rocket, covered in sand, even in his mouth. He hit the tree just behind the group, who could not stop laughing. The wives even started clapping and shouting 'encore'. This was too much for the officer, so with his wife, they gathered up their things, jumped into their boat and to quote TC, "buggered off." When the group got back to camp, TC and Peter called into the guardroom to inspect the book. The officer had signed for the boat he had. No comebacks, 'Sir'.

A couple of months went by and TC was spending all day in camp and out on the airstrip, practising different techniques of embarking and disembarking from the helicopters. These were the Wessex 5 and a new squadron had just taken over and needed to work with the section,

HMS Bulwark Commando Carrier with her flight of Wessex Mk 5's entering the Straits of Singapore 1968.

HMS Bulwark South China Sea off the Malaysian East Coast 1969.

A Giant Tortoise similar to TC's mobile seat.

Waterfall similar to the one where TC rescued one of his patrol and the rifle.

TC performing before the Officer arrived.

Rapid Rope down on deck from 50 feet.

Lining up on deck in sticks waiting to emplane.

Round-up time, a regular scene in Aden South Yemen.

Dockside Aden, HMS Albion the Commando carrier in the Background.

Typical checkpoint and search area downtown Aden.

to secure their needs. These helicopters were based on HMS Bulwark, now at anchor in the Johor Straits. Sometimes, in this part of the World, helicopters cannot always land, so they had to use various methods of 'Rope Downs', from thirty feet to a hundred feet.

There could be times when the helicopter will get close to the ground but not be able to touch down, so they would have to jump out while in the hover, not much more than five to eight feet. Another way for rapid deployment was when the helicopter comes in to land, touches down and keeps rolling forward at taxiing speed. The idea is to jump out and roll away, then as the last man bails out, the helicopter would pull up and away. This is to prevent the helicopter from becoming a sitting target and usually takes, no more than fifteen seconds to offload the troops.

They had to fall in with full kit, including backpack for this training. With a rope down from thirty to a hundred feet, the pack goes out of the door first and then the man follows. One chap decided not to fill his pack with the proper kit, as they were only training, so he put a small lilo in his pack, did up the straps and inflated the lilo, to make it look as though the pack was full. (Big problem). After taking off and flying a circuit, when they came back to the airstrip, out went the rope, first man out, then the packs but this one pack, instead of falling, just floated away with the downdraught of the rotors and when it finally hit the ground, it just bounced and drifted down the airstrip. Although at the time it seemed funny, TC could see how dangerous this could have been because there were other helicopters on the strip and it could have blown up into the Main Rotors or even the Tail Rotor, which spins four times faster than the Main Rotor. The Colonel was livid and demanded to know who the pack belonged to. This chap was severely reprimanded and spent a week in detention, where he was punished every day. He would be taken on extra long runs by PT Staff, extra drill by the instructors, then fatigue duty, which was cleaning the guardroom and his kit, with inspections by the Adjutant and the duty officer two to three times a day – this is beasting.

Some days later, TC had to report in with all his kit, draw weapons and was taken with others, to RAF Changi. There were only about thirty of them, the rest of the unit stayed behind. They were put on a plane and headed off to Aden in South Yemen, to act as security for the main harbour at Steamer Point. The British, who were based there, were withdrawing two units, these were 45 and 42 Commando. They landed at RAF Khormaksar, which reminded TC of Bahrain. They were bussed down to Steamer Point and given live ammunition and told to load up. They were not alone, there were other vehicles in the convoy. There was conflict going on caused by the Front for the Liberation of South Yemen, 'Flosy' and the Marxist Group, the National Liberation Front, 'NLF'. These groups were basically terrorists and the commando's main interest in the area was a huge BP refinery at Ghadir, Little Aden. There were British families posted in the region but they had been evacuated earlier. TC found that it was quite boring for a short time because they did not see anything of the country but it was very hostile.

The two units boarded the ships, as last off the place and the commandos were flown back to Singapore, not a shot fired.

Back at Dieppe camp, TC went to see Sew Sew. This old Chinese lady did all the sewing and alterations for the men. The shorts that were issued to them came down below the knees, so they had them altered, as with their shirts, all jungle greens. She also made a 'zoot suit' for TC, out of parachute material. It was like a modern-day track suit and the idea was, when in the jungle and bivvying-up for the night, TC would remove his wet gear, put this suit on and get a comfortable night's sleep. The only drawback was in the morning, when he put his cold, wet gear on again, remembering to shake it out thoroughly, in case any creatures had decided to make it their home for the night, especially leeches. They came in all sizes and would get in through the stitching and seams in the clothing. When they bivvied-up for the night, it was part of routine to strip down and check each other for leeches. (This is what is called a good mate). The 'zoot suit', once taken off, would fit into TC's pocket or a small plastic bag and was very light. TC paid Sew Sew ten Singapore dollars and thought it was well worth it.

The Gurkhas were carrying out night parachute drops on the airstrip and next morning, word went round that two of their guys landed, rolled up their 'chutes and chatting away, which they always did, walked away and fell off the hangar roof. As the WWII airstrip was laid out with steel sand tracks called Somerfeld Tracking, they obviously thought that they had actually landed on the runway. Both suffered broken bones and concussion but survived the ordeal. They also had a habit of screaming when leaving the aircraft. This was fine normally in fact TC had often shouted 'Oh God', in similar circumstances. (He used to think that as he was much closer to him he would be heard loud and clear). This was not acceptable on a tactical drop onto the LZ (landing zone). TC was adamant in his respect and admiration for these Gurkhas, for their courage and professionalism and they thought the same about the commandos. When doing jungle exercises with enemy, the commandos always used the Gurkhas. They were a formidable force. To quote TC, "They were bloody marvellous."

TC and his troop carried out many exercises and manoeuvres up country and in Borneo, Sarawak and on one occasion, Indonesia, as they had in the past dealt with various conflicts in these places, including Malaysia, during the emergency uprising, which was brought to a conclusion early in 1966. They practised and rehearsed fast deployment from helicopters and beach landings from ten-man Geminis (RIBS) Rubber Inflatable Boats with Johnson 40hp motors and paddles. (These were only used for clandestine approaches to beaches or rocky areas).

They then had a three-week exercise up in Malaya. The enemy, this time, were not Gurkhas as they would have liked but the Singapore Armed Forces. These lads were all conscripts and very skinny specimens. Their uniform was tight fitting with sharp creases (this was their battle-dress). The task was to be flown in by helicopter to a specified LZ and they had to make their way through the Ulu to a FUP (Forming up point) at the edge of a small airstrip, which was being heavily defended by the enemy, the SAF. Just before the light faded, attack, take and secure the airstrip, so that in the morning at first light, the helicopter could come in with supplies etc.

This all went to plan, except when they arrived at the FUP and sent two scouts to observe the size of the enemy and see what weapons they had and also, where the main fire power was. For example, a machine gun nest and mortar pits (if any). The two scouts returned inside an hour to report that nobody could be seen anywhere. It was still daylight and they had about two hours to wait for the attack. TC thought the situation very odd and they decided to do a quick check on the maps and co-ordinates to make sure that they had the right airstrip. Yes, they were correct, so a signal was passed back to 'Mother' (their ship). Subsequently they were told to go in and investigate, as it was confirmed the enemy were there, as ordered. So off they went and spread out as they entered the area. Nothing to be seen, no machine-gun emplacements no mortars - weird. They began searching the few buildings.

There were signs that someone was there, some kit, some food and some of the cook pots were still warm. They had the area covered, in case of a counter-attack but there was still absolutely nothing to be seen and certainly no weapons. Entering the last of the buildings, they were amazed to find that all the soldiers were there, sitting on the floor, hands on heads and their weapons piled up in the corner. These men did not want to get into conflict with the marines, they had been told that they were extremely vicious and as they had Gurkhas with them, who they believed eat people. (A rumour started by the Japanese, when they occupied Malaya and Singapore in WWII.)

The enemy were all collected. The helicopters flew in and transported the prisoners back to HMS Bulwark (nicknamed by all Navy and Marines, as The Rusty B). To quote TC, "These fellows were shitting themselves, as they had never been in helicopters before and certainly never been on board a commando carrier". They had no idea of how big this was but were all subject to 'Light' interrogation and sailed back to Singapore with their captors. On completion of this exercise, the commandos boarded one of the Wessex helicopters and were flown back to 'Mother', which laid about ten miles off the East Coast of Malaya.

As they came in to land, the helicopter shuddered as it touched down on the flight deck, then suddenly jerked upwards off the deck. TC was facing the doorway and almost undid his seat belt, which he was not supposed to do until instructed by the crewman, who was sitting by the side of the door, opposite TC. He would signal this with a thumbs-up but as he did not do this, TC realised that there was a problem and he was right. The helicopter banked sharply to the left (port) and went sideways over the side of the ship into the ogin (sea). TC said that he had a fantastic view of the sky through the hatchway, which was open and the side of the ship, as they plummeted into the warm waters of the South China Sea. There was no panic at this

Flight deck of HMS Bulwark preparing for flying stations, note the forward lift well bringing the helicopters up from the hangar below.

Quick disembark from Wessex onto flight deck.

The only shot I could find of Dieppe Camp in Singapore, home of 40 commando till 1971.

TC's lucky escape from the downed Wessex, early bath time, note the inflatable Ball.

RIB, Inflatable Geminis used for rapid beach assaults powered by outboard engines or can be paddled in for a clandestine approach.

because they had all done these drills, even in the dark, simulating landing in the water, rolling over to disorientate one, then calmly, when all movement had ceased, unbuckle and make one's way out and up. It is important to mention that the Wessex 5 helicopter is fitted with large canisters on either wheel. These burst open and inflate to a large orange ball, about eight feet in size when inflated, which will prevent the aircraft from sinking. The problem in this case was that the port side did not inflate, so the aircraft went under on one side, but not to the bottom. They all carried out the normal drill and TC was not aware of any panic from anyone. They were all wearing assault life-jackets, which, once out of the aircraft, one pulled a cord and the jacket would be inflated via a small bottle of compressed air attached to the jacket.

Everyone was recovered, including the two pilots and the crewman and no injuries were sustained. The training they had, proved its worth. The helicopter was also recovered, along with all the kit and weapons. They later found out that static electricity build-up was the cause. TC thought, "Slightly shaken and stirred."

Singapore / Hong Kong

Having survived the enforced ducking in the South China Sea TC and his section made their way back to Singers (Singapore) Dieppe Barracks and the usual routine of cleaning stores, weapons, and personal gear. After all this, they were free to go home for the weekend and that evening, Corporal James asked if they would all meet up at the Singapura Hotel for a celebration and down a few Tiger beers.

They met inside by the swimming pool. This was in the centre part of the hotel in the quadrangle. It was an open-air pool with rooms around all four sides, rising up twenty floors, with balconies overlooking the pool. To reach the pool area, you would have to walk through the foyer, passing the cocktail lounge, where a white-suited pianist would be playing on a magnificent grand piano. At one end of the pool, a chef would be cooking 'satays' on sticks over open charcoal. The aroma was intoxicating and very mouth-watering. They sat on soft armchairs and were waited on with beers and satay.

They were all having a good time but as the evening wore on and the tiger was flowing, they must have become quite loud, because suddenly a waiter appeared. He was dressed very smartly in a white jacket, black trousers, and a black bow tie. He demanded, "Keep quiet and behave or I will throw you out." "You what?", someone said. As he started to repeat his threat, a hand came from nowhere and pushed him backwards into the pool.

TC remembered some people leaning over the balconies, watching and laughing. Just then, another man came running out. This one was all in black and TC thought he looks like the manager. He was waving his arms and shouting, "You can't do that," as he was picked up and thrown in the pool too. Then, a shout went up, "They've called the Police." Corporal James reacted instantly, "Follow me," he shouted and ran from the pool area with the rest of the section close behind, as it was well-known that the police there were pretty ruthless and pulled guns on trouble makers.

They followed Jamie through the cocktail lounge and as they ran, TC remembered that someone slammed the piano lid down. (He said that thankfully the pianist did not lose any fingers), They ran through the foyer and up to the big glass doors, which led to the street, but now there was a new problem. Standing across the doorway was a huge Indian Sikh. He must have been at least six foot six tall and had a big black beard. He wore a white suit and of course a turban. He was clearly hotel security and immediately assumed a Karate stance and screamed at the approaching marines. Corporal James, without flinching, assumed the same stance (near enough) and absolutely bellowed at the Sikh, who was so shocked, he froze on the spot and at that precise moment, Corporal James punched the Sikh straight in the face. It made his head shoot back, so that he hit the door really hard. He slid down the door and sat down with a look of shock and utter disbelief on his face. He was dragged out of the way and they all made a run for it in different directions, as they could hear the police sirens getting closer.

TC and two others flagged down a taxi that was passing and drove to Bugis Street, which was packed with Service Personnel from the UK, Aussies, and Americans. Later on they met up with the rest including Corporal James and TC told him how impressed he was that James knew Karate. To which he was told, "I don't, I just did what he did but I shouted louder." TC commented, "James was a Physical Training Instructor and a Geordie".

A week later, TC received orders that they would be going to Hong Kong for three months deployed on the Hong Kong – Chinese border, alongside members of 32 regiment Gurkhas. He was in the advance party for this deployment and was soon winging his way to Hong Kong in a C130 Hercules transport plane. It was a very noisy plane and also quite uncomfortable because the seats were no more than canvas deckchairs, (minus the sun, sea and sand), just the smell of Avgas (Aviation Fuel), or Paraffin.

As they flew over Hong Kong Island, TC was fascinated by the landscape. All the mountains with high-rise buildings were sticking out of the side of the hills, like stalagmites. This was, of course, 'The Peak' and as they came round towards the Harbour, heading for Kai Tak Airport, TC could not actually see the runway and thought, where the hell is he going to land this bus? They were flying quite low by now and suddenly he heard the wheels go down.

"Thank God they work," he said. They were so close to the sea, TC wondered if they were going to land in it, as it was just a few feet away. Still with no sign of land and looking up at the High Rises that he had been looking down on earlier, he thought, oh shit, I hope we are not going to ditch in the Ogin and get soaked again. He looked out of the porthole and could only see water. He said, out loud, "What the fuck have we landed on now?" As they started to slow down, at last the tarmac and airport buildings came into sight. He had not realised that the runway went out into the harbour and that was all it was, a strip of land, a few feet above the water and no wider than the runway. What a welcome to Hong Kong.

They were met by two trucks and taken to their new home for the next three months. The

The old Hotel Singapura where TC and his mates legged it, photo circa 1968.

The very famous Raffles Hotel, opposite
the Brit club.

The Britannia club, Beach Road, opposite Raffles Hotel.

The swimming pool Britannia club.

The fruit market and life in general of every day life in the old Singapore, circa 1967.

The old Serangoon market place and Chinese New Year, celebrated with fire crackers.

TC cannot resist a bet to dive in and swim ashore to the island of Palau Senang South China Sea.

The Hercules C130 transporter, TC's air taxi.

Two Pictures of Kai Tak airport, notice how difficult it is to land on this strip. Kai Tak now closed.

Old Sek Kong camp, SNCO'S accommodation on the right and Nissan huts on left. The mountain in the background called Nameless. Apologies for poor quality, the only photo I could obtain.

trucks wound their way up the mountain, higher and higher, into some cloud. Emerging from the cloud, TC caught the most fantastic view of Hong Kong and Kowloon, way below. He even watched as another aircraft came into land. On and on they went, still making their way up the winding road. The engines on the vehicles were working really hard, as the drivers were searching for a suitable gear. Second gear was too low, with the engine screaming, third gear was too high, with the engine struggling. This road was called the Twisk. Over the top they drove and started to descend, down into the New Territories and on to Sek Kong South and another WWII airstrip, all grown over and with Nissan huts, a small parade ground and wooden cabins on one side, complete with veranda. This would become the SNCO'S (Senior Non-commissioned Officers) Quarters. The Coolies (local Chinese) had been working hard connecting electricity, so that the marines would have hot water.

They selected their grots, dumped all their gear and went in search of some well-earned scran (food). They were told that they were being fed by the Royal Artillery camp on the other side of the airstrip. So armed to the teeth with mess-tins, mugs and yaffling spanners (cutlery), they pushed through grass that was up to their armpits, across to the other side, into a brand new camp and found the Galley – oops – cookhouse.

They were now on Pongo territory. Nevertheless, it was very nice compared to what the marines were going to have to make do with for the next three months. As TC entered the cookhouse (he really hated that word) and went up to the servery, he was stunned to see a hotplate with piles of fresh steaks beside it. The men were wondering if they were allowed to help themselves and cook the steak, when a Warrant Officer, all of six feet four inches, appeared behind the servery. He was wearing perfectly pressed whites and a peaked cap in addition and said, "Come on lads, welcome, help yourselves."

They took large steaks and slammed them onto the hotplate the juices were running and so were theirs. A quick flip over was all that was needed and onto the plates. They certainly did not need mess tins, mugs or yaffling spanners, everything was provided. "Very nice," said TC and he started to move along to get some 'chippy chips' (as he called them), when the Warrant Officer said, "Hold on lads, is that all you want? I thought you all had massive appetites." TC was startled and said, "Can we have another steak? We are normally allowed only one." The WO replied, "Boys, you can have as many as you like, so long as I don't see any of them going in the bin." "Well, this is Christmas," TC said, as he took another one.

The following morning, TC was up, showered and trekking across again for breakfast. "Wow," he said, "same again." This time he had three steaks with a fried egg on top of each one, 'beautiful'. Back in their camp, they set to work, clearing out huts, putting up beds and generally tidying up in readiness for the main unit to arrive. They had to man the Guardroom now, as this whole area had been used by the locals to drive around, up and down the runway, flying model aircraft and using it to teach people how to drive (most of them very badly). They actually shared the camp with other residents – cattle, belonging to a local farmer. They were told that the cattle had the right to wander round the camp. TC said, "That was ok with us," because they used to jump on them and ride them across the airstrip.

The Unit was due to arrive very soon and when they did, the advance party would no longer be able to use the facilities over at the Royal Artillery camp. TC was full of praise for the marines' own chefs, when they took over he admitted that the food was extremely good and at least they did not have to walk a mile to be fed, mostly in pouring rain.

Soon TC found himself up country on the Hong Kong Chinese border. His first posting was a small village called Tsoi Yuen Kok. TC said that the situation was quite bizarre because they could see the guards of Communist China across the border between the buildings and they were just yards away. They used to try to intimidate the marines by pointing their weapons at them but the marines had to patrol with their weapons slung upside down, on their shoulders, so as not to intimidate the Chinese.

The gaps between the unoccupied buildings were in neutral territory and TC and his mates would stand there and eyeball the Chinese, then move off to the next gap and the Chinese would follow. The marines would watch for a while, and then move off to the left or the right and the Chinese copied them but suddenly the marines would move back to the same position and the Chinese would end up running up and down, wondering where the marines had gone. This was a stupid game of cat and mouse but it passed the time and to quote TC, "Those poor sods were only conscripts, who knew no better.

A few days later, they had a visit from the 'sin bosun' (padre) and after a tour of the camp, TC walked with him to show him how they wound up the Chinese guards. He thought it was really funny but some children appeared and started to throw stones at them. This was common practice but he said that it was disgraceful on the part of the Chinese guards. As they began to walk back, a stone hit the padre in the small of the back. He said, "Little bastards, sorry God," as he picked up the stone and threw it back, missed the child but almost hit the guard, who was standing nearby. At this point the guard smacked the child round the head so hard, it nearly knocked him off his feet. TC said that if the guard had opened fire at them, he most certainly would have returned fire. This would have created an International incident. They both had to supply written reports and the padre had his wrist slapped. TC said "Good on you padre."

Back at camp again at Sek Kong, TC had some time off and with two mates decided to explore the area on foot. They climbed a mountain, walked across paddy fields (rice fields) and at one point walked along the top of a massive pipe-line about six feet in diameter and supported by concrete piers, ten to twelve feet high. One slip and it was a long way down. They did this, because it saved them walking through some very unpleasant terrain and more paddy fields.

A couple of days they spent on the local bus, down to Kowloon and across on the Wan Chai Ferry to Hong Kong Island. The bus journey, according to TC, was a white-knuckle ride. Going over the top of the mountain from Sek Kong on the Kam Tin Twisk road was hair-raising and the descent, from high in the clouds, with Kowloon and Hong Kong hundreds of metres below, was daunting due to the very narrow road cut into the side of the mountain.

All of that is bad enough but when you see the driver sitting with one foot tucked under him as he puts the bus into low gear and lets it go, using the engine as brakes. TC had to admit that it was very worrying and a relief when they arrived at the bottom. They also had to take advantage of a trip in the cable car, up to the Peak, which was so high up that the view of Hong Kong and the Harbour was absolutely wonderful.

Two weeks later TC did that trip again, this time with his sergeant, who had been in the region many times and knew all the good places to go. Hong Kong of course, was full of bars, restaurants and a multitude of shops. This trip was mainly for a bit of shopping for their wives or 'Mums', as they were known. After a bit of lunch and a few 'wets' (drinks) in a bar called 'Yellow Submarine', they went off to visit one of the emporiums. The sergeant wanted to buy some silk underwear for his wife. The open counters in the emporium reminded TC of Woolworths stores back home in the UK. As the sergeant started to sort and fumble through piles of ladies briefs, the young girl assistants were quite embarrassed and congregated at the far end of the counter, giggling.

Eventually the sergeant chose a pair of pants, screwed them up in his hand and threw them on the floor. TC was most surprised by this action and asked the sergeant what he was doing. The sergeant replied, "Just seeing what they looked like on the floor, that's where I usually see them." TC could not help laughing and his sergeant called to one of the assistants to come and serve him.

None of the assistants wanted to come and serve him, they were all embarrassed and TC did not blame them, he was a little uncomfortable himself and kept busy with choosing silk underwear and a silk nightdress for his wife. When the elected salesgirl came to serve him, the sergeant said "Have you any American pants?" The assistant looked puzzled and began holding up different styles but all the sergeant would say was, "No, no, I want American ones." Two more assistants came to help but he kept repeating, "No, I want the American type." TC wondered what the hell he was talking about, when a female passer-by stopped and got involved. She asked what he meant by American pants and he replied "Oh you must know, one Yank and they're off." Everyone found that very funny and TC had to walk away because he could not stop laughing, though he did manage to buy some things for his wife,

The woman who had stopped to help was also highly amused and slapped the sergeant on the arm saying, "You English are very funny and very naughty boys." It turned out later, that

Tsoi Yuen Kok village on the Chinese border.

TC on weekend guard duty, Sek Kong camp.

TC out for walkabout Sek Kong area Hong Kong. TC climbed 'Nameless' Sek Kong airstrip can just be seen in background centre of picture, the camp is just the other side of the airstrip.

Wan Chai ferry crossing Victoria Harbour. The famous Peak Tram cable car Hong Kong.

she was the owner and 'Mamasan' of one of the bars, where they ended up in the evening. They were there until the early hours, only to find out that the last ferry from Hong Kong to Kowloon had gone, so they had to hire a water-taxi, which was shared with others and had no engine. Basically, it was just a rowing boat, no life jackets. TC found it quite harrowing and was relieved when it reached the other side. Sometimes they would end up having a race with another boat, both throwing water at each other and by the time that they landed, they would all be soaked, including the boatmen. TC and his mates always gave them a few extra dollars. They loved it!

Two days later, TC with others was being flown by Wessex helicopters up country near the Chinese border. His pilot could not help showing them how good he was at contour flying. This is flying in a covert mode, flying very low and following the hills and mountains in the valleys, instead of flying over them, hugging the side all the way round, sometimes the tips of the rotor blades would be just a few feet away from them. TC said he had to admit that those navy pilots knew their stuff. He also said that he was very much on edge, until he saw the crewman sitting in the doorway smiling. He was telling the pilot about the look on the faces of the marines. To quote TC, "Up the navy."

TC's last posting on the Chinese border was at the last railway station in Hong Kong called 'Lo Wu'. The train would arrive and everyone on board would have to have their papers checked, before being allowed to continue across the bridge over the Shenzhen River into Communist South China and the same, when the trains returned. The marine's job was to make sure that no illegal immigrants entered Hong Kong, as there appeared to be thousands of people in China trying to escape. If they were caught by the guards on the Chinese side, they could be shot. To TC, it was reminiscent of the East-West Berlin 39th parallel era.

The last few weeks of his Hong Kong tour, TC was based back in Sek Kong camp and every night, he and his mates would go up the road to the local village and go from bar to bar. The lads from the Royal Artillery barracks across the airstrip would join them and they thoroughly enjoyed each others company and had many a laugh. The bar girls were great fun but as they lived above the bars and their accommodation and food were part of their wages arrangements, they relied on tips. They were very strictly monitored and were not allowed any 'close contact' with the customers. Hugs and kisses were ok, so was dancing but anything more than that and they would be dismissed. This also applied to having affairs outside, even when not working.

On TC's last night in Hong Kong, the female owner of Lily's Bar threw a party for the departing marines. She laid on a massive spread, tables and chairs for the lads and the girls waited on them hand and foot. It was a fabulous evening and the girls were very tearful when TC and the lads left. It was about 0100hrs the usual time that the red caps (Royal Military Police) patrolled the bars, chucking out all service personnel but on this particular evening, as the lads had more than one run in with the RMPs during their deployment, so when they left, TC

TC top of the Peak, Victoria harbour in background Hong Kong.

Hong Kong Junk in full sail, Victoria Harbour.

The bridge at Lo Wu Station Chinese Border.

Chinese guards, yu picture me I picture yu.

British side of Lo Wu station Chinese Border.

HMS Fearless assault ship, helicopters and landing craft on board.

Tasty sea food stall, one of many in Hong Kong.

Water Taxis juggling for parking spaces.

Nathan Road at night in Hong Kong.

Slightly better picture of Sek Kong camp, Hong Kong.

and the lads commandeered their landrovers by sitting in and on them and refusing to get off until they were taken back to camp. They managed to get fourteen marines in and on one of the landrovers. The guys from the Royal Artillery thought this was hilarious to watch and after many requests from the RMPs to get off (to which they all refused again), they were driven very carefully and very slowly, back to camp.

The driver could not actually see where he was going, so the lads were shouting directions to him. TC admitted that at the time, the RMPs were not impressed but back safely at camp, they all shook hands and the RMPs saw the funny side of things. They wished TC and the lads 'good luck' and hoped that they would not return.

TC had been told that while he was up country, two marine drivers had been pulled by the RMPs and reported for speeding. Later the same evening, one of these drivers had been picked on by the same two RMPs, who had been responsible for reporting him. They were now part of the team that were clearing the bars and when this particular marine had an altercation with them, two more RMPs decided to get involved and the result was a punch-up in the street between the five of them.

It ended with the marine being arrested and put in the cells for the night. The following day, he was brought before his own Commanding Officer for punishment. The four RMPs were there as witnesses. All four were showing injuries consistent with being involved in a fight. One had a broken nose the others had cut lips, black eyes, and multicoloured bruising. When the Warrant Officer from the RMPs had finished his evidence as to what had happened; the CO said, "Let me get this straight. This marine has beaten up all four of your lads, causing injuries as shown, with no injuries complained of by this lad. Is that correct?" The WO said "Yes, sir." The CO looked down his nose and said, "Are your staff properly trained in self-defence and restraint procedures?" The WO replied, "Yes of course, sir." The CO managed to keep a straight face and said, "Well, I find it absolutely deplorable that four onto one ends up with all the injuries on the four and none on my lad. All I have to say is get out of my office and in future, leave my lads alone, they are here doing a very difficult and arduous job, so go and pick on someone else."

One job that TC was asked to do before they left, was to drive a Landover and half ton trailer down to the Harbour in Hong Kong and collect some stores from HMS Fearless. TC and his sergeant drove down together and spent most of the day on board having lunch in the PO's (Petty Officers) Mess. They were given a guided tour of the ship and as the American Fleet were also in Harbour on R and R (Rest and Recuperation) from Vietnam, TC went up onto the helipad and was looking across at the American ship that was anchored nearby and watching the sailors working away, when the ship's tannoy burst into life, saying "Now hear this," and just like in all the American films, everyone stopped what they were doing and looked up at the tannoy speakers. Then the announcer said, "Today's ice cream flavour is," (big pause) "stand by, stand by, STRAWBERRY." The sailors all started jumping up and down and cheering, like children. TC could not believe his eyes and was of the opinion that they must all have daily bets on this and everything else. God bless them.

Ten minutes later, while TC and some Petty Officers were still laughing and joking about the Yanks, another message came over the tannoy. TC said, "What is it this time, is it tomorrow's dinner menu?" It was actually about their shore leave in the afternoon and evening. Basically, it was a warning telling them that when they go ashore on the Liberty boat, they will find that there are British Royal Marine Commandos in town. They will not insult them, try to fight them, or try to out drink them. Should anyone attempt any of these, 'they will lose'.

With this last announcement, TC thought, I have really heard everything now. He could not stop laughing. At this point, some of the Americans looked over at TC and perhaps because he was in full uniform, topped with his precious Green Beret, they saluted him. One of the Petty Officers said to TC that they were showing their respect, so TC did the decent thing and saluted back.

TC's Hong Kong tour was now finished and they were all on ships heading back to Singapore. During the trip, TC could not help reflecting on a few incidents that he would always remember. There was the time that his section challenged the SNCO'S to a game of Volley Ball, as this is the favourite game of the Royal Marines and it was agreed that they would all meet at 0500hrs the next morning on the court and the winners would get lashed up with loads of ale for breakfast, supplied by the losers but if only one person from the team of six failed to turn up in time, the game would be void and the losers would have to pay. Well, all TC's team turned out, including a few extra, who came to watch, even though they were all suffering from mega-hangovers from the previous night but sadly, only three SNCOS appeared, so this cost the SNCO'S Mess for a lot of beers. That was their breakfast that morning.

Another incident that was really funny, concerns TC's mate Paddy, when he rounded up one of the cows that they shared the camp with, led it up the steps and onto the veranda of the SNCO'S accommodation, situated at one end of the Parade Ground. He managed to get the cow into the room, making sure that no one was in. He pushed it onto one of the beds but the bed collapsed, so he shut it in, complete with friendly flies and a few droppings. The SNCOS whose bed it was did not find it very amusing at all. TC never returned to Hong Kong but he said, "I can still remember with admiration, all the friendly local Chinese and the beauty of this breathtaking bunch of Islands".

Back at Sek Kong camp, whilst off duty, TC and a small group of friends decided to lie outside their grot on towels, to get some bronzy time in (sunbathing) and TC took his radio out with them. They were listening to a Chinese quiz show called 'The Rado Show', which was sponsored by Rado Watches. When the host read out questions that may be difficult, the contestant would always ask, "Any clues please?" The next question the host asked was, "What is a polopony?" The girl contestant asked immediately, "Any clues please?" The host replied, "Prince Charles rides one," Still the girl had no idea. The host suddenly realised that the idiot who had written the question, had not split the word and it should have read 'Polo Pony', by now TC and his friends were all in hysterics but the radio station kept fading, due to the weak signal, so someone suggested that a length of D10 Cable should be inserted into the hole at the back for an external aerial.

TC did this and to get height he noticed that there were two overhead wires above them, which were held up by telegraph poles, he assumed they were phone wires and this would give a really good signal. He hurled a coil of D10 up and over the wires. The only problem was that when the D10 contacted the overhead wires, there was a blinding blue and purple flash and a very loud bang. TC's radio went off and all the power to the camp as well. TC said "Oh shit." These were not phone wires but power cables and were not insulated. All they were getting from the radio now, was smoke. It took thirty minutes for everyone to stop laughing but it could have been a lot worse had TC not let go of the D10 cable before it touched the power lines, not only that but TC had a metal ladder beforehand, luckily, it was too short, which is why he threw the cable. TC commented, "That would have been an even bigger laugh." Needless to say, his nice new Panasonic radio was completely burned out.

Malaya / Thai Border

After a leisurely trip back to Singers on board HMS Fearless, TC and his company finally ended up in Dieppe Camp and as usual, spent two days unloading stores, equipment, cleaning and returning everything to the stores, ready for the next deployment that would come their way. This is why they have the reputation for being ready for action at a moments notice, anywhere in the world. Their training never stops. They then had two days off, so were able to spend time round the swimming pool at the Britannia Club in Beach Road, run by the NAAFI and situated opposite the Raffles Hotel.

Two weeks went by with training on camp, physical and range work. Every morning they would parade at company lines and the troop sergeant would hand out a Paludrine tablet to each one of them. They had to consume them immediately, as the sergeant kept a book to say that they had all taken the tablets. Paludrine are very small anti-malaria pills and come in tins of five hundred. When the marines went up country to Malaya, they had to take two tablets each day. These pills were dreadful to take and if you tried to take one without water, it would get stuck in the back of the throat and was really bitter.

TC managed to secure a tin of five hundred for himself and one morning, for a laugh, he turned up for parade with his own tin. As the sergeant came to him, TC held out his tin and said "I'm sorry sarge but these are useless, they don't work." The whole troop was looking at TC in surprise and the sergeant said, "What makes you say that?" TC replied, "I've been throwing them at the mosquitoes all night and haven't managed to hit any." Everyone was laughing, including the sergeant, the troop officer and TC himself, even when he was told to get out front and give forty. That meant forty press-ups, while the whole troop counted. TC was not embarrassed at all.

While on guard duty at Dieppe Barracks, the lads used one of the upstairs rooms of the accommodation block nearest the guard room. This room was designated for the sentries to get some sleep for a couple of hours between their patrols during the night. They would be woken by the existing patrol when it was time to take over.

TC was on duty, finished his stint patrolling and had managed to get two hours sleep in the duty room. He was woken at 0600hrs by the last patrol and went to the heads down the corridor, to shower and change into clean uniform ready for the day's duty, which would begin at 0730hrs. All he was wearing was a towel wrapped round himself, flip-flops, and was carrying his wash bag.

In the washroom, he hung his towel on a hook and began shaving in front of one of the basins. He was aware of someone in the showers but at that point, paid no attention. Suddenly the person came out of the showers and to TC's shock-horror, he discovered it was a girl, completely naked. She was towelling herself dry, standing in front of a mirror.

She glanced at TC, gave him a big smile and said, "Good morning," Stunned, he replied the same and tried to look as though he wasn't bothered. The situation got more bizarre when once dry she stood at a basin cleaning her teeth and putting on her make-up, standing very near to TC, still totally naked. TC thought, obviously she spent the night in one of the rooms as somebody's guest. While still shaving, he cut himself three times.

They packed again for exercise, up to Kelentan, Malaya, about 40 miles south of the border with Thailand. Some of the jungle was very hard going and extremely dense. Late in the afternoon, as the light was fading fast, they stopped and camped for the night. TC could not be bothered to make a stretcher-bed, so after making a brew and some food, he found a flat space on the jungle floor, cleared all the dead, rotting leaves away (this is a favourite hiding-place for leeches and small black scorpions) and cut down a few large leaves. He placed the leaves on the ground then opened his shelter top, which is a waterproof sheet about six feet by four feet. He would lie on this but not all night because he had to do a spell of guard duty. TC took off his wet clothes, donned his zoot suit and lay down on the makeshift bed.

There was a large hole in the jungle canopy above him and he was looking up at the clear sky, which was dotted with bright, twinkling stars. He found it absolutely fascinating and was fully relaxed, listening to the night-time jungle noises. He was lying on his back, using his pack as a pillow, when suddenly something cold and wet landed on his chest. He reckoned it must have weighed about one kilogram, it had not crawled on, it just landed – thump. TC could not see what it was because it was so dark and although he had a small torch in his pack, he could not move to get it. He said, "I actually stopped breathing and could hear my heart pounding." He thought that everyone must be able to hear it and kept thinking, what the hell is this? It was very cold and clammy, then, as fast as it landed, it was gone.

The next morning, TC found out from one of the 'old sweats', who had been there before, that it must have been a bull-frog. The following night, while camped up, TC had his spell of sentry duty and then got his head down for a few hours of sleep, lying again, on the jungle floor. The bullfrog incident surely could not happen twice in two nights, however, just before first light,

TC's friendly Bull Frog having Mouse for lunch.

TC's Encounter with this highly venomous creature.

Typical secondary ulu, Malaysia.

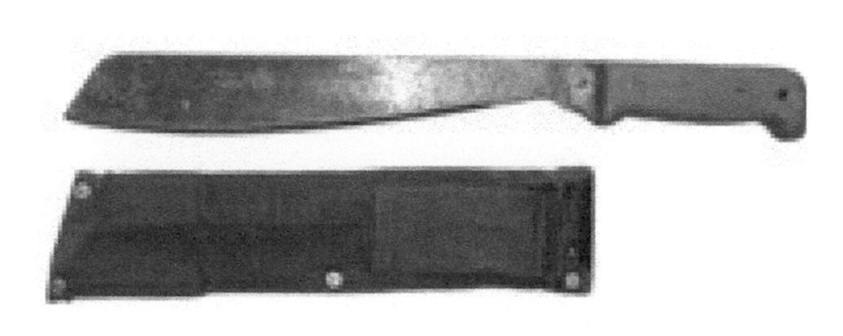

British Army issue Golok and sheath.

Soldier Ant, half inch long and they bite like hell.

TC was woken by unusual warmth. He opened his eyes to see a small fire about two feet from his head. He came to, with a start and seeing George Turner standing there, said, "What the fuck are you doing?" George said, "Look at this motherfucker." TC sat up and as the flames died down, he saw there was a very large scorpion lying there. It was very black and very dead. George said, "I was watching it for a while and it was heading straight for you, so I sprayed it with lighter fuel and torched it."

Later on in daylight, the navy photographer wanted to take a picture of it. He happened to have a pint beer mug with him, which he used to drink his tea from, so he put the scorpion head first in the mug to give it some kind of size comparison. Its tail was hooked over the lip of the glass. It was the biggest scorpion that anyone had ever encountered.

Not long after that, a small German film team joined them. They were making a documentary on jungle warfare and they spent most of the day filming the marines on the move and setting up camp for the night. When the lads set up camp, they showed them how they made a perimeter wire around the exterior of their camp, using vines tied from tree to tree, so that no one strayed outside the camp, getting disorientated or lost.

Just before the daylight faded, they asked the film team if any one wanted to go to the toilet, because then was the right time. Once it was dark, no one could move outside the perimeter wire. Otto wanted to take a shit, so he was given a shovel and told to bury his waste afterwards, as nothing must be left behind. He was told to be sure that he did, otherwise 'Soldier Ants' would carry it off. He found this quite amusing but was assured that this was true and he must go outside the perimeter to do this. So off he went, followed by TC with his shovel. Although close by, he did not see or hear TC at all. Then he stopped, had a look around and thinking he was alone, dropped his trousers and squatted down to do his business. TC pushed his shovel under the rear of him, collected his droppings and quickly withdrew his shovel, then slid back into the undergrowth.

Otto stood up, looked round with his shovel in his hands, ready to bury his business and when he saw that there was nothing there, he dropped his trousers again and checked himself. Not finding anything, he quickly made his way back into camp and couldn't wait to tell all his team what had happened. They all fell about laughing, as they had been told what TC was doing. When Otto left camp, he called TC a few names in German but they did not appear to be derogatory, as he was patting TC on the back at the same time.

Late in the afternoon, they came under fire from the border but as they only had blank ammo with them, they were unable to return fire. Fortunately, no one was hit and they had to depart the area rapidly. The following day, they were airlifted by Wessex onto the 'Rusty B' (mother), where all the information was handed over and disseminated. They stayed on board for two days, then they were supplied with live ammunition and flown back into the Ulu for a search and destroy operation. TC thought that signals must have been going backwards and forwards from the ship to Singapore and the UK.

They were put down in a clearing, which had a small road running through the middle of it. The helicopters were landing on this road, much to the surprise of the locals. Once on the ground, they had a briefing from a Gurkha officer, who told them that there was a bandit camp about four miles north of their position. These bandits were apparently leftover remnants from the 'Malay Emergency', which concluded in late 1966. The marines' mission was to take out the camp and destroy it, arrest and detain any insurgents within.

They moved off with a small group of Gurkhas in front, towards a place called Banggul Binjal, which was a Kampong (wooden huts on stilts). Late afternoon the following day, they arrived close to the target, where they set up three ambush positions, surrounding two sides of this camp and they lay there all night observing movements. Unfortunately, from where TC was positioned, he could not see very much but he knew they were going to hit this camp at first light. The signal would be a green flare fired over the camp.

He had made a decision not to move his position until just before first light and to remain where he was for the night, as discipline told him not to move, in case he was seen and compromise the whole operation, causing unnecessary casualties. While he was lying there, he could not see his oppo (mate) either left or right and he was hoping that he was not too far back or too far forward and risk being shot by his own men - 'blue on blue', as it is called. He said that his mouth was really dry but he could not risk going for his water bottle, he must literally make no movement.

TC was wondering what it would be like in the morning, when they went in. He suddenly heard a thumping noise near him, it seemed extremely loud and wondered if it was coming from one of his oppos nearby. He thought, sod it, this is going to draw attention to my position. He looked at his watch, it was only 2330hrs, and they had been laying there for hours, with hours to go yet. TC was startled to realise that the thumping he could hear was coming from himself, it was actually his heart racing and he knew he had to calm down.

The sweat was running down the side of his face and in his eyes, it stung and he wanted to rub his eyes and get a drink of water, he also wanted to take a piss but could not allow himself to move. He could not hear any movement from anyone else and as he was soaked through with sweat from the day's march, he had to pee in his pants. It was a very strange and uncomfortable feeling, as the last time he did this, he was one year old. Well, he thought, at least that will keep the creepy crawlies and animals away.

He so wanted to get up and stretch his arms and legs and by now, he was very sleepy, his eyes were like lead and sore from sweat and straining to see but now he had stopped sweating and he was beginning to get very cold. TC couldn't wait to see the green flare go up. He knew that the minute he heard the noise, he would be on the move. His head was really heavy now, his rifle seemed to weigh a ton and he felt that if he just rested his head, he would nod off instantly but he also knew that he dared not. He checked his watch again the time was now 0300 hrs, not long to go.

He heard his oppo to his left move slightly, so he had a good idea where he was, just behind him and close by. He was able to make out some shapes of the kampongs, as the light was changing. TC said that he had been longing to get up, as his shoulders, arms, back and legs were getting stiff and very cold. He couldn't wait for sun up.

A short while after there was movement in the camp. A man, dressed in a sarong, with a rifle slung over his shoulder, came from behind one of the huts and went into a small shed, which TC assumed was the outhouse (toilet), about seventy-five yards in front of him. TC got a nudge from his oppos left and right, he could just about see them and he could hear some movements in the foliage around him, as people could probably see what he had seen. At this moment, he was up tight to his rifle and gently clicked the safety catch off. As he did this, he could hear a few more safety's being taken off. They were all ready. What seemed like forever, maybe just a few minutes passed, then with a loud bang, whoosh and pop, the green flare burst over the camp and all hell broke loose.

The GPMG to his right roared into life, as did all of them. At this point, TC could not see a target, so he put a round in the top of the wooden toilet, as he knew there was an armed person inside, thinking that he would run out and give up or try to take a shot and was prepared to take him out with a well-aimed shot but he never got the chance, because the wooden structure practically disintegrated from the amount of lead passing through it, mainly from the GPMGs.

TC had not realised that many lads were firing at the same target, then there was a lot of shouting and some of the bandits came running out with their weapons firing in all directions. As he sighted one bandit, he was about to squeeze one off, when his oppo to the left fired several rapid shots and one of the red hot cylinders ejected from his SLR hit TC on the left of his jawbone and lodged between his shirt collar and his neck. It had cut his jaw and burned his neck. He never got a shot off and dropping his gun, frantically clawed the hot cylinder from his neck. He said that it was bloody painful.

By now, they were up on their feet and moving in. TC saw some bodies lying in the dirt, so they took the weapons away and started clearing the huts one by one. One of the bandits was hiding behind the huts and as TC spotted him, he stood up and was holding a rifle. TC didn't give him a chance to shoot he quickly fired off three or four shots from the hip, as he had no need to take a well-aimed shot because the bandit was only ten metres from him. One of the rounds hit the bandit's rifle, it broke up into pieces and the man went down like a sack of potatoes. TC

Rapid deployment from Wessex dropped into clearing, edge of village.

Knee deep in paddy fields or progress through secondary Jungle?

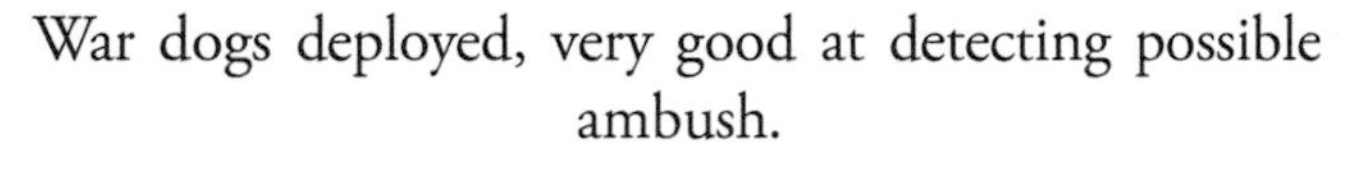

War dogs deployed, very good at detecting possible ambush.

Dogs never get involved in the fire fight.

Kampong Banggul Binjal after the clash.

Same village, at the north end, basic shacks.

The fire team, no matter what the occasion, there's always time for a group photo, taken the day before the attack.

TC and co, the aftermath, waiting for their Wessex airlift out.

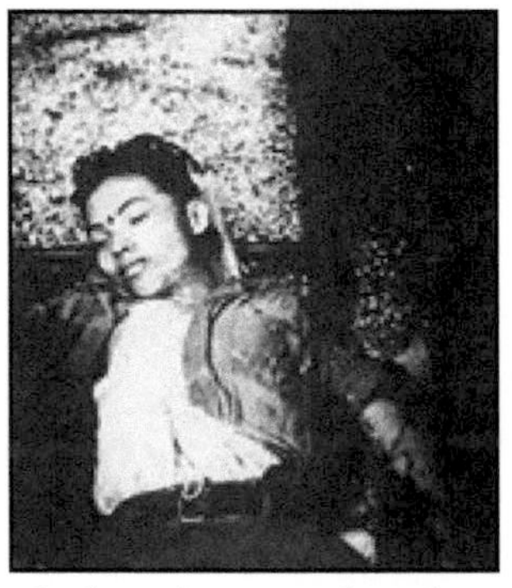

Sad end to one bandit.

One dead, one surrendered.

Meet Horace! 8 inches leg to leg.

was quite taken aback and when he went to check and remove the remains of the rifle, he was surprised to see that it could not be fired again, for it was well and truly mullered. He had an even greater shock, when he saw, after he counted, that there were seventeen bullet holes in the man. The Gurkhas also had him as a target.

There were women and children in some of the huts and they were told to stay there temporarily. Five of the insurgents tried to escape from the North end of the camp towards the Thai border but ran straight into a band of Gurkhas, who had been put there as a cut-off group.

The skirmish lasted about twenty minutes, with no casualties on the marines' side. There were seven insurgents dead and eleven arrested. The Navy photographer had the job of photographing the bodies and the weapons. The camp was then searched for more weapons, of which plenty were found. The women and children were escorted over the border into Thailand and the camp was destroyed. All the weapons were placed in a pit, with plastic explosives on top, covered with earth and blown up.

They eventually moved over to the other side of the camp, where they got some brew going and food, which was very welcome. After this, they walked to another clearing and waited for their air taxi (Wessex) to take them back to mother (HMS Bulwark). TC's neck and cheekbone were hurting, so back on board it was off with his shitty, smelly clothing, a lovely hot shower, clean gear and a visit to the sickbay. His jaw had swollen quite badly and was cut, plus he had a big burn on his neck. Jock thought it was funny but did say sorry and bought TC a beer. 'Thanks a lot Jock.'

Two days on board ship and they were back to Singers again. After a while, TC was put on the JNCO's (Junior Non-Commissioned Officer's) Cadre, held at Nee Soon Barracks. The accommodation was a large wooden hut with no proper windows, only openings with flaps held open on a cord.

Whilst taking a patrol through a rubber plantation, during his JNCO's course and walking through a never-ending avenue of trees, which were planted at equal distances from each other forming a grid. TC saw that all the trees had a 'v' cut into them, with a small cup attached at the lower end of the 'v', to catch the white, sticky, liquid called latex.

As he checked his map and moved off down between the rows, he was looking as far ahead as he could, not knowing if the training team had laid on a surprise attack or ambush. He was concentrating so hard on the distance, that he had not noticed that he had almost walked into a massive spider's web, less than two feet in front of his face. The web stretched from tree to tree but worse than this, right in the middle and level with TC's face, was the biggest, ugliest, dark brown and black spider that he had ever seen. He described it as being the size of a dinner plate, with really long, spindly legs.

TC said that he froze in his tracks. He then signalled to the man behind him and pointed to the spider. He saw that the look on the other man's face showed exactly what he had been thinking. With this, they moved swiftly into the next avenue of trees, to bypass 'Horace', without disturbing him. When TC looked back, he noticed that everyone of the patrol, as they passed the spider, were mouthing something like 'fucking hell'! (Like himself).

This test was to train one to become a Corporal. TC passed this course and was made up to Lance Corporal with immediate effect. He now had one stripe and some responsibilities that went with it, for example, gun controller in charge of the Gun Group (GPMG), TC now had to make out guard duty rosters, acting as Corporal, if he were injured and basically second in command of the section. During the rest of his time, he took part in many exercises, mostly in Malaya but they also went to Kuching, Sarawak and Brunei. While they were in Kuching, they had a base camp in the jungle and worked from there for a week. They had a nine-man tent, which had a metal frame, Navy camp beds and even a six-foot table in the middle, plus some folding chairs. Luxury!

TC said that it was all very comfortable, although on one overnight patrol, when they had to bed down in the jungle, his mate Jimmy decided to cut some bamboo canes to make a stretcher-bed. The bamboo thickets are green and normally about one to two inches in diameter with foliage at the top. They are not easy to cut down, plus what he didn't remember was that sometimes at the top, among the foliage, were 'red ants nests'. Yes – as he started to hack away at the bamboo, a swarm of ants showered down right on top of him.

TC said, "I didn't know that Jimmy was good at Irish dancing at high speed, not only that but to completely undress while dancing the jig, takes some doing. I suppose we could have helped him but it was more interesting to watch his fantastic sideshow." As TC was recounting this story, he felt that he should also mention the unforgettable actions of Jimmy, when he managed to capture a large, green Praying Mantis. He tied a piece of string to one of its legs and took it everywhere with him, He attached the other end of the string to the epaulette on his shirt and whilst on the move, this creature, TC said that he was referring to the Praying Mantis, not Jimmy, would sit on his shoulder or on top of his head.

One day, TC had gone out from the perimeter and dug a large hole to put all their rubbish in and bury it, so as not to leave the area in a mess. The hole was five foot deep and when he climbed out, to his astonishment, he came face to face with a bloody big cobra snake, which reared up and opened its head and neck like it was about to strike. The snake was only four feet away from TC and it was staring straight at him. At this point, TC slowly raised his shovel and smacked the snake across the head with it, which sent it flying. He followed up with another whack and this time, it was dead. TC picked up the snake, by the tail and chuffed with his kill, carried it back to camp to show it off. As he approached the tent, he could hear the lads inside playing cards, laughing and joking. When he got to the tent opening, he could not resist the

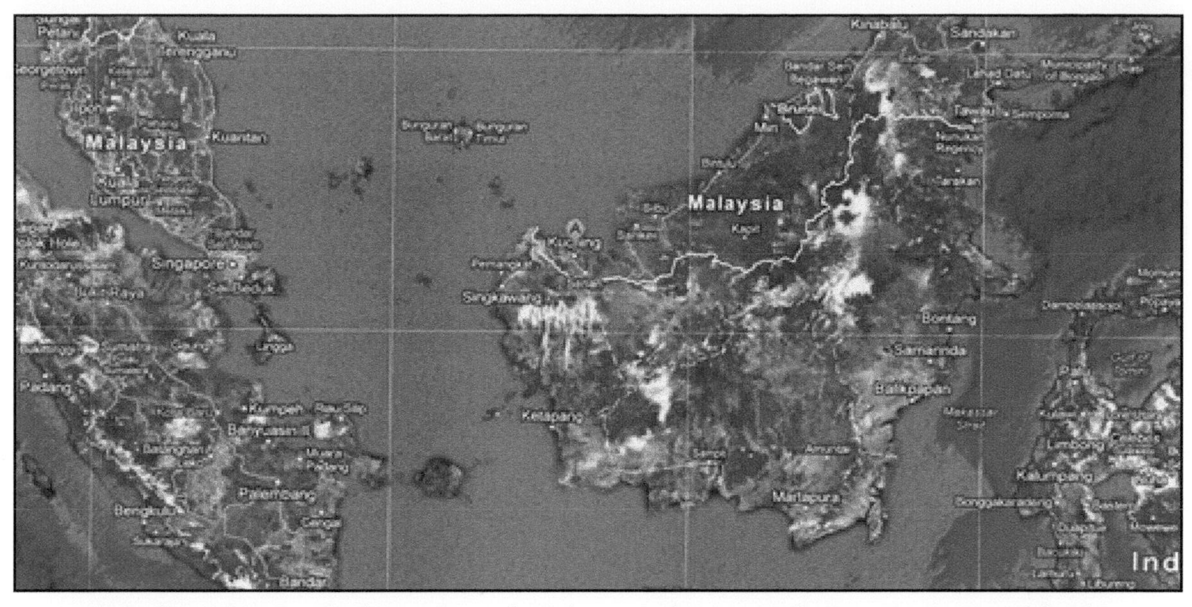

Map of Kuching, which is part of Malaysia where British Forces were involved in insurgency 1966.

Jimmy's little mate, the Praying Mantis.

Malaysian cobra ready for the attack; it wasn't as quick as TC's shovel!

Fairbairn Sykes Commando Dagger.

No need to be smelly and crabby just because you're in the Ulu. TC and team.

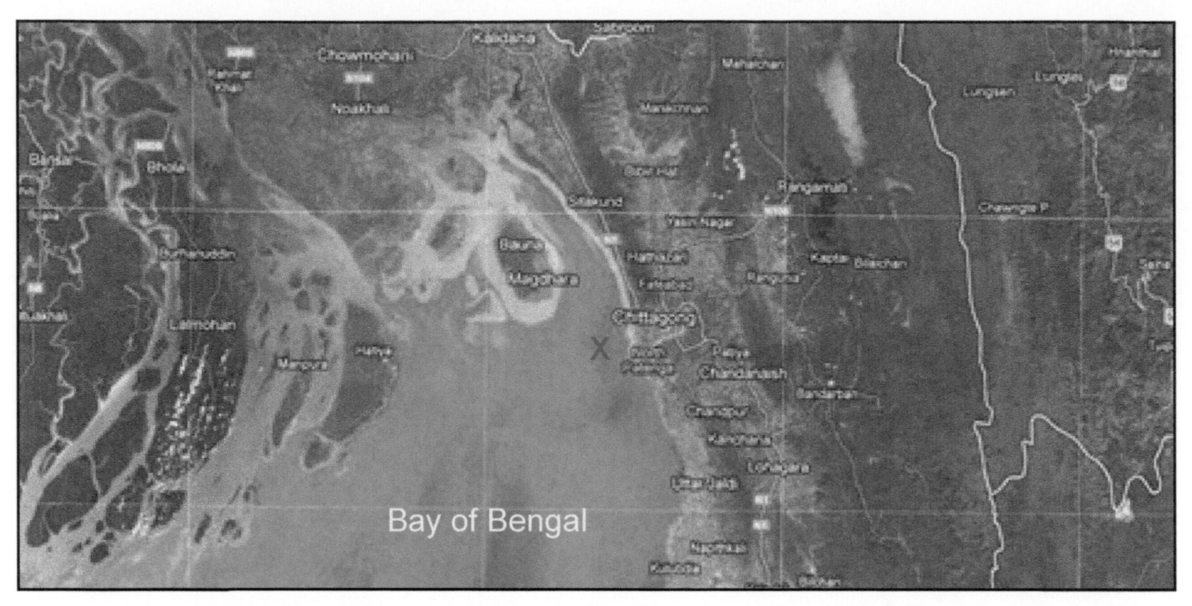

Operation Burlap flood disaster, caused by Bhola cyclone which killed approx 500.000.

River estuary Chittagong, showing South Patenga, now an International airport.

RFA Sir Galahad, sadly now an official war grave in the Falkland's.

Assault Life Jacket and Jacket Inflated.

temptation and threw the cobra in and onto the table. TC said that all he could hear was a loud commotion of chairs being thrown back against the walls of the tent. Then he heard his name shouted out followed by "You bastard!" He said that he had never seen anyone leave a tent so fast. It was quite hilarious.

Three days later, they were on a long patrol and TC was suffering from bad stomach pains. Several of the other lads had the same problems, possibly from contaminated water, which does happen occasionally. He got through the day but during the night, it got worse with vomiting and the runs (shits). Nothing could be done about it until the morning and as soon as it became light, they got on the radio and a Wessex Helicopter arrived overhead. It was unable to land, so a harness on a cable was lowered down through the jungle canopy and TC was airlifted (casevacked) out, along with his back pack and flown out to the ship.

Once on board, he was taken to the sickbay, where a medic gave him a cup of Liquid Paraffin to drink. TC commented "My God, it was disgusting but it did the trick." A bit later, on his mess deck, his pack arrived and he noticed that his black Commando Dagger was missing from where it had been attached to the outside of his pack. To quote TC, "I was really pissed off because it was a genuine Fairbairn Sykes Fighting knife. It had either fallen off during the air lift or, again quoting TC, "Some thieving matelot had it away." He never did find it.

Back in Singers, two weeks went by and they were off again, this time it was to India, 'Operation Burlap'. The marines' task was to provide humanitarian aid to flood victims. They went to Chittagong, Bay of Bengal, on board RFA Sir Galahad. During deployment at Chittagong, they were to be flown into the airstrip at South Patenga, so they had to go to the ship's stores to draw Assault Life Jackets but Taff, who had the top bunk above TC, had spent most of his time sleeping in his pit, other than going to the galley for scran. He asked if one of the lads would collect a jacket for him. Now because Taff had the top bunk and lying down, the deck-head (ceiling) was just above his head. Also overhead were pipes carrying fuel oil and Avgas, plus air ducting for the ventilation via punkah louvres (air jets). He chose this bunk, so that no one would have to climb over him and as it was always hot in the mess deck, he had the fresh air punkah louvres blowing cool air on him.

He was told to get up and collect his own life jacket. They also had to collect weapons, which is why he had to go himself, to sign for them. He grudgingly did this but on his return, while everyone else were checking their weapons, Taff climbed back onto his pit, stuck his pillow behind his head and nodded off once more.

TC could not help himself, when he saw the pull-cord on the life-jacket that Taff was wearing, dangling down the side of him and being dared by the others, he pulled it. The compressed air bottle emptied out into the jacket, which inflated instantly and before Taff realised what was happening, the part of the jacket behind his head, forced his head up against the air duct pipe, also forcing his face and nose into the air pipe. He went into panic mode but by the time he had realised what had happened, TC and his mates had left the mess deck rather rapidly to escape his fury. He now had to go back to the stores and collect another life jacket, explaining that he had accidentally caught the pull-cord on the hatchway to the mess deck. He did not speak to them for ages but when the lads kept laughing about it, eventually he joined in, calling them a 'bunch of bastards'. After that, he never lay around on his bunk again and he never put his lifejacket on until they were ready to leave. TC said "Good old Taff."

Their main job in 'Operation Burlap' was to supply food and medical support to the victims. TC spent a few days roughing it at the small airport at South Patenga, helping to guard the food stocks and being part of a protection party. The whole place stunk of human and animal corpses in the heat and the water, all bloated up beyond recognition. The local Army did not want to touch any of these, so it was also, clean up and burial parties, a really shitty job. TC was more than glad to see the last of this operation and return to normality in Singers.

Back on board the RFA Sir Galahad, TC, having cleaned his rifle and returned it to the Armoury, found himself quite bored. Several of his mates were still on the lower mess deck, cleaning their weapons, laughing and joking about different things. TC recalled that this is one of the strangest things they did, laughing and joking about a lot of silliness or taking the piss out of someone, even each other. He said that this is pure camaraderie at its highest.

He felt very mischievous, so he went to his pack, where he had stashed a thunder flash. This is a large flash bang firework, with a striker on the side. One strikes it, throws it and seven seconds later, there is a big bang and a flash, however, TC thought this would be too dangerous to light and drop it in the mess deck through the upper hatchway, so he cut a hole in the side of the thunderflash and emptied out all the charge – or so he thought and instead of using the striker and fuse, which would have taken the seven seconds, he put a very short piece of fuse in the hole, which would have gone off in three seconds.

TC just wanted to see his mates' reactions when it landed on the deck. He thought it would not go off. They would have seen the fuse smoking and recognised it as a thunderflash and would be waiting for the huge bang and flash, which of course, would not happen. TC knew this because he thought he had removed all the contents - whoops! Standing by the hatchway, TC lit the fuse and dropped it in onto the mess deck, just like the dead Cobra in the tent in Kuching. Mayhem broke out, with people shouting "Oh shit" and other phrases but instead of a loud bang, it was a pop with loads of smoke. TC had not removed all the charge completely, there was enough left to burn a large hole in the jumper, which one of the lads threw onto the thunderflash in panic.

Unfortunately, the jumper belonged to the Corporal, who was not amused and spent the next two hours looking for TC, who kept well out of the way. Later, TC went into the mess deck

TC performing a destruction technique on concrete blocks in front of a small audience.

Shot of the flight deck, HMS Bulwark South China Seas.

Chico shoe shine, they make a good job.

TC's repatriation machine from RAF Changi back to Brize Norton, end of his far east tour.

with his hands up, shouting "Surrender." TC said that they all found it very funny and more so the marine, who threw the Corporal's jumper on the thunder flash. Afterwards, he wore the jumper with pride, as it had a massive burn hole in the front.

During his stint in the Far East, TC had been learning Martial Arts as it fascinated him. He took up Tae Kwon Do, which is Korean Military Karate and went to classes three times a week, in the camp at Dieppe Barracks. The instructor was Korean and TC said that he was 'bloody good'.

On Friday nights, he went with three others down town to a local club. This was run by the Chinese and again, the instructor was very good. When he went for his gradings, he had to go to a big sports arena in the town, where clubs from all over the Island had come together for their gradings. There were at least two hundred people there and club by club, they had to perform in front of six senior judges, who would put them through their paces. TC found it embarrassing at times, when going through his routine in front of all the people, watching him closely. On three occasions, he passed a double grading, so he was made 1st. Dan Black Belt in less than two years. Pretty good going.

TC also joined and trained with the local professional wrestling teams, who were all marines at Dieppe and Simbang camps, 40 and 42 Cdo. Once he had learned many holds, throws and mostly falling properly without getting hurt, TC very much enjoyed this sport and with others, went round the Messes at various establishments in Singapore, usually on Friday and Saturday nights, putting on shows.

They were well looked after by their hosts and once the show was over, they were invited to some of the tables for drinks. Occasionally, they put on shows downtown for the locals, who used to get very excited at the display, because they thought it was all very serious. TC did get a few minor injuries but nothing too bad.

Not long after, it was time for TC to be repatriated back to the UK and his next posting, which would be Deal in Kent – back to where he started his career. He was looking forward to this now, going back, not only as a fully-trained marine but as a JNCO, albeit he was only a Lance Corporal but would very soon be made up to a Substantive Corporal, which would give him his second stripe, or tape, as they called it.

The time soon came to say goodbye to all the friends they had made and TC and his wife wondered if they would ever meet them again someday, then it was down to RAF Changi and a VC10 back home to the UK and Brize Norton.

Although it was April and quite mild, having come from the steamy heat of Singapore, TC said that he remembered being 'bloody freezing' and could not move from the fire for days. It took two weeks to get used to the change in climate.

They lived with TC's parents for a short while, then his in-laws. TC knew that although he had ninety days leave, he would be on the move again when the time was up. Then he would report for his next tour of duty at The Depot Deal Royal Marines.

Chapter 7

Return to Depot Deal

During the waiting period before their flight from Changi to the UK, TC and his wife met a Marine Corporal and his wife. This Corporal was from 42 Commando and was also going to be stationed at The Depot Deal. His name was Frank Wilson. TC and Frank met up again on the same day at The Depot Deal and completed their joining routine together, ending up in the Company Sergeant Major's office, HQ Company. They were both assigned to the Provost Staff. At the time, TC was not happy about this assignment but finally decided to go with the flow.

He found the situation quite bizarre, as having gone through the rigours of recruit training and comparing the Provost staff to the 'Gestapo', TC now found himself heavy-handedly dishing it out instead of taking it. Albeit, when they had to bawl out a recruit for the slightest incident, they did have a chuckle afterwards, as the recruits, were bloody terrified, to quote TC.

Now, on Tuesday mornings, TC had to man the gates during the march round the town of Deal and once they had all passed through the gates, they would be locked and the keys returned to the Guardroom. They had duties to perform as Guard Commander, which was a 24hr duty, from 0900hrs to 0900hrs the next day. There was always paperwork, reports to write-up every day, books for this and that and of course, as Guard Commander, it would be TC's task, when that day's duty was over, to go to the mast and raise the Union flag.

This was done at 0800hrs and was quite straightforward. Frank, who had taken the flag down on the preceding day, had rolled it up ready for TC to hoist the next day on parade. TC took the flag to the Mast, hooked it on to the halyard and hoisted it onto the Masthead, ready to pull the halyard and break the Union flag, on the first note of the bugle, when the bugler sounds the fall-in at 0800hrs. TC had marched out from the Guardroom. The RSM and the Adjutant were on parade, also the Colonel, who had arrived by car and was standing on the dais, waiting for the parade to begin. The RSM called the whole parade up to attention did an about turn to face the Adjutant, who was on his horse and handed over the parade to him. The Adjutant then called to the bugler to strike the bell and sound the fall in.

TC was standing to attention, poised like a coiled spring, ready. On the first note from the bugle, he tugged on the halyard, the flag broke open and TC thought thank God, when all of a sudden, about three hundred tiny pieces of paper, (which had been torn up and rolled inside the flag), came fluttering down like confetti. The morning breeze blew all this paper across the parade ground. TC could see all the men on parade shaking, as they tried to control their laughter. The Colonel and the Adjutant said nothing and appeared not to have noticed.

TC was quite relieved, until the Adjutant dismissed the parade and told him to stand fast. TC's first thought was oh bugger. Ten minutes went by and then the RSM asked if TC had rolled up the flag. TC said, "No Sir." The RSM then told him to find out who had and both of them should report to the Adjutant's office. Frank owned up and they both went over to see the Adjutant. They were marched into his office by the RSM. TC thought, this is starting to look serious. They were both very lucky that the Adjutant just gave them a 'bollocking' and told them to stop larking around, as this was a training establishment and that they should be setting an example.

The following week, TC turned the tables on Frank, as it was his turn to roll up the flag. Frank went on parade with it, confident that TC would not dare to put paper inside it. He was quite right but as he broke the flag that morning, he and the bugler were showered with clouds of broken biscuits. TC had used three whole packets. Fortunately, neither the Colonel, the Adjutant, nor the RSM had seen this, as they all had their backs to the mast at that moment. Obviously by now a certain amount of boredom was setting in and they could not help but keep playing tricks on each other.

There was the occasion when TC took over from Frank in the Guardroom. They had four telephones on the desk and just before TC came on duty at 0900hrs to take over, 'this sod' (to quote TC), swapped all the handsets around and put them on different phones. The first phone call that TC received, he picked up the receiver but it was completely silent. This happened again and each time that TC put the receiver back down, he cut the person off.

TC realised what his mate had done and while he was trying to trace the respective receivers to their proper cradles, Frank had tangled all the cables up and another call came in, this person was cut off too. Eventually, TC had it all sorted out, just as another call came through, this time it was the Adjutant. He was very angry and said, "What the bloody hell is going on? I have been cut off twice." TC told him, "I'm sorry Sir; I've only had this one call from you. There's no problem here." TC got away with it but vowed to get his own back on Frank.

The following morning, when Frank came in to relieve TC, the first thing he did was to check that TC had not switched the receivers over. He was killing himself laughing, when TC told him about the Adjutant being cut-off twice. When TC left the Guardroom, he went straight to the JNCO's Club, just round the corner and phoned Frank. When he answered, TC hung

The four musketeers of the Depot Deal before a ceremonial parade TC second from left.

The official opening of Centenary Gate, North Barracks 1961.

Centenary Gate and Guard Room just after closure and demolition 1996.

Band and formation leaving Canada Road.

March along Deal seafront to Jubilee Gates.

Saluting the Mayor, Jubilee gates to Officers Mess.

41CDO Deal, parading with SMGs in preparation for N Ireland deployment.

Rifle practice, Kingsdown ranges Deal.

up. A short while later, he did the same thing again on one of the other phones and hung up again. TC rang again on another line, when Frank answered this time, TC said, "There must be a fault on the other two phones because I couldn't hear you." Frank laughed and said, "What the fuck are you up to?"

TC returned to the Guardroom about half an hour later and when he saw Frank, he burst out laughing. Frank pointed at TC, saying, "You bastard, you're up to something." Just then the Provost Sergeant came in and started chatting to them.

He was looking straight at Frank and said to him, "What have you been up to?" Frank frowned and said, "What's wrong sarge?" To which the Sergeant said, "I suggest you go and look in the mirror" and started laughing. Frank went to the washroom and they heard him shouting TC's name very loudly, "You bastard, I'll get back at you for this."

What TC had done, was, just before Frank had arrived on duty to relieve him, he poured ink from a bottle onto the ink pad and then rubbed the pad around the ear-piece and speaker end of all the handsets, so he had a very black ear and ink on the side of his face and his mouth. TC said that he looked like he had been blowing up the exhaust pipes of cars.

The pranks went on and on. Frank always had packets of chewing gum and once he chewed up a new strip and stuck them on the arm rest of the chair that TC was sitting in, so that it would stick to TC's shirt sleeve or jumper, he also stuck it to the underside of the phone receivers, so that the receiver buttons would stay down. When TC went to answer a call, the phone would still be ringing. It got so bad, that whenever they took over from each other, they would be checking everything they touched.

One day they ended up together on the same duty and during the late morning, Frank went outside to speak to the sentry on the gate and was leaning against the side of the gate. TC crept up behind him and signalled to the sentry to keep quiet, by putting his finger to his lips. Frank was deep in conversation with the sentry and before he knew it, TC snapped a set of handcuffs on his wrist and the other end on the gate. They both fell about laughing, until Frank asked TC where he got the cuffs from. TC said, "From the bottom drawer." Frank immediately stopped laughing and started to worry. He was absolutely horrified, saying that there were no keys for that set and they were being returned, that was why they were in the bottom drawer. He started to panic now, as it was close to lunchtime and people would be passing through the gate from South Barracks, where the officers were. Their married quarters were at the far end of North Barracks, which was where TC and Frank were. To make matters worse, Frank had no head dress on, so he would not be able to salute officers, as TC had handcuffed his right hand to the gate.

TC could now see the Colonel about 200yds away walking toward them. Panic now set in and

TC said to Frank, "Joking aside, where's the key to the bloody cuffs?" Again, Frank replied, "I'm telling the truth, we don't have one." TC then did the honourable thing that anyone would have done under these circumstances, he legged it and left Frank to it.

Later, TC contacted the Provost Sergeant and told him they had to get the maintenance department to come over and cut him loose. Frank told TC that when the Colonel went past him, he stood to attention as best as he could and apologised for not being able to salute him but the Colonel just smiled and said, "Typical Provost Staff, what are you like?", and carried on walking past. They were expecting another audience once again with their friendly Adjutant but it didn't happen.

The finale to getting one over on each other came to a conclusion one morning, when TC was due on duty at 0900hrs. Entering the Guardroom and approaching the doorway from the entrance hall, he saw two lads in combat uniform, standing against the far wall of the Guardroom, being very quiet and drinking a cup tea. There was no sign of Frank, the Guard Commander and as TC walked into the room, for a split second, he noticed the look on the faces of the two by the wall, signifying that something was not quite right.

Just as TC walked through the doorway, a hand gun was pushed to the right side of his head. Momentarily, there was a blur and some movement then Frank was lying on the floor gasping for breath. The two lads by the wall were horrified, one of them said, "Jesus Christ TC, you almost killed him."

TC looked down and noticed that he was now holding the gun in his left hand by the muzzle. It was a Smith and Wesson revolver. They helped Frank up onto his feet and took him over to the sick bay. Fortunately, he was all right, with just a very sore throat and loss of voice for a few days but what the hell happened? Apparently, as Frank stepped forward from behind the door, he was holding the revolver in his right hand, his intention was to surprise or 'scare the shit' out of TC but this went wrong as Frank had no idea that TC was a 1st Dan Black Belt in Tae Kwon Do and his reaction was so fast that he grabbed the muzzle of the pistol with his left hand, pulling Frank off balance, TC had struck him across the throat with his right elbow. All this happened so fast, as a result of instant reaction. Had the weapon gone off when Frank was off balance, the shot would have hit the wall to TC's left, until TC saw Frank on the floor, he had no idea that he was responsible and at that point, TC realised that he could have accidentally killed his friend.

The gun had been left in the Guardroom over night for safekeeping by the Royal Marines Combat Demonstration Team. Although the gun was real, it had been deactivated and was incapable of being fired. After this, they decided not to play any more pranks, as this last one could have ended up being very nasty.

They did not spend all their time playing around. They had some very arduous duties to perform. They had to go to various meetings, normally with the Adjutant, when, for example, there were VIP visitors due at the Depot. Their main task was the security of the barracks and being available every two weeks, when Mummy and Daddy came down to see their son's pass-out day, ready to go to the next stage of training at CTCRM Lympstone.

A very rare case that TC had to deal with was when an adult recruit was reported to him by a junior marine, for threats of assault to obtain money. This recruit was trying to take money off the juniors. It was alleged, that on one occasion, he threatened the lad with a bayonet and another one had a dart thrown in his foot. An identity parade was held, the culprit was arrested and put in the cells. The end result, was that this adult recruit was found guilty and taken to the Navy Detention Quarters, Portsmouth for 90 days and then thrown out of the Corps. Although the Royal Marines have to be tough and hard, they don't accept thuggery in any form. TC commented that a sergeant he knew in 40 Commando was a drill instructor at DQs, Portsmouth and 90 days in there would have been hell, especially as he was going to be thrown out at the end.

After five months on the Provost Staff, TC was asked if he would be interested in joining the recruit training team at Deal as a GD (General Duty) Instructor. This he did and thoroughly enjoyed his time with the team, teaching Weapons, Fieldcraft, and Physical Training. At the end of their training at Deal, TC would escort the whole squad on to the train at Deal Station, changing at Waterloo, London and then onto Exeter, where, just as he had done, he handed them over to the new training team, waiting on the platform, some of which TC knew and then they would be taken to their new home at CTCRM Lympstone, Devon.

TC's part was now complete and he used to spend the weekend at Lympstone, before hopping on another train back to Deal, ready to take on another squad of raw recruits. Whilst at Lympstone, TC met many good mates that he knew from his recent posting in the Far East and spent time ashore, catching up on all the gossip. By now, the story of TC's near escape of killing Frank had done the rounds and he had acquired the reputation of being the British Bruce Lee. TC commented "What a joke."

During his posting at Deal, TC learnt to ride horses. The Depot had two, both military chargers and the groom taught him very well. They used to go out riding together and once TC was confident, he was allowed to go out on his own. He frequently used the Adjutant's horse, as it was the better of the two and TC would often spend his free time at the stables, just to help out cleaning and looking after the horses in general. Sometimes the groom and TC would go out on a blanket ride. This is to exercise the horses, as they would be exercised twice a day and by only using a blanket instead of a saddle, this would give the horses backs some relief.

This way of riding was not easy because without a saddle, there are no stirrups and therefore

8oz stick of PE4 plastic explosive.

Mk 7 Anti Tank mine.

Box Anti Personnel Mine.

Hayrick shaped charge for cutting through steel girders or rail tracks.

Beehive shaped charge for punching holes in concrete.

The Claymore mine, stand on its legs or secure to a tree, it's full of high explosive and ball bearings.

The Bangalore Torpedo, designed to connect sections together and push through wire fencing.

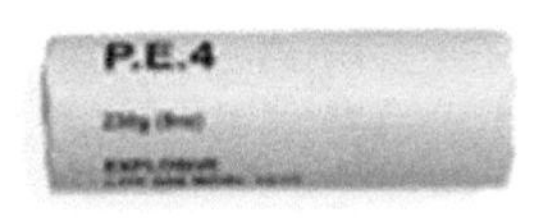

8 oz PE4 Plastic.

Fuse which burns at about 40 seconds per foot.

Fuse instantaneous, this burns at 1000 feet per second.

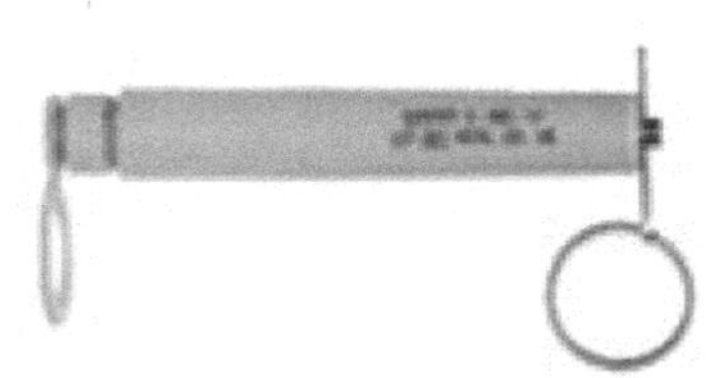

Fuse igniter manual.

Electric fuse igniters.

This is a very small selection of what TC had to become expert in during his AE course.

you had to grip the horse with your legs, although you still had the horse's head harness, a snaffle and reins for a certain amount of control.

The next time that TC had to go to CTCRM Lympstone, he got talking to an old friend, Paul Radcliffe, who was an Assault Engineer (AE's), TC's world, was weapons and shooting, any time any where any weather but hey, this guy plays with explosives. TC thought oh yes, I hadn't thought of that. So once, he had been shown around the AE's Training School at Lympstone, he was utterly sold. It was all about the lifting and laying of mines, demolitions, booby traps and many other skills, water supply being a very essential commodity for the Commando units.

Back at the Depot, TC applied via his CSM (Company Sergeant Major) and off went his paperwork. Two weeks later, he received a positive reply and he would be on the next available course. TC commented that this was one of the best courses he had been on. All the instructors were friendly and in general, to quote TC, "A bloody good laugh." Many hours were spent in the classroom but it was still fun and was really great when they went outside for practicals, most of the time on different locations. At the end of the course, there were the inevitable exams, written, oral and identification of various components. TC was absolutely thrilled, to have passed as Superior.

Back at Deal again, TC was approaching the end of his two-year posting and his paperwork came through. This time, he was able to choose his next posting. First second and third preferences. TC's first choice would have been Singers again but unfortunately, the British had withdrawn from the Island, TC thought to himself, where can I get some bronzy time? Ah, there it is, Malta GC. Yes, he got the posting he wanted.

However, in the meantime he had to carry on with his duties at Deal, as his posting was not immediate. About a week later, his CSM sent for him and asked TC if he would be interested in going on a parachute course for four weeks, as he was the only one who could be spared. Para courses were a limited luxury, even in the marines, unlike the Paras, SAS or SBS where it is a basic part of their training.

TC was off in a couple of weeks and he drove to Abingdon in Oxfordshire, and reported to No.1 Parachute Training Centre. On the course were a few marines and some members of the Navy, Army and Air Force. The marines were in a room on their own, away from the rest. (TC never did find out why). The Flight Sergeant, an RAF Instructor, made sure that he had all the marines on his team. He said that he always chose the marines because he never had any refuse to jump. The one thing that TC was a bit wary about was heights. He was quite happy hanging on a rope, climbing cliffs, ladders or anything of this nature, where he had something to hang onto, that was stable and physically attached to something else but the thought of jumping out of an aircraft in full flight, did concern him a little and of course, the uncertainty of not knowing what it would be like, that first step into nothing.

As usual, the first day opening address was in a classroom, and then they were taken for a run around the site for a bit of physical by their illustrious instructor, who was at least fifty years old. After five minutes, he was unable to keep up. So, he took them behind one of the hangars and out of view of anyone, he sat them all down and had a general chat, a joke, and a laugh. He just loved the Royal Marines. TC said, "He was a great fellow."

Later on, in the first week, after hours and hours of ground training, learning to fall and land properly, jumping off different kinds of apparatus from all different heights. The Fan was the start of it, jumping off 6ft walls onto rubber mats. How to leave the aircraft correctly, from a simulator in the hangar. The Fan, as it was called was 30 ft high and after putting on a harness, which was attached to a cable wrapped round a drum and with fan blades also attached to the end of the drum. One-stepped off the platform and the body weight would spin the drum as you descend. The fan blades would resist the spin, acting as air brakes controlling the speed of the descent.

The highest was the tower at over 70ft. One climbed the steel tower and at the top would be put into a harness again, connected to a cable running up and over a small crane jib. The cable end would be attached to a large piston inside a cylinder full of oil.

As the person jumps off, the body weight pulls the piston through the oil and up the cylinder. This piece of apparatus is called 'The Tower' and it is the last piece of equipment for training, before a live jump.

Having been taught how to prepare and adjust the straps on the parachute, the first two live jumps would be from a barrage balloon attached to the rear of a truck, fitted with a winch. The balloon would only take four jumpers and the Instructor in the cage slung underneath. Once inside the cage, a steel bar would be dropped in place. The parachute static line would be hooked up on a cable on the top of the cage and the winch would be let out and the balloon would go up slowly to 800 ft. The only sound to be heard, would be the wind, whistling through the cables, quite an eerie sound, then the Instructor dropped the safety bar-clank and the stomach did weird somersaults.

One by one the jumpers step out, they can actually hear the ties breaking as they fall. These are strings, which hold together the rigging lines in bunches, when the chute is packed. The chute is automatically opened by the static line, this line remains behind in the balloon. TC commented, "As you fall, there is a tendency for your head to go back, and your feet come up, as though you are going down on your back. This is only for a few seconds, because then there is a sudden jerk when your chute opens and slows you down rapidly. By now, you would have dropped about 200 ft. from the 800 you started with. By the time your chute has opened properly, you only have 40 seconds of flight time before landing." He also remarked, "I have to tell you that the first time you jump, it is harrowing but the minute the chute opens and you

The 70 ft Training tower.

Jumper leaving the tower.

View from the top of tower.

The Balloon jump 800 ft.

Static line drop from C130 1000ft.

Low altitude drop from C130. 1000 ft.

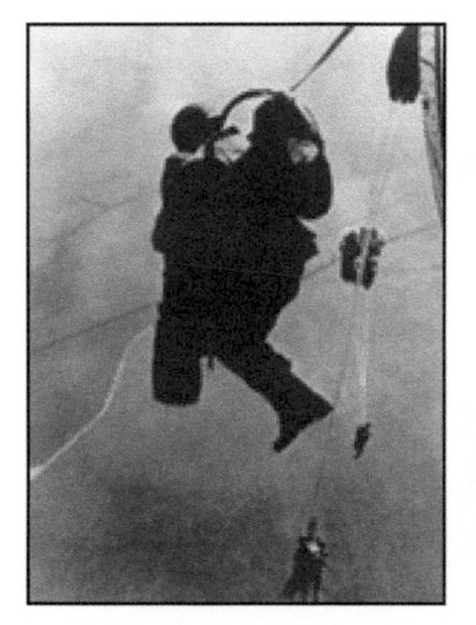

View from the door.

Equipment on line.

Cramped and waiting to jump.

look up at it, wow! What a delightful sensation it is, then back to Earth with a bump."

TC folded up the chute (well, gathered it up), as the proper folding is done by professionals in a hangar, under very strict observation, at every stage of the folding and repacking. It has to be checked and signed off by a supervisor and every chute has its own serial number, so that when you draw your chute from the stores, your name and the serial number of the chute are recorded and you had to sign for it.

Walking off the DZ (Drop Zone), TC was chuffed that he had made it. He took his chute over to the store wagon and was told to draw another one, ready for the next jump. TC thought oh shit, (his favourite words). Well, it had to be done. The course consists of eight jumps before you qualify for your wings, which would be presented to you. To quote TC, "Unless of course, you have a chute malfunction, then you get your wings much earlier."

On one occasion, TC asked the instructor what would happen if his chute didn't open. The instructor replied, with his sick sense of humour, probably from spending too much time in the company of the Royal Marines, "No problem, just take it back to the stores, fill out three copies of the appropriate forms and the person who failed to pack your chute properly, gets a good old-fashioned bollocking, then you draw another chute." Everybody fell about laughing. This old guy had all the answers, due to his long experience.

The following day, with two balloon jumps behind him, TC again went to the stores, this time to draw two chutes. They were going to jump from aircraft. It would be a Hercules 130. Off they went. The DZ was a place called Weston–on–the Green and at 1000 ft, this time. Jumping from the aircraft is totally different from Balloon jumps. For example, when one steps out of the aircraft doorway, the slip stream helps to pull the static line out much faster and the chute opens quicker, thus giving more time in flight, also unlike the balloon, you do not fall like a stone for the first 200 ft.

The course was finally over and TC had loved every moment. Before long, he was winging his way back to Deal, with his well-earned wings. A few weeks went past, by which time, his movement orders came through to join 41 Commando in Malta, so once again he packed up and was off to Brize Norton but this time, not in an RAF VC10 but in an RAF Britannia 4 engine turbo prop. After a few hours, TC arrived at RAF Luqa Malta GC and 41 Commando.

Malta GC 41 Commando

Upon landing at RAF Luqa, Malta, TC was collected by a cheerful sergeant from 41 Cdo, who was from the movement's office and although TC was the only passenger, the sergeant had brought a 4-ton truck to pick him up. TC thought, how much luggage does he think I've got? Certainly no machine guns and bullets at this stage.

TC was dressed in a three piece suit, collar and tie and looked more like a city businessman than a Royal Marine Commando and he knew that he would regret wearing these clothes, as it was midday in Malta and the month of May. It was bloody hot.

The trip took about forty minutes to reach the camp at St. Andrews Barracks, where TC was given the dreaded joining forms again. He had noticed that the camp was very quiet and when he enquired the reason, he was told that the unit was away on exercise somewhere in Sardinia, so apart from TC and a few left behind on rear party, basically, he had the camp to himself.

TC found his accommodation, which was upstairs, one of six rooms, all for JNCOS (Junior Non-Commissioned Officers). They were away on exercise, so he was on his own. He unloaded his luggage and dumped his suit, which was now feeling very uncomfortable. He headed straight for the shower and literally sat in it for twenty minutes. Cold water– bliss.

Feeling much fresher, TC stood outside his room on the veranda. It ran the length of the building and looked across the firing ranges, which sloped down to the edge of the sea and beyond. He remarked, "What a great view."

TC's wife did not accompany him at this point of his posting. She had elected to stay behind in Deal, as she had a good job and both her parents were working on the house, which was bought a few months earlier.

Now he realised that he was very hungry, so went to the galley in search of food, to quote TC, "After all, we men are the great white hunters." While he was in the galley, he met up with a couple of lads from the Royal Marines shooting team. They were there for practice, as the climate is perfect for this sport. They invited TC to come out with them to see the sights, mainly the bars at St.Julians and Paceville.

TC should have begun to get his joining card completed but having found three of the venues that he needed to register with were closed, he went back to his grot and threw the card into his locker, where it stayed for the best part of three weeks.

In one of the bars they visited, TC was introduced to the local wine, called Marsovin. It was cheap at two shillings a bottle, sharp and 'bloody awful' but it took three or four bottles to get used to it, so by then, he could have been drinking water from the drains and he would not have known the difference.

Later they met a Sergeant, who was also part of the team and like them, he was a little worse for wear but they soldiered on until the early hours of the morning. Eventually, they all had to walk back to camp, except the sergeant, who was billeted in the Dolphin Hotel, across St Georges bay from St Andrews, so they had to walk back with him, as he couldn't stand. He was almost incapable of walking. TC wondered what was wrong with his legs, as they kept splaying outwards. Outside his hotel, the doors were locked as it was by now 0230. So they banged on the glass doors and got the attention of the Manager and the Concierge, who were both standing by the desk and waving at them to tell them that they were closed. The lads signalled back pointing at the sergeant to show that he lived there. They eventually came to the door, looked at the sarge and shouted, "No, go away" and that they were closed.

At this stage, TC knew that they had to take drastic action and spotting big brass dolphins as door handles, one on each door, they turned sarge around, with his back to the doors and hooked his arms over the two dolphins, one either side. They hung him there, said goodnight to the unhelpful staff inside and walked away. Nothing more to be done here.

TC remembered walking back to camp, chatting and laughing about poor old sarge and that was all he did remember, because when he woke up, there was a very bright light shining in his eyes. He was lying on his back out of doors. He could make out a large grassy bank to his right, about five feet high and he could hear the roar of occasional vehicles going by. To his left he could see trees and bushes.

He managed to roll over and got up on all fours. His head felt like it did not belong to him and he struggled to get to his feet and scale the bank to see where the hell he was. At the top, there was a road with a couple of large buildings opposite. TC looked up the road, his eyes were now burning and was able to see the small clock tower of the Barracks Guardroom, one hundred yards ahead. He now recognised that the building opposite, was the sick bay and thought, that's lucky. However, he did not go in, as he desperately needed water now. He was so dehydrated that his mouth and tongue were bone dry, like leather. He could not even swallow and his mouth tasted like 'a Nagasaki gravedigger's flip flop', (as the marines say).

TC dragged his way to his grot, showered and drank most of it, dried off and fell onto his pit, the room spinning like a top. He reckons that he must have fallen asleep because when he opened his eyes, it was dark. He got out of bed and needed a pee, so he staggered to the heads and then fell back onto his pit. He said that he literally felt like doggy doo. He did not have a clue, as to what had happened to him or where he had been. TC checked his watch. It was 0200 in the morning? What worried him was, which morning? The next time he woke up it was daylight and the time was 0830.

He was very thirsty and hungry, so he made the effort to get up, shower, and go to the galley for some scran and a big mug of tea, (preferably a bucket full). When he arrived at the galley, he found that it was just closing up. He threw himself on the mercy of the duty chef, explaining that he had been very ill for the past two days and needed food. What a good egg he was, he cooked TC a full English breakfast, with two mugs of tea and several slices of toast.

On his way back to his grot, he saw his two mates again, Tim and Dave from the shooting team and they asked where he had been for the last two days. TC was very surprised that it really was that long and explained what had happened. They laughed as Tim told him that he had walked with him, all the way back and apparently, he had gone up to his grot, which was the last time he had seen him until then.

They later found out that the sergeant was eventually released from the doors of the hotel by the Police, as the hotel staff did not wish to get involved, however, once he was unhooked from the door, the staff were able to open the doors and took him to his room. The staff were not happy with him.

After a couple of days running round the camp trying to register and get his card filled in, TC spent most of his time going down to the Lido, as it was called. It was in St. Georges Bay and there, he met many of the wives, who were married to the lads he would be joining, when they returned. Until then it was swimming and lots of bronzy time. In general, relaxing, sight-seeing on his own and hopping on and off buses. TC swore that, never again would Marsovin pass his lips.

The day before the unit was due back, in the late afternoon, TC was on his way back to camp from the Lido. It was quite obvious where he had been because all he was wearing were his swim shorts, flip flops and a towel, also he was carrying his new radio/tape player, which he had bought from the NAAFI shop. Suddenly, he spotted a tall Colour Sergeant walking towards him, from the direction of the block where his grot was and he was pointing at TC. "Corporal TC, would it be?" he asked. TC answered, "Yes Colours." The Colour Sergeant said, "Right, I have been looking for you for the past three weeks, where the fuck have you been? I can see by the colour of you, you've spent plenty of time at the Lido but you should have reported to me straight away, as you were required to head up a fatigue party every morning, parading at 0800hrs".

TC did apologise to him. It was pointed out that he was his troop Colour Sergeant (his name was Pete Harris). TC did tell him that he had tried to register and walked round camp but all the offices were closed, and then he had been taken ill with food poisoning and had spent the next three days in bed. He accepted this and the next morning TC mustered at 0800hrs with ten marines and two L/Cpls. They just had to go to company lines and make sure all was clean and tidy when the unit would be landing later in the afternoon and they would be required to stand by and assist in the unloading of stores.

When the unit started to arrive back on board, some of the wives and children were there, waiting to see husbands and daddies. The married men were not pressed to get involved in the unloading, so the married men were allowed to go with their families. TC said that on this occasion, fortunately, they did not have to clean the equipment, as this would be done first thing in the morning.

The following morning, they all fell in (paraded) at their respective company lines. TC's was 'G' Coy, (Golf Company) and this would be the first time that he would meet all the company and his section in particular, along with Dave Meadows, the Cpl that he was replacing. He walked TC along the three ranks of marines and L/Cpls, introducing him to them.

The dark sun-tanned colour of his skin must have had an effect on them, as several days later some of them told him that they thought he was a Pakistani. Marines are not racist, by any means. There is a wide variety of colours and creeds within the Corps and all have to pass every tough test, no quarter shown.

Every morning, straight after parading at company lines, it would be a quick change into PT rig and off for a four mile run, out of the camp, up the hill, round the radar station at Madliena and back to camp. This run had to be done in less than thirty minutes. Once back on board and everyone was within the time limit, it would be a quick shower, change into rig of the day and have a short break for tea or coffee. After this, there would be more training, either in the lecture room or outside going through weapon handling, stripping, and assembling and carrying out various drills, like stoppages and malfunctions.

Two or three times a week, they would be on the ranges (TC's favourite place), as the ranges were part of the camp, called HMS Pembroke. These ranges were from 600yds down to point blank, where TC used his skills to hone two of the lads, who were not such a good shot as some of the others, TC wanted them all to be marksmen like himself, so he was able to spend time coaching them all.

TC said that he was very fortunate to have a great bunch of lads, who worked very hard and had many a good laugh along the way to lighten the load. This included the Cpls in the company and he had a good time in the evenings at the JNCO's Club, along with their wives.

Some mornings, TC would take the lads running down to the Lido, where there were a series of floating rafts, about 20 yards out from the end of the jetty. They would run at full speed along the wooden jetty, jump off the end shouting 'Geronimo' and swim to the first floating raft, climb on, run across it, jump off the other side into the water and swim to the next one, which would be 30 yards away then did the same with each raft in turn. There were five of these rafts and were about ten feet square, covered in coconut matting and secured to the bottom of the bay by steel cables. The water depth was approximately 20 feet but very clear and pale blue. Once off the last raft, TC would allow them to have a free swim for about half an hour, before jogging back up to camp, where they would shower and change into rig of the day then get a coffee and an egg or bacon 'banyo'. (Sandwich), before more training.

TC undertook NBC (Nuclear, Biological and Chemical) warfare training, as under NATO, this was part of the marine's responsibilities. The Cold War was still in full swing. NBC requires troops in the field or in the suburbs to wear very uncomfortable protective clothing, with full hood, rubber over-boots, gloves with liners and full-face respirators. The 'Noddy suit', as it was known, was charcoal-impregnated and in addition, they had their battle order on, as well as having to carry personal weapons. While wearing all this kit, they had to perform all the normal duties in the field, digging in as usual and patrolling in the streets of the suburbs, also a 4 mile speed march in the extreme heat, finishing on the ranges and firing onto targets at 100 yds. To quote TC, "Doing all this and with your respirator full of sweat, then trying to shoot at a target, was very difficult. You cannot remove your respirator until the exercise is over and by then you have about 3 pints of sweat in your clothing and boots in particular".

Preceding this practical exercise, there was classroom instruction on the effects of a nuclear and biological blast. Every soldier had to go through this scenario, no matter who or what they were but as TC was nominated NBC rep for 'G' company, he had to do all this several times with different groups, while all the others only had to do it once. This is probably why TC was very fit and trim – all that sweat loss but he tried to make up for it in the evenings by going ashore, usually down to 'The Gut'. The proper name for this area is Strait Street in Valetta and it was probably the busiest street in Malta. There are masses of bars, on both sides and it was certainly Malta's version of Bugis Street in Singapore.

During this era, American warships would visit Malta quite regularly, normally the 6th fleet on R&R from Vietnam, so it was not unusual to see many drunken American Marines or Sailors. After all they had been through it must have been a great relief to be ashore and drown their sorrows.

RAF Britannia in flight, very quiet and comfortable AKA whispering giant.

British soldiers wearing full NBC suits operating the 84mm Carl Gustave Anti Tank weapon, this weapon takes two to operate. The firer and the number two, who is the loader and re-loader.

Rubber Inflatable 10 man Geminis used for beach landings and rapid insertions or silent approach mainly the SBS.

British soldier dressed in full NBC suit, commonly known as Noddy suits, carrying the powerful 7.62mm SLR. TC's comment, British troops won the Falklands war with this weapon, also used in N Ireland and should never have been withdrawn from service, it beats the plastic 5.56 SA80 hands down.

'The Gut' or Strait Street Malta, daytime. At night all these bars are very busy.

One night, TC and his crew were involved in an exercise security testing raid on HMS St. Angelo, Naval Base which is in Valetta harbour. It was a British Naval Base, and the marines were all blacked up and using several RIB Gemini raiding craft. They set off from St. Georges Barracks, which is next to St. Andrews Barracks, home of the Royal Marines. They went out to sea in their raiders, followed the coastline a short while, then steamed straight into the harbour to carry out the raid on RN boats and ships anchored in St. Angelo. All of this caused major panic among the civilian population, as they believed the Island was under attack. Although the Navy was aware of the exercise taking place, someone had forgotten to notify the Maltese Government, so the Maltese Navy were alerted. (Both small inshore boats). Dom Mintoff, the Prime Minister at the time, lodged a serious complaint to the British. It appeared next day on TV and in the newspapers.

After the raid, TC and his crew made their way back to St. Georges Barracks. The small flotilla of Geminis entered the Bay, which is also the Lido. Coming in from the sea, they had to slow down considerably, one behind the other, watching out carefully for the pontoons. As they passed the last pontoon, there were two naked bodies to be seen, lying on the top, a male and a female. The very embarrassed couple laid face down, trying to hide their identities. There was a lot of jeering from the boat crews as they passed by, until suddenly a voice from one of the boats called out, "Good evening Taff". The male, knew he had been recognised, looked up and muttered something like TC's favourite words, "Oh shit".

Once alongside the jetty, they vacated the boats – exercise over. They had to go back to St. Andrews on foot, just a ten minute walk but two of the lads did a short detour and gathered up all the clothes that the lovers had left at the end of the jetty, before swimming out to the pontoon and they took them away. TC was devastated, as he was not part of this 'dastardly deed'.

A few weeks later, they all packed up and were on the move again. This time it was an exercise in Cyprus and they were occupying an old barracks, twenty miles from Famagusta, this was one year before the Turkish invaded it in 1974.

After two days of training, they had the weekend off, so TC, Paddy, Kevin and Simmo Simpson jumped into a taxi and were driven into Famagusta (or as they called it, Fama G.). They spent some time just walking around, then Paddy, who was a Rugby player, bought a Rugby ball and they ended up on the beach for the rest of the day. While on the beach, they met four young ladies, who were nurses from the BMH (British Military Hospital). TC and his mates told the girls, that they were all helicopter pilots of the Royal Marines. They arranged to meet up later that evening at a night club, to which TC and the lads had been given free passes, earlier in the day. Later, they met up again at the club, which turned out to be pretty grim, empty and not very clean. Eventually it got busy and livened up. Paddy was dancing with one of the girls and seemed to be getting on very well but TC and the other two were not interested and quite bored.

They wanted to move on to search out some more bars. Paddy didn't want to leave his lady because he seemed to think that he was in with a good chance. He probably was, until TC went up to him on the dance floor, while Paddy was having a slow smooch and in a loud voice said to him, "We are all going back to the brothel where we were this morning". At this the poor girl, who up to now was in his arms, recoiled in horror and stormed off. Paddy told TC that he had no parents but did see the funny side of it, by punching TC on the chin. They left the club and went round many of the different clubs, until it was 0100hrs, then Paddy decided to play Rugby in the main street, which was almost devoid of traffic. They ran down the middle of the road, passing the ball to each other and rolling around on the ground.

Paddy eventually won the ball and as TC and the others chased after him, he drop-kicked it high and it hit all the coloured strings of lights, which were looped across the road. At this point about six cab drivers who were standing by their vehicles watching and laughing, suddenly stopped being amused, as the shower of glass from the lights started falling on and around them. The lads, being Royal Marines, 'Britain's Finest', carried out the IA (Immediate Action) and ran for it.

Now they had a problem, they could not find a taxi to take them back to camp for the 0800 parade, so they had to walk. They arrived back at 0400hrs to find that the morning parade had been cancelled. They were all shattered from the long trek back and to quote TC, "Thank God, now we can get some serious zeds in, - zzzz."

Later that morning, TC and the lads were required to exercise with the Wessex helicopters, as a new group of pilots (squadron) had taken over. They were using a small, dirt-covered airstrip for this. It was the usual routine, jump in, take off, fly around and land. Get out quickly and do it all over again. TC, Paddy and Simmo all had SMGs, nice and clean and well oiled. After they had completed the last circuit, the three of them decided to walk back to camp taking a short cut across the farmer's well-furrowed fields.

These fields were used for growing melons, although at this time, they were empty of anything except red dirt. As they got halfway across, chatting away, suddenly, one of the helicopters came in fast and low, heading straight towards them. They stopped talking and were watching the Wessex looming in at them, when at the very last moment it banked hard right and the rotor blades missed the ground by a couple of feet. At this point the call went up loud and clear "Fuck", as they all dived to the ground the blades swishing passed just feet away as it went passed, then they got up and started laughing at each other because they were covered in red dirt. It did not help matters as they were wet and sticky from sweat as well. TC was very angry because his SMG was covered in dirt, which had stuck to the oil. His anger only lasted a few seconds, for when Simmo stood up, he was spitting dirt. He had dived head first into the ground and was now absolutely covered in dirt and dust, his big bushy moustache had turned completely red from the earth and he had also lost his SMG as he had to let go of it in the scramble but they soon found it buried in the dirt. Simmo looked so comical, that TC and Paddy could not stop laughing. TC said that he could not believe how close to the ground the chopper pilot came and that it was either a good guess or 'bloody good' flying. To quote TC, "Well, they were all Navy pilots and I would trust them implicitly with my life, in any situation".

Back in Malta again, three weeks went by and the Island became under threat from a terrorist group called 'Black September'. All British installations on the Island were a potential target, so 41Cdo were split into various groups to guard the many installations, such as the hospital at Mtarfa, the Radar Stations, the Airport and Radio Stations.

TC headed his group, who were given RAF Luqa Airport to protect. Luqa was also the civilian airport and was run and operated by the RAF. Along either side of the runway, the Royal Engineers or Sappers had erected sandbag Sangers (gun emplacements) to protect the GPMG gunners, who would engage any hostile aircraft, should it attempt to land. TC's base was about three hundred and sixty yards away and his accommodation was a Nissan hut, overlooking the runway. He had another and his accommodation was a Nissan hut, overlooking the runway. He had another sandbag Sanger built on the roof, occupied by an extra GPMG gunner. They also had to patrol the whole site, day and night, on foot and by Landrover.

At this time, the RAF had Lightning Fighter Aircraft, Shackletons used for photographic reconnaissance and Nimrod AWACS. (Airborne Warning & Control System) These all had to be closely guarded, no one was allowed near any of them without authorisation. ID cards had to be worn and shown. TC and all his crew were carrying live ammunition and their weapons were loaded.

TC recalled that one day he was walking around the Lightning Aircraft, when he was approached by a man wearing a flying suit, but was not wearing an ID card. TC stopped him and asked who he was and why he was not wearing his ID, to which the man said, "I'm dressed in a bloody flying suit, and I am a Flight Lieutenant". TC was not happy about this or the man's attitude, so he told the so called officer that he would not be allowed any further. TC now ended up in an altercation with the officer and told him again that he would not be allowed anywhere near the aircraft unless he produced his ID. The furious officer said to TC "What are you going to do, shoot me?" With this, TC said, "Well, the outcome of your next move, will answer that question". TC then cocked his SMG and pointed it at the man's mid-section.

The officer went pale as he looked at TC's SMG and after a short silence, he said "Fuck you, I'll go and get my fucking pass, you jobs worth, then I will be having you up before the boss and you can kiss your career goodbye, how dare you pull a loaded weapon on me". He turned and stormed away, back to the offices, from whence he came. TC now removed the magazine from the weapon and released the breech block, thus un-cocking the gun, making it safe and then replacing the magazine.

Ten minutes went by and TC was approached by an aircraft engineer. He had seen what happened and he said, "Was he giving you grief?" TC replied, "No, no one gives me grief". The engineer said, "I have to tell you, that guy is a complete obnoxious arsehole". They both laughed and suddenly TC saw the officer coming back. He strutted pompously up to TC, waving his ID card at him, saying arrogantly, "Look, here it is, can you see, I hope you can read". TC just glanced at the card, nodded and said, "Thank you Sir, your plane awaits". As the officer walked away, He turned to TC and shouted, "I bet you wouldn't have fired that gun at me, would you?" TC's answer was enigmatic, "Well you ruined the chance to find out now, Sir". TC heard nothing more from this incident.

A few more weeks passed and TC and his crew were relieved from guarding Luqa airport by an army unit and so they returned to St. Andrews but only for two days because they were then sent down to St. Angelo RN Base to cover that venue, as it was open to the public for a few days. As well as the locals, it was a popular site for holiday makers from all over the world. TC and the lads were all billeted, temporarily, in the Officer's mess. TC thought, very nice.

Their task was to patrol all over the site, giving the impression that there were many of them and all walking about with loaded weapons. This action was more of a deterrent than anything else. TC enjoyed stopping and talking to people from back home in the UK. Some had sons in the Marines and particularly, he liked walking and talking to three WWII RN veterans, who had been in the supply convoys during 1942 when Malta was under siege. They told TC about the state of their ships, when they finally made it to Valletta Grand Harbour, many of them unfortunately fell victim to the German U-boat Wolf Packs, as they were known. Very sad, TC thought. The three old gents were re-living it as they talked. Much respect to these old shipmates, he thought.

After a few days at HMS St Angelo, TC and his crew returned to normal duties back at St. Andrews and 41 Commando. TC very much enjoyed the Royal Marines favourite game of Volley Ball and his personal choice of squash. Due to this, his CSM (Company Sergeant Major), asked if he would like to go on a Volley Ball coaching course at RAF Luqa. Naturally, he jumped at the chance and said yes.

TC commented, "It was a brilliant course and the timing was great, because 41 Cdo were due to have their sports day shortly after that". There was also the 'Round the Island relay Race', in which TC took part. This was an annual event, like the London Marathon but done in relays by teams running round the whole perimeter of Malta, doing three sections each and finishing up at St. Andrews.

Once again, TC had to pack up and embark on the Sir Galahad, sailing from Malta Grand Harbour and heading towards Mainland Turkey to take part in probably the biggest NATO Exercise ever undertaken at this time. It was called 'Deep Furrow' and involved America, New

English Electric Lightning's lined up at RAF Luqa Malta.

Wheels down Lightning coming into land RAF Luqa Malta.

Nimrod line up RAF Luqa.

Nimrod landing at RAF Luqa.

A Shackleton RAF Luqa.

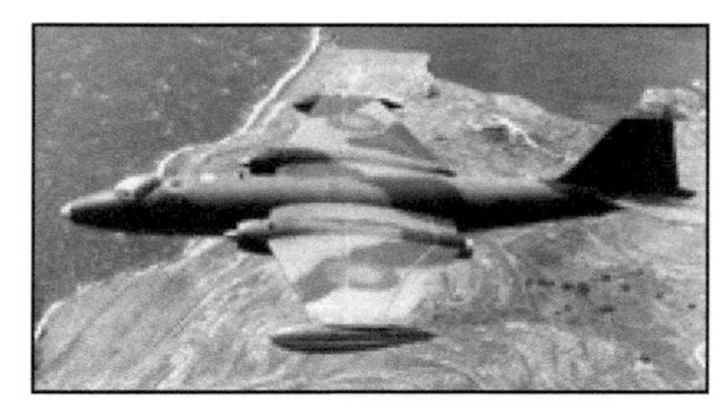

English Electric Canberra PR9 reconnaissance over Malta.

'Operation Pedestal' SS Ohio badly damaged limps into Grand Harbour Malta 1942.

Melbourne Star entering Valletta Harbour 1942 during the siege of Malta.

Brisbane Star torpedo damage Malta 1942. She still made it with cargo intact.

Entrance to Grand Harbour Valletta Malta. St Angelo Fort, centre left, was a Royal Naval Base. AKA Stone Frigate.

Zealand, Australia, Greece, Turkey and Italy. Winding their way through the Aegean Sea, they passed many small islands, until finally dropping anchor at Saros Bay. TC remembers what a spectacular sight to see all those multi-nation Navy Warships, as far as the eye could see. It was like a re-enactment of the D-Day Landings, except they were not under fire. Military jets screamed overhead and heavy transport planes dropped parachutists by the hundreds.

Then it was time to disembark from the Sir Galahad, climbing down the cargo scramble nets, which had been slung over the side of the ship and onto the waiting landing-craft, that were American and made of fibreglass. The problem here was that they were not manned by Royal Marines but by Americans and the coxswains were having trouble keeping them under control. They could not hold them tight against the hull of the Sir Galahad, so that when the troops clambered down to board the fibreglass landing-crafts, they found that there was a gap of four or five feet between the two vessels. The coxswains had to manoeuvre back and forth this took too long. If it had been a proper tactical landing, under fire, they would have been 'sitting ducks' or 'a turkey-shoot'. TC and his troop finally managed to get aboard and off they went.

The procedure now is that once the crafts have collected all the troops they move away from the Mother ship and circle up, like a wagon train, then all at once head into the shore side by side for the landing. The idea is that they all hit the beach together in one big wave. By the time that TC and his troop joined the circle of other landing-craft, a thick black cloud of smoke began to emanate from the engine and eventually, the engine died completely. It took ten minutes before another craft came along side to take them off but by now, all the other crafts had left the circle and were headed for the beaches, leaving TC and his men following up behind by about 200 yards.

The American coxswain slowed right down as he approached a small sand-bar, which he was aware of when being briefed. He was going so slowly, that when he hit the bar, the craft came to a grinding halt. The other landing-crafts cleared the sand-bar by going at speed and going over the top landing all their troops on the beach, a dry landing but TC and his group were stuck on this sand-bar, so the coxswain dropped the ramp. The first two Marines went out and disappeared up to their necks in water. TC recalled hearing a disturbance at the back of the craft and when he looked round, he saw his Sergeant Major, who had removed his beret and was beating the American coxswain around the head with it, the American was cowering in the corner, This seemed very funny but not so when at the start of the exercise, they were all soaking wet up to their necks and once ashore, had to do a 60k yomp inland to their RV, particularly not good when your boots and pockets are full of water.

As it was a very hot day, they did not take long to dry out once they were under way and eventually arrived at their destination, which was on the side of a large hill, where they had to dig in and hide under camouflage. The purpose was to observe a road, about 500 metres away from their location but could be seen up to 2 miles away, as they would see the dust trail in the distance long before seeing the vehicles. Just before last light, a helicopter dropped water and rations. They settled in for the night. It was much cooler now, for the sun had been baking during the day, in excess of 40° with no breeze.

The following morning at sun-up, a young shepherd boy, dressed in a bright red tee-shirt, appeared on top of the hillside, high up behind their position and just stood there for hours, until he got told to 'emshi' (fuck off), as apparently he was sent there to mark their position by the Turks who were playing the enemy. Another long hot dusty unbearable day passed, but cooler once the sun went down and also with a steady breeze. So much better now as they were able to move about freely.

At about 0300hrs, four American soldiers stumbled into their camp. They were lost and had not had any food for two days and were also out of water but what made it a complete joke was that these men were America's finest Reconnaissance or Recce. Patrol, so TC and his troop had to split rations with them, including water. They also had to show them where they were on the map. It turned out that they were over 80km from where they should have been. Once again the Royal Marine Commandos came to their aid.

At first light the next morning, they 'lifted and shifted', making their way along the bottom of a ravine to another RV. After about half an hour, two Turkish armoured vehicles arrived on the plateau above them. TC and his troop instantly froze and went to ground, as they knew that the Turks were looking for them and now standing on top of their vehicles, scanning the area with binoculars. The Turkish troops spent about twenty minutes scouring the area, at this point, the troop officer got on the radio and called in an air-strike on the armoured vehicles.

Within minutes, two Jaguar Jet fighters came in low and fast, right across the top of the two vehicles, then pulled up almost vertically and put their afterburners on.

There was an awesome bang and the ground shook when they did this. TC noticed that one of the Turks fell off his vehicle and as there was an umpire with them, it was game over for the two vehicles and a brilliant display by the two Jaguar pilots.

TC and his men spent one more night under 'Mother Nature's blanket', (TC's own words), then at first light again, made their way back to the beach, now some 40km away. There was a hive of activity on the beach when they arrived, due to the fact that this part of Turkey was suffering from a 'Foot and Mouth' epidemic and all personnel and vehicles had to be decontaminated before being allowed back on board the ships. TC had noticed many tortoises whilst in the wild but everyone had been warned not to touch them (because of the foot and mouth) and Royal would have been going back on board with dozens of tortoises in their packs. Malta would have eventually been awash with them. On the beach, everyone had to remove all their clothing, which was then pushed into long polythene tubing and burned. Then, after scrubbing down, they were issued with clean gear, before stepping aboard their landing craft and ferried back to their respective ships, ready for their return to Malta.

Back at St. Andrews, the stores were unloaded and cleaned, before securing for the day. Next morning, on-going training as usual, out for runs, weapon handling and live firing down on Pembroke ranges, TC's favourite sport. Shortly after this, TC decided to apply for the 'SBS' (Special Boat Section, as it was referred to back then). He had to complete an aptitude swim and dive test, which was carried out at Manoel Island just off Sliema, which was a WWII Royal Navy Submarine base. TC was already a competent and very good licensed diver anyway and happy that he passed this test but little did he know, to quote TC, "The shit that was to come" should he get in.

TC was informed that as his SQ (Special Qualification) was AEs (Assault Engineers), it was unlikely that he would be allowed to go for 'SBS'. Not long after this, he was transferred from G Company to the AE's troop of 41 Cdo. AE troop is part of Support Company and along with heavy weapons, mortar troop, anti-tank troop and reconnaissance troop (or recce troop).

TC knew most of the people he would be working with but those he didn't certainly knew of him and he now did more training with his section. One task they were given was to build a kiddies' pool down by the Lido. The site was to be set back about 50 yards from the sea and the jetty, it was all volcanic rock, so digging out would have to be by explosives. They set to work drilling holes for the charges and then plastic explosives were tamped into the holes in several sections, ready to blow. The Dolphin Hotel situated across the bay was informed to make sure all their windows were open, when the blast came. The charges had been set for point four of a second between each one, to create a ripple effect, instead of all going off together. This went well and was carried out several times during the next three days. Then it was dug out manually with some local tradesmen being hired to screed off the inside and line it with mosaic tiles.

TC and his crew made steps leading up to the pool side and the day before it was opened officially, they used a mobile water pump to pump water from the sea and fill the pool. The project took three weeks to build from start to finish.

On the morning of the opening, the local media were present, as were the CO, mums, dads and the kids. The kids were longing to plunge in, also there was TC's Company Commander Captain Reynolds. TC and his team were standing beside him and Captain Reynolds made a speech thanking TC and his crew for all their hard work etc. etc. Captain Reynolds, immaculately dressed in nicely-pressed shirt, lovat trousers and Green Beret declared the pool open. At that moment, TC nodded to the kids, who had been briefed earlier and together they tried pushing Captain Reynolds into the pool but he resisted. TC being TC, placed a hand in the middle of the Captain's back and – whoops. TC said that he didn't think Captain Reynolds was very amused but as everyone was laughing and clapping, including the CO and the kids all jumping

The American 'Higgins Boat' landing craft, mostly made of plywood, very little protection.

LCVP of Royal Marines Mk10.

American amphibious assault ship receiving landing craft via the stern ramp. OP Deep Furrow.

USS JF Kennedy, Deep Furrow Turkey 1973.

Ariel view of Saros Bay and landing beaches OP 'Deep Furrow' Turkey 1973. Note, Anzac bay and the '**A**' in the red bubble indicates Gallipoli scenes of fierce battles during WWI involving The Turks, Australians and British.

in and splashing him, he had no choice but to accept it as a joke.

Shortly after this, news came in, that the Turkish Army had invaded the Northern tip of Cyprus, the Kyrenia area in particular and that many Europeans were trapped, mostly on the beaches. HMS Hermes was at sea in the near vicinity of Malta and 41 Cdo were mustered, with orders to embark immediately. Helicopters were used to shuttle the unit on board. At this point, TC and three others from the unit were asked to go back to the UK on a Greek language course, which they did.

The four were billeted in the Royal Marines Barracks Eastney in Hampshire. TC palled up with a sergeant from the Army and they worked together. The course was very intensive and was conducted at Portsmouth University, near Gosport, in a language laboratory. TC said that it was four weeks of non-stop headaches. He had to sit all day in a small cubicle, wearing headphones and every now and then the teacher would stop the tape machine and correct any miss pronunciations.

At the end of each day, the teacher would give them a tape machine to take away and practice in the evenings. She asked that they would spend at least three hours each night working with it. To quote TC, "My ARSE". At the end of the course, there was the final exam, part written and part practical. The practical involved sitting in a room with two Greek teachers. One of whom only spoke Greek and the other only spoke English. The teachers asked questions of each other through TC as interpreter and although he found it quite difficult, TC and the others all passed.

The four of them were then flown back to Malta, grabbed all their kit and flew on to Cyprus and to Polymedia Camp, which was on the Northern edge of Limassol, where TC joined up with his troop and 41 Cdo. The camp was pretty awful, as it had been the old GNG (Greek National Guard) Garrison and as these were only conscripts, the quality of life compared to the Royal Marines was pretty basic and disgusting.

Cyprus Hill 171

On the second day in the camp, TC had to draw a Landrover from the motor pool. This was an FFR (fitted for radio). The radio was a C41 and was fitted in the back of the vehicle. The vehicle was painted white with UN roundels and decal. It had a large UN flag on the side pole. TC reported to the IO (Intelligence Officer) for a briefing, along with his crew, Peter, Tony, Cass and Steve. Steve was the signaller and would be in charge of the radio.

Their task was one of humanitarian aid once again, just like Chittagong but thankfully without the flooding. They were given several villages to visit and assess displaced persons, report on medical aid needed and quantify the food supply. It was the first chance for TC to try out his newly-acquired Greek language. No worries, he was very confident.

When they came to the village, they were aware that all eyes were on them. TC approached two of the women and asked politely, "Where is the Mukhtar (head of the village)?" They just shrugged their shoulders, looking at TC as though he was from another planet. He moved on to the centre of the village, where there was a cantina. TC and his crew decided to stop for coffee and chat with the inhabitants for a while.

The inside of the cantina looked like something from a 'spaghetti western' film. There were a group of men all sitting round an old cast-iron, pot-bellied stove and all chattering away loudly. The marines entered. It was obvious they were all carrying loaded weapons. They ordered coffee, sat down and started talking amongst themselves. All the while, TC was trying to pick up on the loud conversation from the locals seated round the stove. He had difficulty trying to understand what they were talking about and could only pick up the odd word.

Eventually, TC went over to the men and asked if they would like a drink, in English, of course. One of the men now took the lead and asked the others, in Greek. They all agreed but looked as though they did not understand English. TC ordered a bottle of brandy and glasses. The local brandy is cheap and as TC said, "If you don't like drinking it, you can always use it to clean the drains or as paint stripper". Now, the Greek men are smiling but still chatting away in Greek.

TC had noticed that as they drove into the village, there were a few buildings with 'EOKA' daubed on the walls. This is Greek for 'Ethniki Organosis Kipriakou Agonos' in English, 'National Organisation of Cypriot Struggle' 1954. The British were involved in this conflict during the fifties, which still leaves very bad feeling among some Greek Cypriots. Although TC and his crew were dressed in UN rig, blue beret etc they still had 'Royal Marine Commando' flashes on their jumpers. This was a give-away that they were British and could possibly come under attack.

After a while, Cass said to TC, "Can you understand what they are saying?" TC replied, "They are talking about us five Englishmen." Suddenly Cass stood up and said to the Greek men, "There are only four Englishmen here, I am Scottish." The place fell silent and TC pushed Cass back into his seat and told him to shut up and not to be a fool.

Now TC spoke to them in Greek and apologised for Cass and said that he, TC, had just come off a Greek course but was not very good at the moment. All the time, TC was thinking, let's get the fuck out of here pronto, when surprise, surprise, one of the Greek men stood up and offered his hand to TC, then in perfect English said with a laugh, " Well done for making the effort to learn our language." They all started laughing then, as they all spoke English.

The one who stood up was, in fact, the local school teacher. His name was Georgiou and he would become good friends with TC and still is today. He is retired now and is a property owner in Cyprus. He told TC that actually, his Greek was very good, although it would be better if he had been taught colloquial Greek. The reason he could not understand much of what the men were saying was because in Cyprus, they use different dialects in different parts. Georgiou told TC that his Greek was absolutely perfect and if he was on Mainland Greece, particularly Athens, he would be considered very posh. TC thought typically, "Me posh, fuck off."

As the day wore on, TC and his crew visited many more villages. Before the next one, TC took Cass on one side, out of earshot of the others and read him the 'riot act'. Cass apologised and assured TC it would never happen again. Village after village and TC's Greek was getting better, after his earlier experience, thanks to Georgiou. They were now collecting and collating information from all the villages, as to refugee movements, medical needs, food supplies and warm clothing, as the evenings and nights were quite cold. Back at Polymedia camp, TC and the lads were able to relax for the evening, although TC had to report to the IO (Intelligence Office) to disseminate all the information he had collected during the day.

Two days later, TC and his crew received more villages to visit. The last one of the day would be up in the Troodos Mountains and mount Olympus, which is the highest point in Cyprus at 6404 feet. It was a gloriously warm, sunny day, so the sides of the Landrover were rolled up and the men were all in shirt sleeve order. Off they went to the first village of Palodia then Spitali, Gerasa, Kalochorio, rising up to Zoopigi, Agios Loannis and finally up to Troodos itself. They were driving on a zigzag road, through pine forests, up and up and getting colder as they went. It became very cold, as they went through some cloud and the lads in the back wanted to stop and roll the sides down, which they did. Unfortunately, they had no jumpers with them and the heater in the vehicle was useless.

As they rounded a bend in the road, to their shock, they spotted small patches of snow at the sides of the road. It definitely got colder, the higher they progressed the more snow they saw, until after a few minutes, there were flurries of falling snow and then, it was snowing hard. The windscreen wipers were on full but not very efficient and TC and his crew were now driving in 6-8 inches of snow and blizzard conditions. The lads were all shivering, cursing and swearing but TC, typically, was laughing about it. Eventually they reached the top, pulled up outside the cantina and rushed inside.

A group of men were sitting huddled around a stove, the whole place was lovely and warm and as TC and the lads came in, the men all moved away from the stove, inviting them in, "Please come in and sit," they said. TC thought that they were probably thinking, how stupid coming out in shirt sleeves in the middle of a snowstorm.

These villagers were very friendly towards the lads and the cantina owner came over with a bottle of Brandy and some glasses. TC asked for another bottle of Brandy and glasses for everyone. Once the glasses were filled, they all stood up and toasted everything and everybody. TC followed this by ordering full English breakfasts, double everything, as this was the last village on their list and they would not get back to camp in time for the evening meal. The second bottle of Brandy went down as well as the first – alcoholic central heating.

TC's Greek language was getting better all the time but he regretted not knowing that Troodos had a ski resort called Mount Olympus. At this time, the Turkish invasion was in full swing, so of course, there were no holiday-makers around, nor any traffic on the roads, other than military vehicles, mostly UN and Greek National Guard but not many of them. He also, had not known that Troodos had totally different weather to the rest of the Island.

This was not mentioned at the original briefing but to quote TC, "Life is one big learning curve." Even today, if he is sent to any foreign country, he will study everything about that country, climate, people, traditions and in particular, it's history. This is why he is so good at what he does, preparation is everything.

Two weeks went by, then TC and ten men were sent to a vulnerable village on the edge of the Attila Line or Green Zone, where the Turkish Army had dug in on a broad front, only several hundred yards from the village of Athienou. He was requested to make a base camp on Hill 171, which was east of the village and only two hundred yards from the Turkish trenches. All the high spots along the front were occupied by UN personnel from all different contingents,

View of Troodos mountains, note the golf ball on top of Mt Olympus, the highest point in Cyprus 6404 ft.

The golf ball on Mt Olympus this was a British long range radar station now run by the Greeks.

Troodos village and Mt Olympus Ski Resort.

Very beautiful scenery but not ideal weather for shirt sleeve order.

Typical UN refugee camp in Cyprus 1974, one of many for 200,000 displaced persons.

UN Ferret car on standby at observation post.

Austrian, French, Belgian, Dutch, Australian etc. The Turkish army had been halted at this point by the UN but still had intended to take more ground, if they could, without firing on the UN.

TC and his crew set up tents and made themselves comfortable. He had his men dig in on the forward edge of the hill, facing the Turks, who had their trenches dug for them by a few JCBs which were all digging continuously across the whole front. Those poor buggers, thought TC, living in the trenches day and night, with very little food or warm clothing.

TC took the 4ton lorry next day into Polymedia camp on a 'raid' with his men, he collected empty 40 gallon oil drums, paraffin heaters and some fuel. They 'appropriated' an old sentry box made of wood, collected a full tool box from the AE's stores – picks, shovels, hammers, saws, nails and a couple of UN flags on 12 foot poles. As they were being fed by the Austrian chuck wagon that visited three times a day, TC explained that the food was 'shite', for example, lunch every day would be a huge ladle full of mashed potato with either beetroot or strawberry jam. Once again, to quote TC, "Well, sorry folks, my men are not eating this crap."

Fortunately, one of TC's crew, Chris, was a chef in Civvy Street, so they went to the rear of the galley at Polymedia camp and had a word with the Colour Sergeant head chef, whom he knew very well and told him what the Austrians were feeding them on. TC came away with catering tins of steak and kidney pie filling, flour, oil, baking trays, fruit and a whole leg of pork – bread, jam, bacon, eggs, and steaks.

Back at Hill 171, TC and the lads set to work. They painted the sentry box white and placed it fifty yards to the right of the camp with one of the flag poles and UN flag flying. The second flag and pole were put in front of the camp. Sandbags were filled and placed along the front of their fire trenches. The oil drums were placed side by side in a square, with one missing at the front to allow access in and out.

The missing one had the top chiselled off and holes made in the sides. This made a brazier, as there were heaps of logs and chopped wood all around. Just below the hill, behind their position, was a small abandoned gypsum works with a kiln to fire the rocks and a small shed with a corrugated tin roof. The roof was removed and put on the oil drums and painted white with the letters UN in blue painted on the top. The brazier was put in the middle of the shack now 'Shack TC', as the lads had named it.

Apart from the 4ton Bedford lorry, they also had a Landrover and trailer. The Landrover was an FFR for communication, as radio checks had to be made every hour on the hour also a sentry had to be posted on a one hourly basis. These were part of TC's responsibilities, also to make sure that everyone was on their toes at all times.

Between Hill 171 and the Turkish trenches was a mine field, believed to have been laid by the GNG but as it was laid in a hurry, it was not mapped. The mines were mainly AP (Anti personnel) M14 – M16. These mines are American built and they also supplied the Turkish forces. The M14 mine is placed a couple of centimetres below the surface and when you step on it, it explodes, taking off your feet or legs. The M16 is commonly known as the 'Bouncing Betty' and again, is buried. This has three prongs protruding from the top. If you step on it or catch one of the prongs, it sets off a small charge which fires it into the air and about head height, explodes. There are also mines that don't need to be buried, these are the VS50, called clams or oysters and can just be scattered by the hundreds on to the surface, either from the back of trucks or even from aircraft. They fall in brush or grass and because they come in camouflage colours, they are difficult to spot.

By the end of the second day, the camp was completed this included a 'Lazy Man Boiler' and a built-in oven. TC was well-pleased to have hot water on tap all day and all night and proper hot food in the field. The lazy-man boiler was made from an empty 40gallon oil drum and the oven from a small metal locker found at the gypsum works. TC had taken the trouble to make a sketch of both and how they work. The boiler is called Lazy because in order to draw off a pint of hot water, it is necessary to put in a pint of cold water. The idea is that it can never run dry, you can only get out what you put in but of course the fire has to be kept going all the time, night and day.

No problem as this would be one of the responsibilities of the Sentry on duty. That evening TC and the crew dined very well on spit-roasted leg of pork, followed by fruit pie. TC commented, "It was great, my compliments to the chef."

TC took the Landrover into the village of Athienou, which also had a UN post on top of a building with a water tower. He found a shop there like a mini-market, which sold almost anything. It was very quiet as now the only customers were the locals and a few UN soldiers. TC began using his Greek Language, much to the surprise of the owners and soon it became known that TC and his crew were between the Turks and the village. The Greeks were very grateful for this.

TC also found out that all the women who worked in the store were of the same family. TC bought some milk, wines, a few cases of beer for the lads, chocolate biscuits, cheeses and other groceries. He was invited back in the evening after the store had closed, to take tea and cake with the family. Very nice he thought, so he went back later. They all sat in front of the shop by the window, the grannies and aunts were chatting and knitting.

Two of the young granddaughters, one of whom had made the cake, sat talking to TC, telling him that they both had been to school in England and had many friends there. They also told him that they were very scared of the Turks and that many of the villagers had packed up and

Small village of Athienou with Kyrenia mountain range in background, Cyprus 1974.

TCs friendly store, centre of Athienou.

Sentry post lookout Hill 171 Athienou.

Larnaca to Nicosia Rd, with turn off to Athienou 1981. But in 1974, this was the site of a temp GNG check point where TC had a face off with Major Stavros of the GNG.

Below are a few sketches TC made of their camp on hill 171 Athienou.

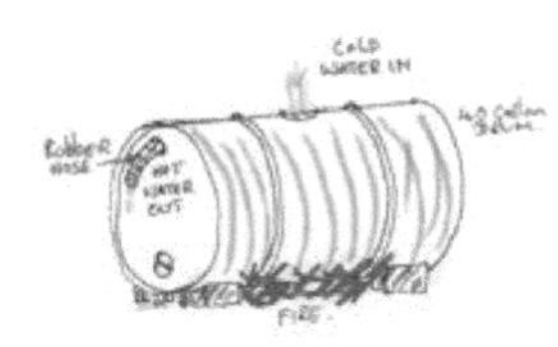

Lazy man boiler.

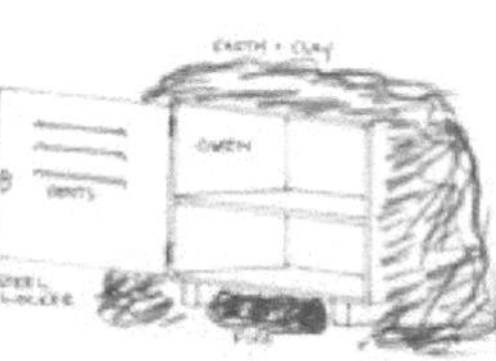

The oven, made from a small locker.

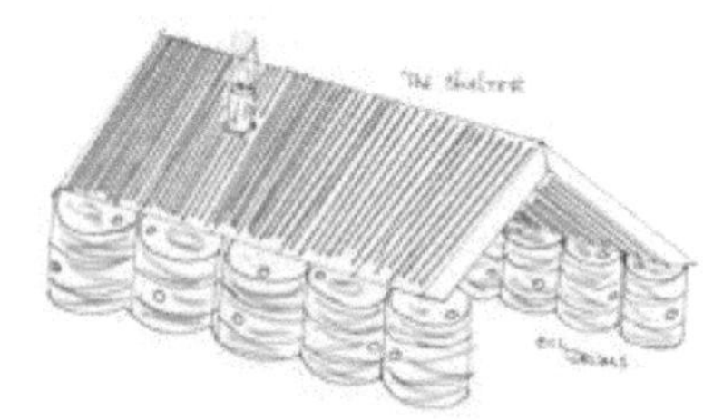

Accommodation, 'Shack TC'.

The Brazier

Pete cleaning his SLR after the muzzle had been up a GNGs nose 1974.

left. They asked TC if he would take them to the hill and show them where the Turks were but TC advised that it would not be a good idea, for reasons of security.

Every few days, TC would take two of the lads and drive down to Polymedia camp to collect provisions, get a decent shower and a change of clothing, then report to the IO and hand in any data. He would then go to the motor pool to get fuel, after which, he would return to the hill. One or two nights earlier, the sentry had spotted some Turks, who had left their trenches and tried to get into the camp, presumably in search of food but TC had set up an early warning device, by putting a low wire entanglement across the front. This is a series of wires, criss-crossed at ankle and knee height with empty baked bean tins and a few stones inside, hanging on the wire, so, if the wires were disturbed, they would rattle.

One day, TC returned from Polymedia and stopped at the store in Athienou to collect some beer and wine then on his approach to the Hill, he could see his camp at the top but on this occasion there seemed to be something different that TC could not recognise. As he drove closer, he was horrified to see that there was a person hanging from a gallows on the edge of the camp. By now, he was really worried, what the hell had happened, he thought but on arrival, he realised that the lads had made a wooden gallows and hung a dummy, dressed in military uniform and facing toward the Turkish lines, this was an idea that Cass had in order to deter them from trying any more attempts to infiltrate their camp area. TC had it removed immediately as this could have created an International Incident. He need not have worried so much because this little stunt of Cass and the lads worked but a few days later TC was involved in his own International Incident. The hanging dummy appeared to be immaterial to what he was about to be involved in.

TC had to go to UN Headquarters in Larnaca, so with three of his team, off he went. He had to collect a wallet containing restricted documents and then deliver them to the Austrian UN Post in the centre of Athienou. On the way back, up the Larnaca road, TC had to pass through two GNG road blocks. As he approached the first one, the guards had stopped a taxi and were searching it. TC was in a marked UN vehicle, therefore, not only did he not have to stop but the GNG never did stop UN vehicles, so TC drove around the knife-rests in the road and onto a small service track, which went round the road block.

A mile up the road, they came to the second and last road block on the Greek side before entering the DMZ (Demilitarised Zone or Green Line) this is the zone that only UN forces may enter and the turning off to Athienou, a trip he had done many times in the past. There were two armed Greek guards standing in the middle of the road, holding up their hands to stop TC, which he did. One of the guards stood in front of the vehicle, pointing, what TC described as a rusty old British made Sten sub-machine gun. The sun was shining off the weapon, making its colour look bright orange with rust. This weapon was a WWII relic, very unstable and very unreliable, even in good professional hands but these fellows were only conscripts.

One of the guards stepped forward to TC and ordered him and the rest of the crew to get out of the vehicle. TC refused, telling the guard that he had no jurisdiction to stop UN vehicles, particularly as they were in the middle of nowhere and in mountainous country.

TC was aware that atrocities happened not just between Greeks and Turks but many UN soldiers had also paid the ultimate price in this conflict and that TC was making sure he was not going to end up as another statistic. He noticed via the left door mirror that another guard had casually walked down the left side of the vehicle to see what or who was in the back. At this point, TC was still arguing with the guard and still refusing to get out, when he noticed in the rear view mirror, the other guard, who was standing at the rear of the vehicle actually had the muzzle of an SLR, stuck up his nose. Peter in the back, was holding the SLR. The guard froze.

The argument started to escalate when the guard told TC he was only a corporal and how dare he argue with a Major of the Greek army. At that point, TC asked for his name as he would be filing a report about this incident. The Major told TC that his name was Major Stavros. TC wrote down his name, then told him to stand aside, as he intended to drive away and if he was prepared to get into a fire fight, that he should just read TC's shoulder flashes first, which stated 'Royal Marine Commando', following up with a comment, "Do you want to go down this route, because if you do you will die here and now, maybe I will as well but I am prepared to take the risk, how about you?"

While this argument was going on, TC was trying to get his SMG out of his draw-string bag, which was down beside his left knee, also in the bag was one magazine loaded with 32 rounds of 9mm ammo. Taff, who was sitting next to TC in the front, gently pushed TC's hand away and took out the weapon. By now, Major Stavros had removed his sidearm, which was a Colt 45cal from his holster and was resting it on the top of the door in a threatening manner.

Just then, TC heard the satisfying sound of the magazine click on the SMG, as Taff snapped it on the weapon, Major Stavros hadn't noticed this, as he was shouting at TC. Again, he blustered, "How dare you talk to a Major like that, you're only a damn corporal" but at this point, Taff, enraged at this, leaned across in front of TC and shouted back in the Majors face, "Yes but a corporal in the Royal Marines is much higher than a fucking Major in the GNG or 'Fred Karno's fucking Army', you piece of shit". At this point Taff had cocked the SMG and pushed it into TCs hand, the Major totally unaware of this and quite taken aback, as was TC. TC then swung the SMG over and put the muzzle in Stavros' face.

All three of TC's men cocked their weapons and Taff pushed his out of the vehicle side window and pointed it at the guard standing in front, the look on the guards face said it all. These guards had no stomach for a shoot out at close range. Stavros then lowered his weapon and replaced it in its holster. He asked TC for his name. TC told him saying, "You will be reading it very soon, when you are standing in front of a UN tribunal. TC then revved up the vehicle and drove

The M14 anti personnel blast mine.

M14 No need to bury it.

The M16 bouncing or bounding anti personnel fragmentation mine.

M6 Anti Tank mine, this is buried just under the surface and is pressure sensitive.

Italian VS50 Valmara anti personnel mine also known as the Clam or Oyster. These are 3 inches in diameter and normally just scattered.

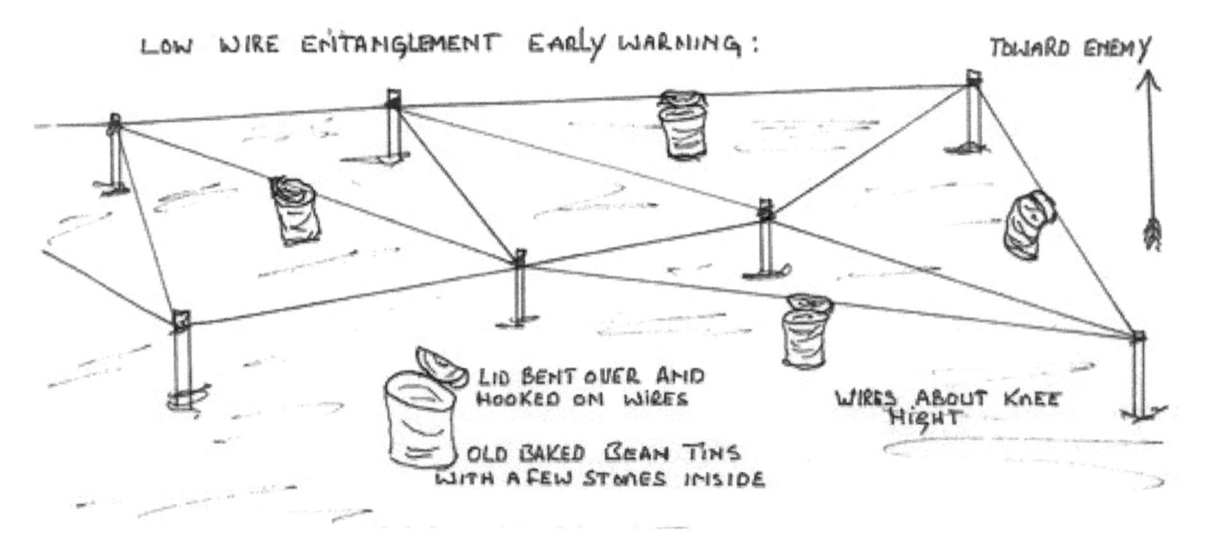

TCs low wire early warning system, another sketch by himself. One touch on the wires anywhere and the stones in the tins rattle. TC had set this system up across the front of their camp area but further out to give early warning of intruders approaching. This works well. TC apologises for the drawings, he's no artist but then can't be expert in everything!

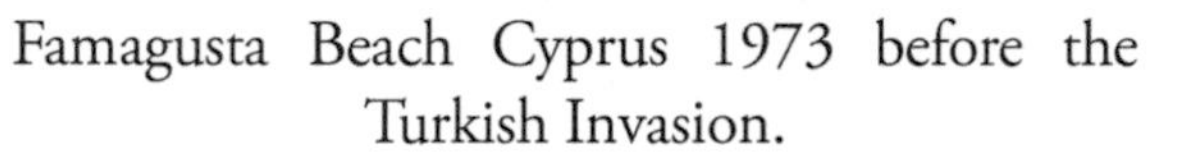

Famagusta Beach Cyprus 1973 before the Turkish Invasion.

The Beach as it is today since 1974. Famagusta is now known as ghost city.

Before and after, same street. Taken 2009.

Remains of hotels along Fama G beach 1974. Taken 2009.

British Nationals being evacuated by Wessex back to HMS Hermes, 'Operation Mercy' Cyprus 1974

Waiting anxiously for that airlift out of Kyrenia.

Royal Marines preparing to go ashore from HMS Hermes off the coast of Kyrenia Cyprus to assist with evacuation.

away. The guard in front jumped out of the way, and then just stood looking on. When TC arrived back at the hill, he had to contact UN HQ by radio and also send a message to 41Cdo HQ at Polymedia to pass on his information. This was done by using coded messages called Slidex Message System. The configuration changes every 24hrs, so it cannot be intercepted and decoded. During the evening, TC was informed, that a message had been received telling him that a group of Top Brass from the UN along with TC's CO from 41 Cdo would be arriving on their location next day to interview TC and the lads, who were with him when this incident occurred. TC thought that the UN was taking this action very seriously.

The next morning, TC put the section to work, sprucing up the camp and arranged with the chef to supply steak and kidney pie for lunch. The large table was put outside with benches borrowed from the old workings at the bottom of the hill. Everyone put on clean uniform and TC went down to the village and borrowed some plates from the shop and bought a few bottles of wine. The chef mentioned to TC that he would like to get on an advanced catering course but there was a long waiting list. TC said he would see what could be done.

Eventually, the sentry informed TC that there were UN vehicles leaving the village and making their way to the Hill. As they approached the camp, TC and his section were all lined up. TC called them to attention and saluted the Officers. The senior officer then shook hands with TC and asked him to stand the section down, which he did. TC had asked the chef to offer the visitors tea or coffee, then they requested a tour of the camp.

TC took them up to where the sentry was during daylight hours. The sentry then showed them the area map and pointed out where the minefield was and the trenches that the Turks were living in. Back at the main camp, one of the UN men asked what the lovely smell was, so TC took them to see that chef was baking a pie in the oven. The visitors were stunned, especially when they asked what the oil drum was for. At this point TC's CO stepped in and gave his explanation of how it worked. Not only that but he gave them some water in a cup and let them see for themselves. The whole group thought it was brilliant.

They all sat round the table for lunch and chef's pie was a great success. Then TC and his crew were interviewed one by one. At the end, TC was approached by his CO, who expressed his personal pride that TC and the section had impressed the UN visitors so much. Before they all left, TC mentioned to his CO about the chef's wish to go on an advanced catering course and the CO said that he would look into the matter when he returned to Polymedia Camp.

TC did not hear any more from the UN about the incident and although he had to pass both GNG Checkpoints, every time he went to Polymedia Camp, he never ever got stopped again, nor did he ever see Major Stavros again. He did stop once or twice and ask for him but as the faces changed all the time, he just ended up with a shrug of the shoulders but as TC explained, "These guards were all conscripts and did not really want to be there, so there was no real interest."

Sometime later, TC was informed that they would be getting relieved the next morning by a section from the Army, or Percy Pongo, as they called them. They packed up after the last breakfast on the Hill and TC made an inventory of all the equipment they had, most importantly, the amount of live ammunition and that for the Carl Gustav 84mm anti-tank weapon.

Before long, the relief arrived and TC was horrified to see that as they all bailed out of their transport, they dumped all their kit on the ground and started making coffee and helping themselves to the food. TC asked the corporal in charge to check the inventory with him for the hand over but the corporal was busy trying to get food and just said to TC, "Give it here, I'll sign it." TC said that he should at least count the ammo but the corporal was not interested. Lastly, TC asked that his sentry needed to be relieved and was told, "Just bring him down, I'll send someone up later." TC was disgusted with the corporal's irresponsible attitude but he could do no more, so he and his section got into their vehicles and drove off.

When he got to the village of Athienou, he stopped to return their plates, said goodbye to them all and thanked them for the gracious hospitality they had shown over the past weeks. The trip back to Polymedia took about an hour and once they were back, TC had to report to the IO and be de-briefed. The Officer asked TC what time they left the Hill, because less than an hour after he had left, the Turks left their trenches and had pushed forward taking Hill171. TC was gutted and said that he cursed the corporal who had relieved him, for his unprofessional behaviour.

TC has never returned to Athienou. And after three days in Polymedia Camp, he was told that he and his section were being sent out to Larnaca, as escort for some Turkish refugees, taking them down to RAF Akrotiri to be repatriated back to main land Turkey but apparently they would then be flown strait back to Northern Cyprus, by the Turkish where they were given houses and land, most of which originally belonged to the Greek Cypriots. TC said, "This is why the Greeks were so angry, especially with Britain, it's not surprising really."

Next, TC received a warning order that he would be going on another static posting, up to a place west of Nicosia Airport, called Pano Zhodia, where there was a factory owned by the Co-op. It was a box factory for crating up Citrus fruits for dispatching all over the world.

Cyprus Pano Zhodia

At 0800hrs next morning TC and seventeen of his men collected a Landrover and two four ton trucks from the motor pool, loaded all their kit, equipment along with personal effects in preparation for a long stay up at Pano Zhodia, the Co-op Box Factory on the border of the DMZ (De-militarised Zone). TC was driving the Landrover, as they drove from Limassol north towards Nicosia. On the way through Nicosia, it became apparent by the severe damage to the buildings and private dwellings, how bad the fighting was. It was an eerie feeling passing through empty streets, which once would have been bustling with people and traffic but now, it was only TC and his men in three vehicles.

From time to time, they would pass by UN Posts, where they would be saluted and give a return salute of respect. This was done under the United Nations. TC did a slight detour and drove into Nicosia Airport. This was totally deserted and was in no-man's land as it was referred to. The Airport showed signs of a ferocious battle, as the Turkish and Greek Commandos fought each other for possession of this strategic few acres. The location was very important to the Turks, in particular. The end result was a mass loss of life on both sides, then the UN stepped in and unfortunately, there were some loss of life among them too. The Airport, then became under the control of the UN and to this day, the Airport have never been used again.

TC saw three British Airways Trident aircraft on the runway, two of which were badly shot up and severely damaged. The third one was completely broken in half. At the far end of the north west runway was a small road, just outside the perimeter of the airport. Beyond that, were fields and in the nearest one, was the burned out wreckage of a Turkish fighter aircraft. TC believes that it was an RF-84F Thunderflash.

Back on the road again and eventually they arrived at a small road surrounded by fields full of citrus fruit trees. It seemed like the middle of nowhere. By the side of the road there were large sheds with a water tank on top of a concrete tower. This was just inside the main entrance. The whole property was fenced off with an 8ft high chain-link fence and on the road outside was a UN check point and a sentry box. There was also an OP on the top of the water tower, this was surrounded by a wall of sandbags to protect the occupants on duty. 400 yards further up the road was a village called Morfou which had been a Greek occupied village but now in the control of a Turkish Armoured Division. This village is now called Guzelyurt Ovasi. TC and his men unpacked and set up accommodation within the factory, now known as the Orange box factory and owned by the Co-op. As the whole area was surrounded by citrus orchards of oranges, lemons and grape-fruits, the box factory was where all the fruit would be packed into crates, bound with wire, ready for the stores or to be exported.

The problem here was that the Turks had control of most of the orchards and the fruit was ripe and falling from the trees therefore they needed the factory to box it up, however, the UN had denied the factory to them, even after several attempts of negotiations. During TC's occupation of the site, some Turkish top brass approached them to try to negotiate and on one occasion, actually threatened to attack and take the factory. The Turkish officers informed them that they would be coming into the site by tanks, at 0400hrs the next morning. TC informed them that if they did this, they would be met with serious force and anti-tank weapons and asked if they wished to be personally responsible for this escalation against the UN.

The Turkish Officer in charge, had noticed the Commando flashes on TC's jumper and commented that he had done the Commando Course at CTCRM Lympstone and having realised how difficult it was therefore had the highest respect for them and had no intention of crossing swords with the British Commandos, and asked that TC and his men step aside, when they came in, so as not to cause any casualties. TC politely told him, that any threat of aggression would be met with force. The Turkish officers then muttered between themselves, saluted and drove back up to the village.

TC sent a signal back to camp at Polymedia and also to UN Blue Beret camp at Nicosia, hoping for some serious backup but none was forthcoming, no support at all, so TC had to rely on what was available there. Attached to the camp was a Lieutenant in charge of two Ferret Armoured cars, with 50cal machine guns. These were no match against tanks but still useful. That evening, they lit braziers all round the perimeter of the camp, fuelled by hundreds of wooden pallets, which were stacked up at the back of the factory. The two Ferret cars were positioned, one on each Northern corner of the factory, facing the village of Morfou Plain. Every man was at stand-to all night.

At 0400hrs the silent, peaceful night air was suddenly shattered with the noise and vibration of many tanks starting-up and revving, albeit the sentry on the top of the OP on the water tower was unable to see any movement. TC and his men were now poised for action, the two 84mm anti-tank weapons were loaded and ready. These would take out a tank although once fired, would there be time to reload, especially if the shot missed? The only answer was to move position immediately. The GPMG's were trained on the road. They would be no good against tanks but would deter foot soldiers, as would the two Ferrets 50cal machine guns. TC's extra

Nicosia Airport, raging battle here between Turkish and Greek Commandos to seize this site. UN stepped in and denied the area to both sides.

Badly damaged Trident on runway. There was three British Airways planes destroyed.

View from outside airport through fences. Airport has never been in use since 1974.

RF 84 Thunderflash Fighter Turkish Air Force.

Abandoned dwelling since 1974 UN Green zone. Picture taken 2008.

Aerial view of Pano Zhodia Co-op Box Factory (now called Astrometis Border Crossing) with surrounding citrus plantations. Four grave sites marked that TC uncovered 1974. The red line 'Buffer Zone' was half a mile further back when TC was here 1974.

surprise was that he had planted explosives on all the machinery in the factory ready to blow with one press of a button. This would deny the Turks, the use of the factory.

The engines roared for an hour or more but the sentry still could not see any movement from the village. TC went up the tower several times and also walked around the perimeter chatting to all his men but still no movement, then suddenly, the engines stopped, followed by a ghostly quiet. The time was now 0530hrs daylight. Fires had now burned out. Cook lit up the petrol Hydros and started making tea and cooking breakfast. TC thought, what a fantastic smell of frying bacon first thing in the morning, when you have been up all night.

The explosive devices were made safe and the 84s were unloaded. Everyone stood down now and resume to normal duties. They posted four men on the road block outside, two in the water tower op, plus three pairs on wandering patrols of the outer perimeter. Those who were not needed got their heads down for a few hours but TC insisted everyone slept with their full kit on, including boots.

A few days went by with nothing unusual happening. There was a large concreted area, the size of a football pitch at the rear of the compound and lots of empty 40 gall oil drums laying around and these were placed all over this open area, to stop any unauthorised helicopters from dropping in. They could move the drums to allow any UN or Naval helicopters to land, as this would be the case later on.

Early one morning, a patrol reported hearing someone or something outside in the north end of the orchard. Could it be a person or possibly an animal? TC took two of his men and went out to the rear of the compound to investigate. As dawn was just breaking, the grass between the rows of orange trees was covered in morning dew. Then two hundred yards out from the north perimeter, TC could clearly see footprints and a trail leading to within fifty yards of the perimeter fence, then stopping. The trail had come from the Turkish village. TC and his men followed the trail back towards the village but by now the dew had gone owing to the rise in temperature. So TC, using his binoculars, started scanning the forward edge of the village, which now lay only 150 metres away TC was still in no man's land and within the UN jurisdiction.

At that moment, something moved on the edge of the village and caught TC's attention. He zoomed in and saw a Turkish soldier looking back at him through his binoculars also. It was now apparent that the Turks had been venturing into the UN controlled zone during the night but for what purpose? TC wondered whether their intention had been to gain control of the factory from the rear fences and on foot, instead of using tanks for a noisy approach.

TC and his men returned to their base and informed the signaller to notify UN HQ and Polymedia camp as to his findings. In order to do this and because of the great distances between Pano Zhodia and Polymedia camp at Limassol also with the Troodos Mountains between, they had to relay their messages via another radio station. At this point, TC decided to climb onto the highest point of the factory roof, punch a hole through it and lower a cord down to pull the aerial up on a long length of co-axial cable and mount the aerial up on the roof.

This was connected to the C41 Radio in the Landrover down below which was parked inside the factory. Surprisingly this worked perfectly as the range was only supposed to be around 10 miles and now they were able to talk direct to Polymedia, as the relay stations were mostly very busy all over Cyprus.

Later in the afternoon, TC headed a small working party and went back out into the orange groves, about one hundred yards out and began setting up his low-wire entanglements, only this time, instead of using empty bean cans with stones, he used 'Trip Flares'. These are pyrotechnics attached to a metal stake in the ground and connected by trip wires. The wires can be pulled or cut, either way the flare will activate giving off a loud bang and a very bright powerful light, which burns for about a minute. It is a magnesium flare.

TC was walking back to the compound, down the middle of a row of orange trees, when he suddenly spotted the tip of a brown shoe protruding out of the ground. Thinking this was a bit odd so he stopped and started to dig it up with his bayonet, only to discover that it was attached to a foot and leg. Immediately he stopped digging and looking around with his binoculars, he noticed that he was being watched from the village by the Turks again.

TC marked the spot and returned to the compound, where he sent a coded signal reporting the possible finding of mass graves as these were being discovered all over the island at this time. The next morning, TC took four of his men, armed with a couple of shovels and went back out to the spot and began exhuming the body. Before they started digging TC placed three of his men a bit further out toward the Turkish lines to act as lookouts or sentries. TC and Jake started digging. It was a very smelly gruesome job uncovering this poor sod's remains and before long they discovered that another body was in the same grave. There were several empty brass bullet cases of 5.56mm scattered around the area. This was the ammunition used by the Turkish troops who were armed with American M16 colt Armalite Rifles.

TC then received a radio message that several UN top brass and his CO were on their way by chopper to his location so the landing area had to be cleared of 40gall drums. By the time the party arrived and escorted out to where TC and Jake were working the two bodies were nearly ready to be lifted out of their resting place.

Both deceased were males, dressed in jacket and trousers. One had brown shoes the other had brown sandals with open toes and wearing socks! TC remembered that he shuddered to think that

One destroyed plane, Nicosia airport. Type unidentified?

Water tower UN OP orange box factory Pano Zhodia.

OP on top of water tower orange box factory. Turkish occupied village on skyline.

View from OP toward Turkish occupied village. Note the UN road block and chicane on left.

Life inside the box factory 'BRITCON', galley in foreground. TC talking to Jake over by pallet stacks.

TC, kneeling left by the GPMG and the crew, as he said, "Always time for a photo session to send back to Mum."

someone could actually wear socks with open toed sandals or Jesus shoes, as he referred to them!

Now, there were several blue capped High ranking UN officials standing around watching and holding handkerchiefs over their noses and mouths as the stench of decaying corpses hit the air. TC and Jake had begun to lift the bodies out, which were not buried very deep in fact only just below the surface and were quite badly decomposed and ripe (smelly).

TC and Jake decided to lift each body out separately, so with one on either side of the grave TC put his shovel under the right leg and Jake under the left leg but there was something not quite right as the foot on TC's side had a brown brogue shoe on it and Jake had a sandal on his side. Apparently the bodies had been placed in the grave beside each other and their inner legs had crossed over one another. The shoes and sandals were mixed up.

TC and Jake, totally oblivious of their audience, were deep in conversation, trying to sort things out. It went something like this, TC, "You have the wrong leg there Jake." Jake, "No I haven't, you've got the wrong leg, this one's mine." TC, "No, mine's got the shoes, you've got the sandals, you should have my other shoe over there." Jake, "Well I have one sandal, why don't you get my other sandal and then I will get your shoe after." Even this was wrong so TC said, "No, you can't do that because the legs are crossed over, you have to get my other shoe first." At this point, they stopped what they were doing, looked up at each other and suddenly realising what they must have sounded like and seeing the looks of disbelief on the faces of their audience. They cracked up, dropping their shovels and walked away in hysterics.

After they settled down, they started again but lifting out the bodies was difficult as they just fell apart and the stench was sickening. However, both bodies were finally laid out and searched. TC found a daily newspaper in one of the pockets, also enough papers to identify them. They had both been shot in the head. Later it was revealed that both men were Greeks, on their way to work. Their car was later found in the village apparently they had been stopped on the road and taken into the orange grove, executed and placed in this shallow grave.

During the following early hours of the morning, one of the flares was activated, so at first light, TC and two of his men went out to the orchard to check and replace the flare. Sure enough, there were the footprints and a trail in the dewy grass, leading to and from the village. These prints were very near where the bodies which TC and Jake had exhumed the previous day. They replaced the trip flare to a new position just in case the intruder had marked where it was. TC had the body remains put into a couple of wooden orange crates and brought just inside the compound but away from the buildings, because of the awful smell. They were collected a few days later by UN undertakers.

Now every morning, small patrols were sent out into the orchards, to let the Turks know that the marines were well and truly aware of them and their little secrets. TC was then informed that one of the patrol thought that they may have discovered yet another body in a field nearby. TC went out to meet them, about 300 yards from the north side of the compound. Upon arrival, he was shown a scattering of empty bullet cases on the ground and again, these were 5.56 mm. A cursory search of the area discovered another shoe cap just protruding from the ground. TC sent for a working party to come out with shovels and wooden crates. A signal was sent to UN HQ regarding the second find.

Shortly after this one of his men called out to TC from 200 yards away in the middle of an open field that he had discovered yet another body. Both of which were eventually exhumed and crated up for removal. TC now ordered a very thorough search of the whole area, right up to the Turkish lines ignoring the fact they were under very close observation but no other bodies were found.

Two days went by now without any more incidents and life was relatively normal. As the marines had previously taken over this site from an army unit, the first thing the marines were aware of was that there were no washing facilities, as the building was in essence a factory. TC wondered how the previous occupiers had managed to keep up hygiene and cleanliness but then it was not really a surprise to him as he had his own agenda about army and hygiene.

Some of the lads from TC's section got to work straight away and rigged up a shower unit, using 40 gallon drums, while the cook got on with very important work, rigging a proper galley area and getting the tea going, not forgetting the bacon banyo's (sandwiches). They had two hydros for cooking, which are like large petrol blowlamps, pressurised and very efficient.

Apart from day to day duties and patrolling, when off duty, they set up a volley ball court at one end of the warehouse, (as this is the marine's favourite game). One evening they were standing around chatting. It would have been about 9pm and cook had made tea, coffee and some filled rolls, this is known as 9 o'clockers and is part of Naval routine. Suddenly, this young army officer in charge of two ferret cars that were attached to support the marines approached TC and Jake.

He was a 2nd Lieutenant and he asked them both if there were any sentries out on patrol. He was told yes, there were three pairs out. At this point, Cass, who was standing nearby noticed that this officer, who at the time was puffing away on a Sherlock Holmes-style pipe and was literally blowing his smoke into Jake's face while talking. This annoyed Cass and he stepped in to listen to what the officer had to say.

The officer informed TC and Jake that he had walked round the whole perimeter of the buildings but could not see anyone. TC pointed to the duty rota pinned on a board beside them and told the officer that although he couldn't see them, they really were there. Cass could not help butting in and blurted out, "Excuse me sir but you look after your Tonka toys and leave the

The Co-op factory from the UN OP showing the front side and stacks of wooden pallets.

View showing the rear perimeter fence and helicopter landing pad "**H**".

Aerial view of factory showing UN check point, water tower OP, citrus groves to right, former Greek village occupied by Turkish army top of picture.

Petrol Hydro cooker now obsolete, as these were considered dangerous, basically a bomb.

Trip flare activated, showing how bright these are. This one has been set off in the daytime.

real soldiering to us sir." TC's heart sank, as the officer glared at Cass, and puffing furiously on his pipe, he turned and stormed off.

TC and Jake just burst out laughing but after TC did tell Cass off for his outburst. He was thankful that no action was taken by this young officer. They were eventually relieved of their post by yet another army unit and returned back to Polymedia Camp.

TC was once again chosen to go on more mobile patrols to various villages and his Greek language was getting much better now. One morning, TC with a driver and two marines were to drive the Imprest officer Lieutenant Davies under armed escort to Dekelia British Sovereign base, to collect the units payroll.

Imprest office is the accounts department and paymaster. They left Polymedia camp in a Landrover, with TC in front with the driver and the officer, with his brief case chained to his wrist in the back with the other two marines, Jock and Carl, all fully armed. They drove down through a small housing estate to get to the main road into Limassol called, Archbishop Makarios Avenue leading to the coastal road but as they turned left into the main street they were suddenly confronted by about two hundred people mostly students, apparently taking part in an anti British protest meeting and sitting in the road.

There were two reasons for this protest, one was because the RAF were flying terrified Turkish refugees out from RAF Akrotiri based on the south coast of Cyprus, back to mainland Turkey, then apparently, Turkey were flying them back to Northern Cyprus, now under Turkish occupation, where they were given land and homes, which had belonged to Greek Cypriots.

The second reason was due to an accident that occurred days before when a British vehicle convoy were escorting Turkish refugees through Limassol on their way down to RAF Akrotiri, when students and locals, incensed at what was taking place, attacked the front of the convoy and brought it to a halt. At this point, a small armoured vehicle, believed to be a Saracen, broke away from the rear of the convoy and raced to the front in order to render assistance but in doing so, knocked down one of the protesters and killed him. The newspaper next day referred to them as 'British Murderers'. Now TC and his crew were caught right in the middle of these angry protesters.

TC's driver had quick reactions and tried to do a U-turn but two civilian cars attempted to ram him, so he mounted the wide pavement and put his foot down. TC's comments were, "It was just like a scene from the Michael Caine film 'The Italian Job', smashing through all the tables and chairs outside the restaurants and coffee shops with people diving into shop doorways for cover". It worked, so ducking into a few back streets they managed to get away. The officer in the back stopped the driver after a short while, to decide whether or not they should turn back and asked TC for his opinion.

The general feeling was against the idea, so TC advised Lieutenant Davies that he knew many back roads in order to get to Dekelia and back to Polymedia Camp, and avoiding the protesters. (Limassol to Dekelia and back would take about four and a half hours along the southern coastal Road). They did manage to do a round trip without any more trouble.

One day they were passing near Troodos again, when TC noticed that there was an asbestos mining area in the vicinity, so they decided to pay a visit. They were received very well by the site manager who told them how asbestos was mined and processed. It was blue asbestos and at that time, no one realised just how dangerous it was.

After his visit, TC called in to have coffee with Georgiou, the school teacher. While in conversation, TC was quite shocked when Georgiou showed him the front page of a newspaper, picturing four men who had been shot by the Turkish Army. One of these men had been Georgiou's elder brother. The four dead men were the same four that TC had exhumed at Pano Zhodia. According to the paper, the four men were in their car heading to work near the village, when Turkish troops stopped them, took them into the orchard and shot two in the head. The other two apparently had tried to escape and run for their lives but eventually also were shot. All their remains were buried in very shallow graves.

About a week went by when TC once again, was sent to another village. This time, it was a very small village, occupied by Turkish Cypriots just outside Limassol. It was called Moutiaka, (now called Mouttagiaka). TC with his section occupied the school in the centre of the village. The concept was to protect the inhabitants from any threats from the surrounding villages, which were all Greek. These were called Armenochori, Germasogia and Foinikaria. Again patrolling the village day and night and on a few occasions going over to the Greek villages, which were just over a mile away.

During the evenings, TC would light a small fire on the waste ground in front of the school and the men from the village would join the marines. They would bring some beers, local food and they would sing songs and chat. This is what is known as hearts and minds. TC collected a vast amount of information from these evenings.

He would always call in to the local cantina when on patrol and he was again, shown great hospitality. He found out that these villagers had been very close friends with all the surrounding villages, until the invasion and now, they were just very frightened people.

One day, TC with three of his men, went to Germasogia, to make their presence known. While he was there, he visited a shop he knew, which stocked some very old wines, this interested TC, so long as it was not 'Marsovin' under a different name. As he approached the cantina, he noticed a group of men sitting outside playing a game of backgammon, (the favoured game of the Greeks).

TC stopped in his tracks, as he suddenly recognised four of the men playing were in fact, from Moutiaka, where TC had just come from. TC thought, "What the fuck is going on here?" These men had been good friends for many years in spite of the mixture of Greeks and Turks, so TC was wondering why they had been posted there to protect these people from each other. He thought that it was a very confusing situation but they were sent there to do a job and they did it supremely well. TC was invited into the back of the shop to view the racks of very old wines covered in dust and debris. He chose two bottles, which were well matured and very good, considering it was a local wine.

The school in Moutiaka was a very old, small building with only one classroom. At this time, during the troubles, the school was closed and the children, very few because it was such a small village, sat outside everyday but were not allowed inside because the marines had weapons, ammunition and radio communications set up in a small cupboard in the corner. One of the children, a cheeky little boy, nine years old and called Alli, arranged for his mother to wash and iron all the men's clothes for a few pounds including their bedding twice a week.

She and Alli were the only ones allowed in the classroom under strict supervision, to clean it. She did very well from all the marines and to show her gratitude she and some of the other women would cook a meal and bring it to them but they were not allowed to stay. The men stayed in the evening but not the women. That was their way of life and to Quote TC, "It was not for us to interfere."

After a few weeks of nothing happening, TC and his crew were ordered to pack up and return to Polymedia. This time it would be an airlift by helicopter, which landed at the school on the children's playing field, much to the kids delight and amusement. The pilot disengaged the rotors leaving the engines running, while TC's men ferried all the equipment from the school to the playing field, about three hundred yards away.

The kids were all round the helicopter, as they had not been so close to one before and the pilot allowed them to sit inside for a short while. One of the men from the village came up in his pick-up truck and helped TC with all the stores and equipment and just for a laugh, TC stood in the back of the truck with the GPMG perched on the roof, and he was driven slowly through the main street to the waiting helicopter.

All the people were waving and laughing. It ended up with a large crowd around the helicopter and when it was all loaded, TC and his men went round shaking hands with all the villagers. Then with two of his men, TC stood by, keeping everyone away, while the pilot started the rotors. TC then got the thumbs-up signal from the pilot and waved to all the villagers and boarded the helicopter. As it lifted off, he could see them all running forward and waving, some looked quite upset and tearful so he thought that they must have made a good impact on them. He had hoped so.

Back at Polymedia Camp fifteen minutes later, they unloaded the helicopter and returned the stores, then it was off to their grots to shower, change clothes and make their way to the galley for the evening meal. They had a break for two days in camp then once again, TC was sent as armed escort to the Sovereign Base at Dekelia, again to collect the unit's payroll. This time it was without incident.

TC and Pete became very good friends with John (or in Greek Yanagi or Yan), a Greek Cypriot who ran the camp shop where you could buy all kinds of goodies. John invited TC and Pete to a Greek wedding. His Daughter was the bride. TC and Pete had to get permission to go in uniform which was granted. The wedding took place in a church, just on the outskirts of Limassol. It was Greek Orthodox and surprisingly, TC could read the writing on the walls and on the icons inside the church.

After the service, they all went back to the house, which belonged to the newly-weds, bought and built by the family. All the men sat at a very large table and the food was served by the women. TC noticed that there was a bottle of local brandy between every two people.

The food and wines flowed and the meal took about two hours, after which, all the men went outside to chat and smoke cigars, while the women sat and had their food. After all this, the music started and the bride paraded in front of everyone, while they pinned money on her dress. She then handed out little parcels of sugar-coated almonds to all the guests. TC and Pete were made to feel very welcome and had a really good day. TC learned much this day.

After a few days in Camp Polymedia, there was fitness training every day. As TC said earlier, "It never stops" and three more weeks went by, again visiting and monitoring many various villages then it became time for TC and 41 Cdo to withdraw from Cyprus back to St Andrews Malta job done.

After two months, TC's two year posting in Malta came to a close and he was flown back to the UK for a couple of months leave before reporting to his new posting Depot Deal again, this time with the 'Training Teams'. He did not mind this, as he got to spend time on the ranges and out in the field, with the Nods, (recruits) teaching Fieldcraft camouflage and concealment. He also taught map and compass work. He thought at the time, that he should have taught the lost Americans, in Turkey, during exercise 'Deep Furrow' and although it was not recognised then, it is believed that the Turkish Armed Forces probably could have used that exercise, as part of their own preparation to invade Cyprus, which they did less than a year later.

SBS Selection (Special Boat Service)

After about 6 months had passed, TC received a signal via his CSM (company sergeant major), that he had been invited to attend RM Poole in Dorset for selection training into the SBS. His CSM asked if he was absolutely sure that this is what he really wanted to do, as the CSM put it, "It's a bastard of a course and you would have never done anything like it in your life so far, nor ever likely to do again". TC was adamant that he was all for this and his CSM stood up, shook TC's hand and said, "Break a leg, oh sorry wrong words". They both stood there laughing.

Four days later, TC was on the train with all his kit en route to sunny Costa Del Dorset and the Royal Marines camp at Hamworthy, Poole. This is also the home of driver training and landing craft training along with many other courses. On arrival at the main gate and Guard Room as it was then, TC reported to the Guard Commander. It was Taff, his old mate from 40 Cdo Singapore 'B' company. Back then they were both marines and now both Corporals.

When TC told Taff why he was there, Taff stood back and at the top of his voice and in front of the rest of the Provo staff who were listening with interest, said, "SBS, You must be out of your fucking mind. SB fucking S, shit." They both had a good laugh and Taff said, "Seriously TC, have you any idea what these poor bastards go through here? We see them nearly every day going out of the gates and returning hours later, half of them can hardly walk and they get kicked out of bed at '0' fuck double fuck". This is Marine terminology again for very early hours of the morning, usually at about 2, 3 or 4am, hence '0' 2 00, or '0'300 and so on.

Taff offered to walk with TC to the SBS offices, to report and sign in but on the way they were so engrossed in conversation, that TC had no idea where he was but eventually they arrived. Taff returned to the Guard Room, not before they had made arrangements to meet up sometime and have a few wets together. Little did TC know then, that this would not happen, as when he began his training, there was barely enough time to take a breath, let alone going out on the town.

TC was taken to a room where more cattle were congregating waiting for the slaughter to come, so they all got chatting and introduced themselves to each other, having a jovial joke, putting their kit away in their lockers and checking the notice boards for info and possibly a timetable, as to what the following weeks would bring. Nothing at all, this is secrecy at its best.

They were left alone until one of the instructors came in during the evening and told them to be outside in the morning, at 0800hrs for opening address and to meet the team. This is usual procedure on any course, just to let you know what to expect. So having been addressed by all and sundry, followed by lectures on the history of the SBS, of which most of them would already have known, the day went by reasonably quickly with no shore leave. Before long TC was tucked up in his pit, wondering what the next day would bring.

No sooner had they all got off to sleep, or so it seemed, the door burst open and the lights were banged on when this very tall thin instructor bellowed, "Outside, 5 minutes in PT rig" TC had recognised this instructor from the briefing only hours earlier and looking down at his watch, thought, "You must be bloody joking", It was just after 0400hrs, still very dark and bloody cold.

Once outside, the call, "Follow me gents", rang out. TC thought, "Oh that's very civil, maybe this course is not as bad as people make out, after all, we are well-trained, seasoned soldiers and long since being called Nods (recruits in training).

Off they all went down the drive toward the main gate and past the guard room, TC gave a glance to see if his mate Taff was on duty but he didn't see him. On they went for some time, until everyone was now puffing and panting, sucking in as much of the early morning fresh air as they could, lungs now working very hard. Soon they came to a grassy clearing not far from the sea, as TC caught a glimpse of it between some trees and he thought to himself, "I know where we are going, down to the sea and a freezing cold swim.

The instructor spread them all out on a grassy area and started with press ups, followed by sit ups, then star jumps, not happy with this he made them all squat down and hop like bunnies. TC remembered from his recruit training days that this really hurts after a while as it plays havoc with your thigh and calf muscles and soon you feel the lactic acid taking effect. This went on for some minutes until TC lost his footing on a small rock and fell over sideways.

TC burst out laughing at himself and thinking about all these guys hopping around in the grass early in the morning. If anyone should have seen them, they just wouldn't have believed it, unless they were local, then they probably would. The Instructor was not amused at this and shouted at TC, "What the fuck do you find so funny, you can't even stay on two feet, what the fucks up with you"? To which TC replied instantly, "Just completely run out of carrots sarge," with this everyone started to laugh. This only antagonised the sarge even more, so he got them to their feet and began running again on and on. Suddenly they came to a lake filled with dirty brown water. As they stopped at the edge, the sarge shouted to everyone, "Why have you all stopped, I never told you to stop, now get in and swim to the other side. I will meet you there and if I get there before you, stand by for the run all over again and no breakfast".

Before he had finished talking, most of them were in the freezing cold shitty water. God knows what else may be in there fortunately God did know what was in there, as he didn't join them. TC thought the sarge was going in as well and it would be some kind of race to get to other side. It would be around 200 yards but he carried on running around the perimeter of the lake.

They all made it in time and sarge ran them all back towards the camp. Now daylight was just coming up and TC was ready for breakfast, a big breakfast but in the back of his mind, he kept thinking that this is not the end. It's a mind game, just as you think you have finished that little stint and believe you're going back for breakfast, they would change things. Apparently, this is what they do all the time playing with your mind, to see if you crack up and leave the course.

On this occasion, TC had it all wrong and they did go back to camp, so he thought after this, forget trying to pre-empt what is going to happen, as you can never win. Back in camp after a long hot shower and a mega breakfast, ready to continue the rest of the day. TC learned later on in the day that four candidates did not join them for the morning run but stayed in bed. Unfortunately they had gone, RTU'd (returned to unit), before the rest got back from the run.

As the weeks went by, physical every day, swimming in the huge swimming pool and learning about the different types of breathing apparatus. Most importantly, the laws which govern pressures and how different depths affect the pressures. TC had a job getting his head around the calculations, as it was quite technical but also imperative to life and survival under the water. If you got it wrong, you're in serious trouble and death would not be far behind. They did many tests in the swimming pool, to see if anyone suffered from claustrophobia, under water and in a very tight, dark confined space, as now would be a good time to find out and leave the course.

Unfortunately several had disappeared by now and the numbers were going down rapidly. With diving nearly every day, they were introduced to the famous Klepper Mk 2 canoe and TC had been waiting for this moment. How it's packed up into two sections, in order that a two-man team can mount them on their back packs and carry them overland. Once they had mastered how to put them together and in quick time as well, which comes from practice and more practice. Then in the water with them, learning how to control them and carry out the righting drills after a capsize.

In addition to this, how and where to stow all your kit, as there are two of you and these little canoes, surprisingly enough, can hold a lot of kit stores and ammo. First thing is, the seat gets left out as your back pack becomes your seat, so you sit low down making a smaller silhouette on the water. When dismantled and packed up in two sections, the skin is one part and the skeleton or ribs the other.

TC was halfway through the course when he was called before the boss to be given an assessment of his progress so far. He was told that he was doing well and as he spoke a second language and was also very advanced in Explosives and Demolition Techniques, plus he had been Para trained as well (this would be upgraded later), he would be an asset to the Section, (the name was later changed to Squadron). He was told once more, that he possibly might be a little too old. TC thought, too old at 27?

You cheeky sods, I'll show you. TC would always rise to a challenge, he could never ignore it.

Back to work and more diving, using a re-breathing set. This is also known as a closed circuit re-breather. This was the LAR V Draegar which is fitted to the front of the diver and uses a loop system, so that when one breathes out, the exhaled breath is passed through a carbon dioxide 'scrubber', where oxygen is added. Breathing in and out passes through a loop and into a canister of soda lime. This must not come into contact with water otherwise the diver will end up with what is known as a 'caustic cocktail'.

The first moment that a diver realises there is a leak, is when he gets a chalky taste and sometimes a mouthful of foam, similar to a 'sherbet lemon' bursting in the mouth. If this happens, the mouth must be washed out with either water or vinegar. Neither is very pleasant.

The advantage of this equipment is that it does not give out any tell-tale bubbles and does not make a noise like the Scuba System. It will also give you 4-6 hours of work time. This is ideal for covert beach reconnaissance or in harbours at home or on foreign grounds, examining the underside of shipping, especially war ships. Unlike the Scuba sets, where the diver can control his breathing to conserve air, the closed circuit or re breather set, one has to keep breathing as normal, in order for the system to keep working and replenishing the air.

Next came working with submarines, as these were the main vehicles to collect and deliver SBS teams on their deployments, therefore it is very necessary to practice entry and exit techniques, whether on the surface or most importantly for clandestine deployments, while the submarine is submerged, usually about periscope depth. This is much more difficult at night, when the visibility under water is nil. While being transported in the submarine, the teams normally occupy the forward torpedo rooms, along with their weapons and equipment. These rooms are very cramped and smell of diesel, hydraulic oils and sweaty bodies.

TC trained and operated up in the Scottish lochs with submarines, normally the 'O' class types, operating out of Faslane on the west coast of Scotland. Faslane or Clyde was home to the submarines in Gare Loch and TC's first encounter with HMS Oberon working in Loch Long, which was situated next door to Faslane. This comprised of loading and unloading stores on and off the craft via the forward torpedo loading hatch, also launching from the submarine, either over the side or in the Gemini rubber inflatables or canoes, sometimes practicing 'float-

SBS badge and motto.

Mk 2 Klepper frame.

Canoe's in use. These take about 10 mins to assemble and half that to disassemble ready to back pack.

Open circuit scuba diver. Note the give away expelled air bubbles, plus once the air in the tank has gone, 30 mins, that's it, quick ascent to the surface.

Diver wearing oxygen re-breather set.

Oxygen Rebreather

offs'. This is when the boats sit on top of the sub's casing or decks and the submarine submerges, thus floating off. This can be quite dangerous when the sub blows her ballast tanks to dive.

There are many techniques that the swimmers have to master when entering and exiting a submerged sub via the various airlocks. These are waterproof compartments on board, in which the swimmer enters and once locked in, the compartment is flooded and pressurised equal to outside pressure. On completion, the outer door is opened to allow the swimmer out. While the swimmer is in the airlock, he can breathe via the on-board breathing tubes known as umbilicals then once outside he can use a Raba. This is a small compressed air bottle with a fixed mouthpiece and will last about ten minutes. The swimmers RV at the 'lurking area' on the casing, where they can change to the sub's air supply and also recharge the Raba via the umbilical cords from the on-board high-pressure tanks.

TC had undergone classroom work, not only map reading but Morse code which he thought was not used any more but it's still very much in use. Morse code is a bit complicated to start with but once mastered, to quote TC, "It's easy".

Part of TC's selection course involved carrying huge backpacks loaded with stores, equipment and sometimes, half of a Klepper canoe on the top, then Yomping for miles across country. This of course was not new, as Royal Marines are well-known for being self-sufficient and Yomping for many days and nights, covering miles and miles but still be ready to fight at the other end, as they proved during the Falklands.

TC realised that this was a bit different, as these packs could easily weigh 130 to 140 pounds and as everyone who has done anything like this will know, that after Yomping for several hours with a heavy load on your back, when you stop for a breather and set down your pack, there is a weird feeling of light-headedness and a floating sensation.

Getting the pack back on again was not so easy. If there is someone to help, that's fine but TC found that by himself and by lying on his pack backwards, strapping it on himself, then by rolling over on his side, then on to his stomach, from there he could push up to the kneeling position and finally onto his feet. Certainly it was difficult but he could do it. During this phase, he recalled that three of the students had to give up. Two could not cope with the weight and the third developed a knee injury. If anyone wished to leave the course, they were never encouraged to stay, unlike recruit training, this was all totally voluntary.

Added to this, the students had no idea where they were going, how long they had to get there or the distances involved. TC remembered that at one point, he thought he might also have to give up, due to the fact that his left hip was becoming very painful and he did not wish to end up with permanent damage, which would certainly mean that he would not only fail the course but even worse, have to leave the Royal Marines altogether. This, he could not even contemplate. As TC commented, "Another play on one's mind" but then to TC's relief, the yomp eventually came to an end.

In fact, TC had dug a bit deeper into his psyche and managed to suck it up, in spite of being in considerable pain, he never divulged this to anyone and so passed the selection. To quote TC again, "I passed by keeping my head down and my 'smart arse' mouth shut". Now he was an SC3 (Swimmer Canoeist 3).

At last he had the following weekend off and had been contacted by his mate Slim, a Corporal from 'G' Company, 41 Cdo Malta, where they had worked together. Slim had found out from Taff, when visiting the guardroom from 42 Cdo at Bickley, Plymouth, that TC was on the SBS Selection course and so he invited TC to spend the weekend with him and his family at Plymouth. Slim's father had been an RSM in the Royal Marines and now owned a pub in Plymouth called 'Noah's Ark'. TC stayed there for the weekend and had a brilliant time.

Back to work with the SBS at Poole, the first few weeks were strange, getting used to a new life almost as no one appeared to be wearing uniform, there were no parades and some were told to grow their hair and stop shaving. A month had passed with more training, plus another two weeks of training with different styles of parachuting and using different types of chutes, this included leaving the aircraft with various amounts of kit and equipment, personal kit would be stowed in a large waterproof valise with their weapons attached and the valise strapped between their legs.

Obviously it would be impossible to land like this so, once out of the aircraft, a release pin on the side of the harness would be pulled and the valise would fall away and hang 15 feet below on a rope as it was with the basic course.

At night, this would be a good indication of where the ground was, by watching the pack when it hit the ground first. It was also very useful when doing a water jump, as the surface is almost impossible to focus on, this can be dangerous, because if this is misjudged the chute and rigging lines could drop on, or around your head, trapping the swimmer under the water. The drill was that, just before landing, to release one side of the emergency chute attached across the front of the harness, which covers the main release mechanism twist lock, then sit back in the harness and release the twist lock. Hang on until about 30 feet from the surface, as the valise splashes down you slip out of the harness and drop into the water, away from the chute. The chute will fall slowly away to one side, then swim to it and recover the kit, which will float.

TC and a few other team members were placed on standby for a short deployment in Northern Ireland. Up and till this time, he had not met any of these men before but as they were not on his course, he assumed that they had been SBS for some time. In other words, well seasoned.

2-man Klepper in use for sneaky beaky operations.

Special Forces operating from sub using a Zodiac rubber inflatable.

Diver using a Raba, emergency air system.

Special Forces fast insertion onto a beach or ship intercept by Zodiac craft.

Two Oberon class diesel electric submarines known as 'O' boats, used by the SBS for clandestine ops, they can switch to electric for silent running onto their specified targets. Picture right is actually HMS Oberon SO9.

Two weeks later, TC was given the heads up and the 'Job' was a go, so kit and equipment were packed after several thorough checks and off they went to RAF Brize Norton, hopped onto a Hercules C130 transport plane and flew across the Irish Sea, landing at RAF Aldergrove, Northern Ireland. TC, Ken, Vinnie and Brian all SBS, waited to meet two more guys and after a short wait, they were introduced to Terry, an SAS trooper and Frank who was also SAS but also 14 Det. They switched to a Wessex Mk5 helicopter that was on standby and flew them all down to Bessbrook Mill, near Newry, then a British Forces Base.

This was a very large military garrison with a very busy heliport and choppers flying in, day and night. They spent the night and most of the next day there and were eventually called in for a briefing by an officer from 14 Intelligence Detachment, (Nicknamed 'The Det'.), whose HQ were based at RAF Aldergrove, Nr. Belfast. The operation that they were being given came under the control of the Det, at County Fermanagh. The Det was responsible for the South of the country, which included Enniskillen and TC was aware that the Det was also part of the SAS.

TC had always referred to the SAS as them up there, meaning geographically situated at Hereford and the SBS were referred to by the SAS as them down there in the south at Poole. Although the SBS and SAS have always bad-mouthed each other it was always done with a degree of respect as they are both part of UK Special Forces and now here in Northern Ireland, they had to work side by side and support each other.

TC and his team were given a surveillance task, which would require TC working along with a trooper from the SAS, called Terry. They would be operating in a bad area of Crossmaglen, well known as bandit country by British forces. This is because the PRIA (Provisional IRA), would cross the border from Southern or the Republic of Ireland and carry out hit and run tactics, bombings, shootings or collecting arms and ammunition from various hideouts, then disappear back over the border to relative safety.

At 0100 the next morning, TC and his team were driven in an old blue VW van with side sliding doors down to their safe house. It was not actually a house nor was it safe but an old disused water mill, right on the border, and passing through Forkhill, which was known as an IRA hot spot. It was about 0215, when the driver stopped in a deserted lane. He had turned the vehicle lights off previously and was driving on a 'night scope', plus the van was fitted with a switch, which would cancel out the stop lights. The driver was another SAS trooper as was his partner, riding shotgun in the front seat with him. As they stopped, all the windows and side doors had been opened some way back, not for fresh air but most importantly, for observation purposes.

With the engine switched off, it was deadly silent and they sat there for a minute just listening. Eight pairs of ears and eyes straining in the pitch black and dead of night for any sound at all, a twig cracking, a vehicle approaching, footsteps on the road or even a strip of fence wire

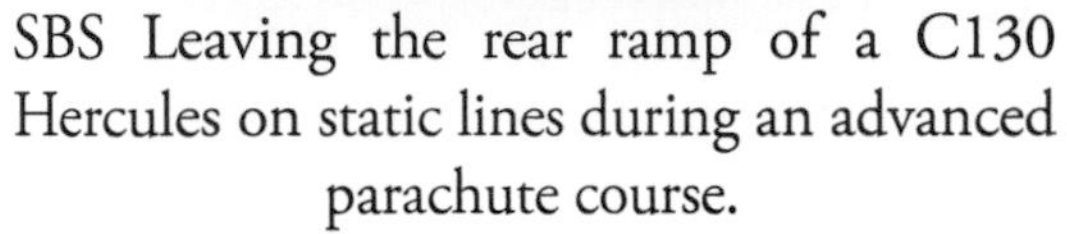

SBS Leaving the rear ramp of a C130 Hercules on static lines during an advanced parachute course.

Specialist free-fall jump from the rear ramp believed to be, a Chinook helicopter.

Parafoil guidable chute with weapon valise hanging below on cord.

Halo jump, free-fall from about 25,000 feet. High Altitude Low Opening, he is wearing oxygen, you do need this at this height.

The awesome Chinook work horse lifting a RIB from the water, this can also be delivered to divers already in the water dropped by chutes or by Helocasting, (Jumping from the aircraft).

SBS rapid rope down onto ship or oil platform for anti terrorist exercises.

twanging, usually when someone climbs over or under it.

The night was clear but with no moon and just a slight breeze which moved the tree branches and a slight rustle of leaves, if there was anyone out there they were as quiet as mice. After about two minutes, nothing, so very quietly, everyone was out with their kit and loaded weapons at the ready. A nasty surprise they didn't need.

TC was carrying his M16 Assault rifle and a Sig Sauer P226 Pistol. The M16 was a derivative of the early American Colt Armalite AR15, commonly used during the Vietnam war. This was the same weapon that TC used in Singapore and Malaya, only then, it had a straight magazine, which only held 20 rounds, now modified with a curved magazine it held 30 rounds.

This weapon was very light and easy to handle. Ideal for close combat as it can be fired semi auto (one round each time the trigger is squeezed) or fully auto (keep the trigger pulled and it will keep firing until the magazine is empty). This was TC's primary weapon of choice. His secondary weapon or back up, was the Sig Sauer P226 9mm Pistol, ideal for covert ops, easily tucked down the back of the trousers or in a pocket.

This was a Swiss made hand gun with a magazine of 20 rounds and can be fired all day long, without any malfunctions, unlike the Browning Hi-power 9mm, which was much heavier and prone to jamming. This is TC's personal opinion and had happened many times to him on the ranges. He used both weapons many times.

Once everyone was out of the vehicle, the doors were left open, so as not to make any noise, it would be closed later, away from the 'Drop-off-Zone'. The driver would roll the van down a slight gradient away from the team and using his night-vision, until about 60yards away before bump starting the engine and driving off.

Meanwhile the team had disappeared through a small gap in the hedgerow and went to ground a few yards away, remaining still for forty minutes before moving off to insert into the safe house. Eventually, once their vehicle was on its way, the driver would step on the brake for a second and the kinetic energy would slide the van doors shut.

One at a time, they moved off with Terry, the SAS Trooper in the lead, as he had been involved in the original set up of this operation. He knew the area quite well, so with a large gap between each other, they moved very slowly and quietly along the tree line and with absolute caution. They could not possibly afford to run into any 'Boyos' (IRA suspects) as this would result in an immediate contact followed by a shoot out. If this did happen the whole job would be compromised. It was also well-known that the IRA lay booby traps near gateways into fields, which is why that method is never used for entering or exiting fields.

Soon they came to a river, where they waded close to the edge. The water was only 12-18 inches in places and so they stayed in the river until they reached a small road bridge. They went under it and Terry told them to wait, while he did a quick recce on the old mill on the other side, which would be their safe house. Vinnie went with him to check it out. After fifteen minutes and no sound of gunshots, a low voice came over the radio headset with the words, "All clear, come on in."

One by one, they moved in, taking the upstairs rooms. There were no window frames in the building, just the openings, which made for a good 'OP' (observation post). The openings downstairs were covered by non-explosive early warning devices, just to warn them of any prowlers or even kids.

From the window apertures, they looked across to open farmland with fields divided by tree lines and hedgerows using their night-vision binoculars and over toward where they would be going to lay up and watch a farmhouse, which had a large outbuilding.

This was a suspected IRA meeting place and safe house, plus possibly an arms cache. The farm was about half a mile away but partially blocked by trees, so looking through the binoculars, they referred to the maps and aerial photos, to check the best route to and from, as this would have to be changed frequently, in case any boyos or farm hands found footprints in different directions and possibly could lay an ambush or an IED, (improvised explosive device).

Having studied the photos and maps, it was decided that TC and Terry, would use one of the routes, which led to within 40 yards of their target farmhouse, so at dusk the following evening they set off. Crossing the river under the bridge and going up the bank, over the small country lane and in through a gap in the hedgerow. They then followed a large tree line between two fields. At that point, Frank and Ken, from 14 Det, had followed TC and Terry to give them cover, especially while they were crossing the lane, then they went to ground and stayed put.

After a short stop, to look and listen, TC and Terry moved off again to the top of the field, crossing through a small ditch into the long grass and eventually came into sight of the south side of the farmhouse, which actually was the rear of the building. Just to the right of the farmhouse was a small yard with a large barn and next to this was a large haystack, covered in a black plastic sheet covered with old car tyres hanging from the sheeting to keep it in place from the wind and rain.

They made a drawing of the building, from as far as they could see, however, later in the early hours they intended to venture round the other side of the property, in order to gain a complete detailed drawing of the whole site. They crawled further forward and came to a small duck pond, which was not shown on the photos or map, so this was drawn in too. The pond had tall bulrushes to the south side, which made a perfect hide so when they belly crawled forward into the bulrushes they had a very good view of the buildings and the yard. Now Terry informed Frank, on the radio that they were on target and they lay there watching and waiting. On hearing this, Frank and Ken withdrew back to the old mill.

During an operation of this kind, the local forces, including the RUC, are informed to keep away from a specific area. This was always a bone of contention between the friendly forces, as the IRA possibly could get tipped off. The truth was that their way of intelligence gathering was usually very good and they had an abundance of friendly informants.

If the IRA was informed that the area was subject to a 'no-go zone', it would have been obvious to them that 'sneaky beakys' were at work there and this could have had various effects. One, they could keep well away, or two, they might set up ambushes, or IEDs and possibly a few may even be brave enough to go out on patrols, looking for the SAS or SBS. This would almost certainly end in a fire fight if they encountered an OP.

However, the thought that information could leak out and make their job even more dangerous, made them tread very quietly and carefully, this was the reason why they never used gates or the same tracks including gaps in stone walls, in case the IRA had set booby traps there.

The farmhouse was in darkness, very quiet and with no movement. The wind began to get up now and the bulrushes swayed and rustled. The trees behind them were also becoming noisy. This was not too bad, as this would hide any noise they might accidentally make but also could have the adverse effect by not being able to hear anyone approaching. That night, again there was no moon but rain, which was brilliant for them. TC had noticed that the skyline was extremely cloudy and overcast.

At 2330, a car drove in from behind the farmhouse and into the yard. They kept their heads down as the car's headlights raked the darkness and shadows danced about. The car stopped and the lights went out but it was a while before the car door opened but when it did out stepped a woman. She stood there looking around, then suddenly both rear doors opened and three men got out. They all went to the rear door of the farmhouse. While the woman was unlocking the door, the three men stood with their backs to her, looking in all directions, obviously on the alert. TC thought they definitely are in a cautious mode and he wondered if they could have been tipped off.

The door now opened and all four went inside. When the light was switched on, it flooded out the windows and doorway into the blackness and TC could see Terry laying just a couple of feet from him but after the door was closed, the woman drew the curtains. They could not see the registration number of the vehicle nor make model or colour of the car, as it was parked sideways on to them.

Terry whispered very quietly into his radio headset to Frank and informed him that there were four possible tangos (targets), on site with a vehicle also that they would move their position later, to gain more information. Frank's voice came back softly, "Ok, be careful. Out".

They lay there, very still and it started to rain. This is great for moving about as it helps to hide any noise but when one is laying like a stone or a dead tree trunk, it can become very uncomfortable when icy cold water penetrates the clothing and runs down your neck and back. This situation is nothing new to TC and Terry, they had suffered it many times in their careers but it did not mean that they enjoyed it. Quite the opposite!

The time was now 0055, and they could still see a small glow of light, which showed between a gap in the curtains. Suddenly the door opened, let out the light and illuminated the woman, as she came out. One man stood in the doorway, watching her. She got into the car and started the engine. "Oh bollocks", said Terry in a low voice, "She's fucking off. Crap! Now we can't get a fix on the car. Who the fuck is she?"

The car reversed and once again, the headlights flashed through the night sky. The back door of the farmhouse closed, as the car was driven out across the yard between the house and the barn. At that moment, both TC and Terry caught the back of the car in their night-sight binoculars and obtained the details of the vehicle. It was a dark blue Humber Sceptre but TC was unable to divulge the registration for security reasons. Subsequently, they found out through their radio, that it was registered to a Mrs Pat O'Donnelly (not real name) from the Forkhill area. Apparently she was well-known to the Det, although the three men left in the house were yet unidentified.

After one hour passed, the lights all went out in the house. The rain and wind got stronger, so TC and Terry decided it would be a good time to take a closer look round the other side of the buildings. They crawled away to one side, disturbing two nesting moorhens, who fortunately did not make any noise, then just as they stood up, the back door of the house opened and one man came out, without putting on any lights. TC's first reaction and thought was, Shit, we've been compromised. They froze where they were, watching the man at the door.

He was looking about him, then, he switched on a torch and began to shine it around. TC and Terry quickly sank down onto the wet soggy ground and did not move. The thoughts were tumbling through TC's head, why is this guy hovering about with a torch? What has he heard? What is he looking for? Is he expecting company? All these questions needing answers. One minute earlier and TC and Terry would have been caught in the open that would have ruined the whole operation, TC's heart was thumping and the adrenaline was coursing through his veins as he was prepared to shoot to kill. His thumb was on the safety catch of his M16. One tiny flick and that would be it. Restraint, restraint, this is where the best training in the world comes into force, discipline, no indiscriminate shooting.

They were now confident that they had not been discovered, as the man kept on shining his torch in one direction in particular, TC's thumb now relaxed off the safety catch. This went on for about fifteen minutes, when suddenly, two dark figures loomed out of the night, about seventy yards ahead and to their left they walked towards the building across the yard. The man at the back door switched off his torch and they all went inside.

There were no lights on at all now. TC's mind was in over-drive. He was thinking, who the hell are these bad bastards? They were definitely up to no good, although they did not appear to be carrying any weapons, such as rifles. Of course, they could have had pistols about their bodies but at that stage, who knows?

TC and Terry remained still for about three hours, as they did not know whether any more boyos would come calling and the possibility of the other two leaving at any time, either on foot or if a vehicle came to collect them, so many questions did create a dilemma. Their decision to stay put was due to the fact that it would soon be dawn and that they had to start moving out of there very soon.

At 0500 a soft voice came over their radio. It was Ken, telling them to withdraw, which they did very quietly. They made their way back, this time down the other side of the tree line. Much to their relief, the rain had now stopped and as they came to the edge of the lane, Ken's voice came over the radio again, to advise them that he and Frank were on the other side of the lane, to cover them.

Back at the Mill, after hot tea and some welcome food, they were able to get much-needed sleep. Later that afternoon, TC and Terry made a detailed report of where they had been, for the benefit of the next two out. This was Brian and Frank. They had to use a different route in and out and the rest of the lads remained on immediate stand-by, in case of any trouble.

The next three nights there were no movement or sightings at all, on the fifth night, again nothing happened, so Vinnie and Frank moved around the front of the farmhouse, updating the drawings, including the long track, which led from the house up to the main road. This was only a 'B' road. Night six, TC and Ken went out and by the time they reached the farmhouse, a light was on once again. As before, they lay, watching and waiting. At 2230, a car approached from the track and as it turned into the yard, they were able to see that it was driven by Pat O'Donnelly.

She got out of the car and went into the house. TC's brain was whizzing round with questions, who is in the house with her? How many of them are there? What are they planning? What the hell is this meeting all about?

Ten minutes later, the back door of the farmhouse opened and Pat came out with three men.

They looked like the three that she had in the car before the first time TC saw her. All four went across the yard to the haystack and appeared to be doing something to the side of it. TC could not see properly, so he decided to move position to get a better look. Now he could see that they had removed a bale of hay from the side of the stack and having reached inside, brought out three large wooden boxes. He watched, as they carried the boxes to the car and put them in the boot. The woman was carrying what looked like a couple of rifles. These were put in the boot too.

At this point, another car came down the track and into the yard. There were two men in this car and when they got out TC recognised one, from having seen him on the first night. They all went into the house and shut the door, leaving a chink of light showing through the curtains, where they had not been drawn properly.

TC and Ken lay there for about an hour, still no movement, so TC went round to the back of the haystack, where he could see the second car. It was a green Vauxhall Viva. He relayed this information in a whisper over his radio. Ken was now ready with his gun, covering TC, while TC crossed the yard to the side of the house. Ken whispered into the radio, "What the fuck are you doing TC?" To which he replied, "Wait out". Then he quickly moved past the door, ducking down under the window.

He slowly came up the other side and peered through the gap in the curtains. He could actually see them all but there were two extra men sitting at a kitchen table, with their backs to the window. They were drinking, smoking and laughing loudly. TC spotted an old Lee Enfield No.4 rifle leaning against a Welsh dresser. This weapon was used in WWI and WWII, a ·303, very accurate and very powerful.

TC had now pushed his luck enough and moved away, back to join Ken. They relayed this information back to Frank at the OP. Shortly, back came the info that the driver of the second car, the Vauxhall, was unknown, as the car had been stolen three days before. It was now certain that this was an active team and looked very likely that they were getting ready for a hit somewhere.

TC and Ken were then informed to keep watch and update any movement, as the RRF, (Rapid reaction force), would hit the house at first light, about 0530. This would be by two Wessex Mk.5 helicopters dropping onto the field at the front of the property. TC and Ken were at the rear and were joined by Frank and Terry, as goal-keepers to stop anyone escaping from the back. The lights went out in the farmhouse at 0210 and all was still. At 0430, all four spaced themselves out and waited.

At 0500, the call came in, "Aircraft airborne." ETA, twenty minutes. The night began to fade away and shapes and shadows started to appear. They could now see each other and the house very clearly. Before long, from the distance, came the faint beat of helicopter rotor blades cutting through the morning air.

TC, Frank, Ken and Terry now stood up and spread out further so as to cover a wider area, as the two choppers came into sight with 20 Royal Marines on board, probably all chomping at the bit ready to get stuck in. TC said to himself thank God it's our boys. The noise was getting much louder, as the aircraft were just one minute away and coming in low and fast both choppers swept in together, down like two massive birds of prey, swooping on their early morning breakfast. The marines were out in seconds, formed up and made their way to the front of the house, apart from two on either flanks. TC could not see the rest however, there was a loud crash and shouting, as the front doors of the farmhouse were smashed open and a rapid entry was made.

Within seconds the back door flew open and two men came running out, both in a state of undress. They were trying to get to the Vauxhall where the stash had been put but TC and Frank both opened up with their M16s hitting the front end of the vehicle. There were pieces flying off it and both tyres exploded. Instantly, the two men stopped where they were, cowering and put their hands in the air, shouting, "Don't shoot, Don't shoot."

At that moment, four marines came running round the side of the house to see what the shooting was about. Frank put his thumbs up, when they saw four armed men, all dressed in black. This is a sign for 'friendly forces'. The marines knew that the rear of the house was covered by SBS and grabbed the two men and took them inside the house. Frank and Terry went with them to inform the Officer in charge of the raiding party as to where the arms cache was hidden.

TC and the team made their way back to the OP to join Vinnie and Brian, who were waiting with tea and bacon banyos. They were all relieved of the successful outcome of the operation but also still very aware that boyos could be in the area. At 0725, they were informed that they should be at a specific location, not far from the OP and to pack up, clean up, leaving nothing behind. They were eventually picked up by the same blue van, which had delivered them. After the long drive back to Bessbrook Mill, they cleaned up and got some very welcome food, before going in for a full debrief. They were all well-praised for the success of this job, as it rendered eight prisoners, all of which were well known and wanted by the UDR, especially the driver of the stolen Vauxhall, as this was Kevin O'Donnelly, Pat's husband, who had been on the wanted list for a long time. He was apparently a very good bomb-maker.

Along with the prisoners, there were also a huge cache of assorted arms, ammo, Semtex, Det. Cord, fuses and grenades, in fact, a small arsenal. The team spent two days R&R around Bessbrook, waiting for another job, which never came, then TC, Vinnie, Brian and Ken were ordered to return to Poole, SBS lines again. Terry the SAS Trooper and Frank from the Det stayed behind.

Bessbrook Mill encircled, Newry N.I.

Wessex Mk 5 dropping in at Bessbrook Mill.

TC's Primary weapon of choice. The versatile 5.56mm M16A4 Assault rifle fitted with the 30 round curved magazine. Both mags on right are 20 and 30 rounds respectively.

Pair of Wessex Mk 5's on patrol over Crossmaglen Northern Ireland.

TC's choice of secondary weapon, the Sig Sauer P226 9mm 20 round Pistol.

Beautiful countryside of Crossmaglen N.I but then during the troubles, this was known as dangerous bandit country.

Terry and Frank tried to talk TC into transferring to 14 Det but TC decided that he would stay put for the moment, as he very much enjoyed what he was doing and with such a brilliant bunch of lads, it was like being part of another family. Everyone was laid back and there was none of this saluting everything that moved. They were all on first name terms too and TC said, "This is where I belong."

SBS Gibraltar

Two weeks passed by, practising beach reconnaissance in and around Poole Harbour, followed by a trip to Loch Long again, doing wet jumps into the Loch from a Hercules. Once in the water, they were picked up by a Zodiac RIB and put on board a submarine. From the submarine they practised more entry and exit drills while submerged and swimming ashore in the dark. There were more exercises while ashore and then a swim back to find the Submarine.

TC now found himself, along with three teams, on board a Hercules C130 en route to Gibraltar for a two week training exercise, using a new technique to board moving vessels in daylight and also during the night. At 1600hrs they were rigged for a HALO jump, (high altitude, low open). They had passed over Gibraltar at 22,000 feet, about seven miles east of the coast line and were given the 'green light'. Off they went, out of the rear loading ramp and into free-fall, over the Alboran Sea. At 1500 feet all chutes were opened and following the team leader, George Wright, they glided down toward a small Naval vessel, which turned out to be HMS Birmingham, also known as the Brum, a type 42 Destroyer. TC commented, "Well, at 1500 feet up, it looked very small. One by one, they all descended into the warm waters of the Mediterranean Sea, where they were collected by two of the ships' boats and taken on board with all their kit.

After a short sailing and some refreshment, they arrived at Gibraltar Naval Base, where they were escorted to one of the large hangars, which had been selected for their stay. Camp beds were laid out and a cook was assigned to them. Two lorries arrived with more equipment, which had been flown in on board the C130, from which they had previously jumped, along with the two drivers and two passengers, who were actually marines. They would be attached to the teams. Three of them would be driving the RIBS and one would remain in the hangar as Security.

Later that evening, after all the equipment had been unloaded, it would be thoroughly checked and double-checked again, including personal gear and weapons. TC and a few of the lads went out of the base and across the road to a pub for a few 'bevies', although not too much, as work would start at 0700 in the morning, after a quick briefing.

That morning, they were all out at 0500 for a run round the base, then a swim out to one of the buoys and back for tea and bacon 'butties'. Next, they were rigged in diving suits, for the swim out to where the HMS Brum was anchored, to conduct a thorough scan of her underside, from bow to stern and beam to beam, charting her size and working out her displacement. This was for exercise only, as members of the crew were alerted to the presence of the marines, so much so, that the ship's divers were in the water but by the time they had rigged up and were over the side, the SBS teams had finished and were on their way back to shore. (Not that the ship's divers would be willing to challenge the SB teams).

The following day, they set sail again in HMS Brum with all kit on board, including three RIB Gemini raiding craft, out through the straits of Gib, heading West, past the north coast of Tangiers. After two hours sailing, they kitted-up in black rig but with no diving equipment. The ship slowed to about twelve knots and the Geminis were put over the side. With them went TC and the rest of the SB teams, plus the three Royal Marine Coxswains. The RIBS pulled away from HMS Brum and took up a position 100 yards astern of her and followed her at the same speed.

While the Brum continued at twelve knots, the three SBS teams now closed up on the stern, with two RIBS side by side and the third keeping back for emergency purposes. As the two RIBS closed in to the ship, this is the moment it can get quite dangerous. The prop wash from the Brum, (she had two of these), could tip the RIBS over if the Coxswains get it wrong but to quote TC, "These guys are the best of the best".

They were testing new equipment and techniques to board the stern of a moving ship, the Brum and carried out a clandestine boarding. The ship's crew knew this was happening and a couple of hands stood by in case it went wrong but it didn't. Once the first two teams were on board, the third team moved forward and also boarded successfully.

HMS Brum slowed to a stop while the SB teams went back over the side back on the three RIBS, then off they went again carrying out the same manoeuvre, again and again. After five, complete boarding exercises without any hitches, they all boarded HMS Brum and she sailed back into Gibraltar. Back at Gib all equipment was once again unloaded and checked thoroughly for any damage.

Early in the evening, after a meal, they were called together in the hangar and given a de-brief on the day's exercise, whereby one or two changes were made regarding the new equipment and techniques used, which TC was unable to reveal, due to security reasons. With that, it was over to the pub for a couple of quiet bevies, once again warned as they were, not to overdo it. TC thought that was a sure sign something was brewing in the pipeline.

Royal Navy submarine in one of the Scottish Lochs during training exercises.

Splash down, on a P9 chute during a static jump into Loch Long.

They made their way back on board at around 2130, as they were told to gear up again. They were off on a night exercise at midnight. They set off in the three Gemini RIBS from the harbour and went out to HMS Brum, which was anchored about half a mile out this time. Weapons were carried with full kit. They had to board the ship, again from the stern but now the ship was not moving, then they carried out the same manoeuvres as before.

Once aboard, they made their way down both sides of the ship, taking over the bridge, the comms. room mess decks and engine room. There was no resistance from the ship's crew, as they were expecting this as part of the exercise. The boarding was very difficult in the dark and visibility very poor but nevertheless, it was successful. Once the exercise was over, it was into the RIBS and back to shore. Again, they had to check and double-check all kit and equipment. By now, TC was definitely convinced that something was coming, these exercises were part of normal training but this one appeared to be a little different.

During the following day, they were all pulled in for a briefing. TC's suspicions were about to come to life. They were informed that they might be required to board a rogue vessel, possibly carrying arms and ammunition and could be bound for Northern Ireland. Later that night they would be doing a night boarding on HMS Brum while she was on the move. This would be the final piece of training before the real thing.

No shore leave now, as they were all kitted up again on board HMS Brum. They set sail at 0130 and as the lights from Gibraltar faded and disappeared from view, they were totally alone in the sea, no other ships or land in sight. HMS Brum slowed down as before and the RIBS were once again put over the side, followed by the three SBS teams. They pulled away from the Mother ship and dropped back while the Brum picked up speed to around twelve knots, then apart from her navigation lights, she switched all her deck lights to infra red. TC thought, oh bloody hell, this is going to be a challenge, as he could not see 'bugger' all.

As they approached the stern and started to close in, it began to get very bumpy and they were getting thrown around, while the coxswain tried to find the right line. They could now see the clear phosphorescent glow emanating from where the two props were thrashing through the water, disturbing the micro-organisms. This acted like a pathway, leading right up to the stern of the Brum.

With the skills of the coxswains now closing up, the rear of the ship came into view, with the black outline of the stern rising up into the clear night skies, steady now. The caving ladders went up and attached to the railings. It was nearly a thirty-foot climb to the top. Looking back down, TC could see the three RIBS riding the ship's wake below, showing up like black silhouettes against the white foam.

With three more of his team below him on the ladder, TC peered along the deck line to make sure all was clear then made a quick leap over the rails onto the deck. He moved to one side and covered the rest of the team as they came over the railings alongside him. They moved off slowly and quietly in complete darkness, making their way up to the bridge. The three empty RIBS closed right up tight at the stern, so that they could not be seen. This went perfectly and so the final exercise was over. The ship slowed down again and the RIBS were brought on board. They now made their way back to base in Gib. The time now was around 0500hrs. Once again, check for damage of equipment and get some well earned sleep. The rest of the day was their own apart from a short de-brief, which went off without any problems.

Later, in the afternoon, TC went off for a short tour of the Island, which was quite breathtaking, especially from the top of the Rock, and the Colony of Monkeys, trying to pinch things from people, like glasses, purses, handbags or basically anything that wasn't tied down. He was looking down onto the harbour and could see the Brum out at anchor then he noticed a submarine entering the harbour into the Naval Docks. Later he found out that it was HMS Otus, another 'O' class Diesel-Electric.

The next morning, TC went along to the quayside to look at Otus. She was just wallowing in the sunshine in the clear blue waters of the Mediterranean Sea. She reminded TC of a huge black sleeping monster waiting to be woken up and to turn into one awesome weapon of destruction. The next two days were spent on board Otus, carrying out entry and exit drills while submerged and it made quite a change to be able to see clearly under the Med, as opposed to the Scottish Lochs or the freezing and rough English Chanel. TC thoroughly enjoyed it.

The only downside on any submarine is the cramped accommodation, not just for embarked UKSF (United Kingdom Special Forces) but even for the crew, who have to share bunks and sleep in shifts. TC remarked, "It was bloody awful". He made it very clear that with all he had done and may have to do in the near future, he would not do that. It was bad enough sharing a confined, smelly compartment with Mk8 Torpedoes for any length of time and trying to dry out clothing.

As well as entry and exit training, they carried out surface launches in the Gemini RIBS. These would be passed up through the forward torpedo loading hatches. At this point, they would be deflated and folded up. The craft would be laid out on the casing with a large manifold attached to the several valves and connected to the on-board compressed-air hose, which would inflate the craft in about 15-20 seconds. Once inflated, the wooden, folding decking would be inserted, then the 60hp outboard engine would be attached to the transom and fuel tanks placed inside at the rear, by the engine. These craft always carried wooden paddles, not only for emergency in case of engine failure but also to paddle into shore during a clandestine operation for silent approach.

When launching these craft from a submarine, this would be done with it surfaced and one of

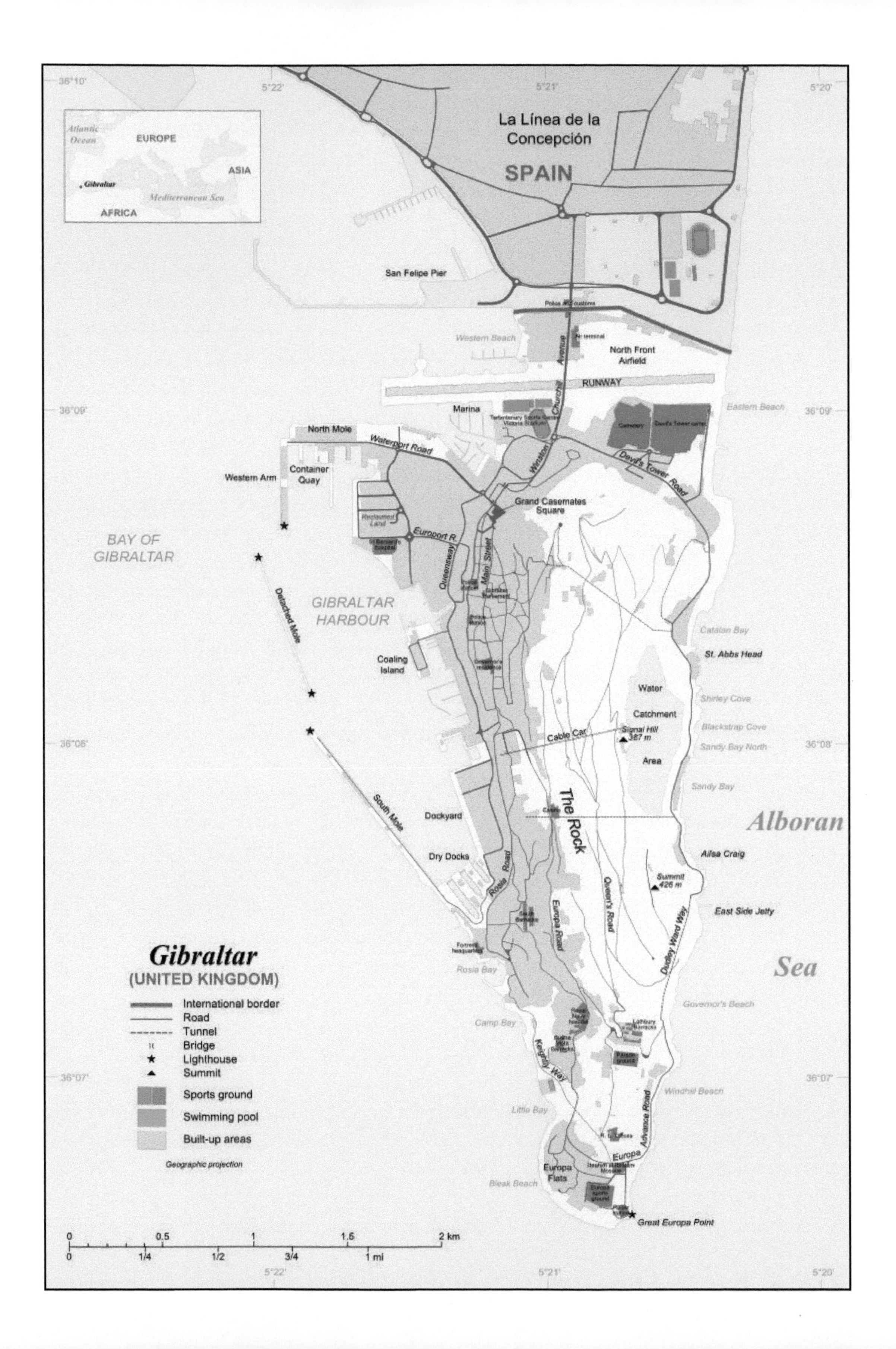

La Línea de la Concepción
SPAIN
Atlantic Ocean
EUROPE
ASIA
Gibraltar
Mediterranean Sea
AFRICA
San Felipe Pier
Western Beach
North Front Airfield
RUNWAY
Winston Churchill Avenue
Eastern Beach
Marina
North Mole
Waterport Road
Devil's Tower Road
Western Arm
Container Quay
Grand Casemates Square
Reclaimed Land
Europort R.
BAY OF GIBRALTAR
Queensway
Main Street
Detached Mole
GIBRALTAR HARBOUR
Catalan Bay
Coaling Island
St. Abbs Head
Water
Catchment
Area
Shirley Cove
Blackstrap Cove
Cable Car
Signal Hill 387 m
Sandy Bay North
Sandy Bay
South Mole
Dockyard
The Rock
Alboran
Sea
Dry Docks
Ailsa Craig
Rosia Road
Queen's Road
Summit 426 m
Europa Road
East Side Jetty
Dudley Ward Way
Gibraltar
(UNITED KINGDOM)
Rosia Bay
International border
Road
Tunnel
Bridge
Lighthouse
Summit
Sports ground
Swimming pool
Built-up areas
Geographic projection
Governor's Beach
Camp Bay
Keightly Way
Windmill Beach
Little Bay
Advance Road
Europa
Europa Flats
Bleak Beach
Great Europa Point
0 0.5 1 1.5 2 km
0 1/4 1/2 3/4 1 mi
36°10'
36°09'
36°08'
36°07'
5°22'
5°21'
5°20'

two methods used. One is putting the RIBS over the side and climbing aboard in the normal way. This is done when there is no direct threat to the sub. The other method is known as a float-off. This is used in order to give the sub the very minimum amount of time on the surface, as this is when she is most vulnerable. The RIBS would be inflated as normal on the sub's casing, while it is surfaced, then the teams board the RIBS, once ready to go, the sub blows her tanks and disappears beneath the waves, leaving the RIBS to float off.

This technique can also be used in reverse to recover the RIBS, once the submarine has been located. As it slowly surfaces, the RIB coxswains manoeuvre the crafts above the casing, forward of the conning tower and attach the RIB's bowline onto one of the sub's cables. As it rises, she picks up the RIBS on the outer casing. This is the same technique as with the canoes.

Once more, these drills are practised over and over again, as this is just as important for the sub's crew and Captain to get it right every time, as it is for the SB teams. Speed and accuracy are paramount, this includes day and night operations. There is no room for error, as any of these drills, not carried out perfectly every time, can lead to very serious injury or death. This is why training is always ongoing at every opportunity.

Back at base in Gibraltar once again and after unloading, washing and checking equipment, there was time to get some serious 'bronzy time' in and for anyone who wanted to go and swim. There was a small, single engine motor launch that would take them out of the harbour and lay off half a mile out, away from the shipping lanes, where it was clear to dive over the side and have a good swim normally larking about with a polo ball. It was basically, chill out time for TC and his team but it was also quite evident to everyone, by now, that something was definitely brewing and that they had not been sent out there for a jolly.

The next day, they were given a piece of electronic equipment to play with. This was made by Marconi and its function was like a transponder, which gave off an electrical signature. This could be picked up by submarines or aircraft, once they were tuned into the correct frequency. It was similar to a hand-held, two-way radio, with a short aerial. It would enable the sub or any craft to locate swimmers in the water. The frequency to identify the signals would only be given to individual operational craft, unlike the SART System, (Search and Rescue Transponder), where the emergency signals can be picked up by any craft.

Once again, off they went on board Otus out into the Med and were put over the side in the RIBS, powering away together. The teams were kitted up in diving suits but this time, with air tanks, (open circuit) sets, scuba divers, as opposed to closed system re-breathers. The sub had slowly slipped beneath the surface, leaving the teams in three RIBS floating in the middle of nowhere. They had shut down the engines and tied the three craft together by the bow lines. After half an hour, the teams went into the water roped to each other. They then switched on the transponder and every now and again, surfaced within sight of the three RIBS, which had their respective coxswains on board.

Divers on way to recce the hull of a ship, notice the 14ft rope between them, this is a Buddy Line and also used to measure the hull from bow to stern and beam.

Three Geminis in formation practising to board the stern of the Brum.

Training exercise, ship boarding, seizure and control by UK Special Forces.

Barbary Macaques on Gibraltar rock, RN Dockyard and Airport below. Spain in the background.

One out all out. Good day for a free-fall jump into the warm blue Med.

Using a Parafoil chute to steer in from a HALO, High Altitude Low Open. The HALO allows the operative to be dropped some 30 miles away from the target.

Royal Navy Type 42 Destroyer HMS Birmingham, known as, The Brum.

They were about three hundred yards away from the RIBS, when the sub's periscope appeared out of the water about a hundred yards away. The submarine had found them. They swam back to the RIBS and boarded. The sub was now on the surface and stopped within one hundred yards of them. The sub's crew were out on the casing and helped the teams aboard. The transponder had worked perfectly with a range of about fifteen miles, so it was back to harbour once more.

That afternoon, the Captain and two senior officers from the submarine joined the teams to discuss the equipment, which turned out to be excellent. TC and a few members of the teams tried to elicit a little information from these officers but they were tight-lipped. In truth, the teams were well aware that something was definitely brewing, so they kept a strict watch on all the daily news reports, trying to find out what they could possibly be getting involved in but were unable to pinpoint anything obvious.

The next three days went by with the usual fitness training, swimming every day and checking equipment twice a day. Weapons were constantly stripped cleaned and reassembled every day as a matter of course. On day four, all three teams boarded the Brum and sailed out of the harbour, into the Med., heading south west into the open waters. After a few hours, a target was put out on a raft and towed from the stern of the ship, about one hundred yards behind.

The SBS teams lined up and spent an hour shooting and testing weapons. The ship's crew, except for a couple of officers, were kept away. TC could have spent all day there many of his team would have done so also. Sailing back into Gib harbour once again, TC spent his time stripping, cleaning and reassembling his M16 and 9mm Zig Pistol.

Back in Gibraltar, about 2100hrs, they all went across the road from the base to the pub for some well-earned drinks and once again, they were informed of not drinking to excess, as a live operation could be impending. At last, thought TC, I knew there was something in the pipeline but where and when? All evening the lads could think of nothing else but sat in one corner of the pub, out of the way of prying eyes and ears. Later, TC and a couple of his mates walked around Gibraltar in the warm evening air until 0100hrs then made their way back to their grots. There, the marine who was on night security watch made them a cup of fresh tea. He told them that there was an O group at 1100hrs in the morning. O groups are Orders. A briefing. Unfortunately, the marine had no more information than that. TC thought, I wonder where we are going and what the hell could this be about? Well, all will be revealed at 1100, in only a few hours time.

SBS Operation

TC woke at 0600hrs and went for a quick run in the cool morning air. On his return he showered and downed a big breakfast, after which with his teams they got down to business by checking every item of their kit. This was absolutely vital to routine. Each man was responsible for all his own equipment and never touched anything belonging to another person, for any reason.

There was much speculation as to why they had been sent there, as this did not seem to be the usual practice for an ordinary exercise. It appeared to be more serious for this particular group. Every member has to be up-to-date with world current affairs, because any situation could arise, which would involve the SBS in particular, at any time.

TC and three of his mates wandered out of the naval dockyard afterwards and went to the nearest pub, the Tartan bar, which was just opposite the main gates. They sat at a small table in the far corner again well away from eavesdroppers and began to discuss in very low voices what could possibly be the reason they were preparing for. At this stage it was a complete mystery. They quietly examined everything that was going in the world, which could possibly involve them.

TC came up with a fantastic idea of getting into a taxi somewhere and asking the driver as they, like many other taxi drivers from around the world, always seemed to know what was going on. They all fell about laughing saying, "Oh bugger, why didn't we think of that before?"

Two days had passed, while they waited around the base, when eventually news came in that they would be having an update and 'O' Group (orders) at 1500hrs in the north hangar. They assembled in the far corner of the hangar, with a couple of the Royal Marines by the main door for security.

The SBS teams were informed that they would be required to intercept and board a rogue ship, which was carrying arms and ammunition, apparently bound for Northern Ireland. The

Intel (Intelligence) was accurate and that the operation had been fully authorised. The ship in question, had to be boarded quickly and quietly in the early hours of the morning, somewhere in the Med. She was allegedly carrying diesel generators, various machinery and parts but hidden amongst the cargo, were weapons and ammo. The ship was called 'Narfoss' and believed to be registered in Tripoli, Libya.

This was not her real name, for security reasons. Her last port of call was Sirte, on the north coast of Libya and heading for Warren Point on the south east coast of N. Ireland. The ship had to be seized and taken into Malta, with the crew, who were believed to be 10–12 persons of mixed origin, including the Captain. They were unsure whether or not there would be any resistance from the crew, so were advised to take all necessary precautions.

A helicopter fast rope down in the middle of the night would be inappropriate, as surprise and speed are paramount for a covert boarding. They would board from the sea on to the ship's stern, on the move and in the dark, which was exactly what they had been preparing for. The three teams would be airlifted by a C130a Hercules and dropped into the sea at a designated co-ordinate, where HMS Otus would locate them and take them on board, delivering them into the intercept area. Narfoss was being tracked by an RAF Nimrod.

HMS Otus had left Gibraltar the previous day. TC had noticed it leaving the harbour. Zero hour would be 0700hrs next morning, when the teams would be taken to the airport. Their heavy equipment and RIBS were already on board HMS Otus.

At 0700hrs next morning, they were ferried down to the airport in two lorries with all their tactical equipment. The huge C130 was waiting on the tarmac. They were kitted up with their parachutes and emplaned. The four big engines of the Herc roared as the plane moved slowly off. Everyone was strapped in and gave the thumbs up, so the crewman could let the pilot know it was good to go. The engines were literally screaming now and the plane was shaking. The brakes were released and this vast monster accelerated from a standing start, like a sports car, it hurtled down the runway and in less than half way, it was airborne, wheels up and heading west.

It gained height quite quickly, then banked over to the left and as it did so, Gibraltar was clearly visible from the port windows, at about 2000 feet below. They were given the thumbs up to undo seat belts, now they could relax for a while. After an hour, everyone was given the order to check equipment and check each other. There must be absolutely no mistakes.

They were ten minutes away from the drop zone, (DZ). Their height was now about twelve thousand feet. This was not going to be a HALO jump, just an ordinary tactical jump at low level, about two thousand feet. The weather was very clear, no cloud, just water as far as one could see.

Map from memory of the Narfoss intercept and sinking area in the Med.

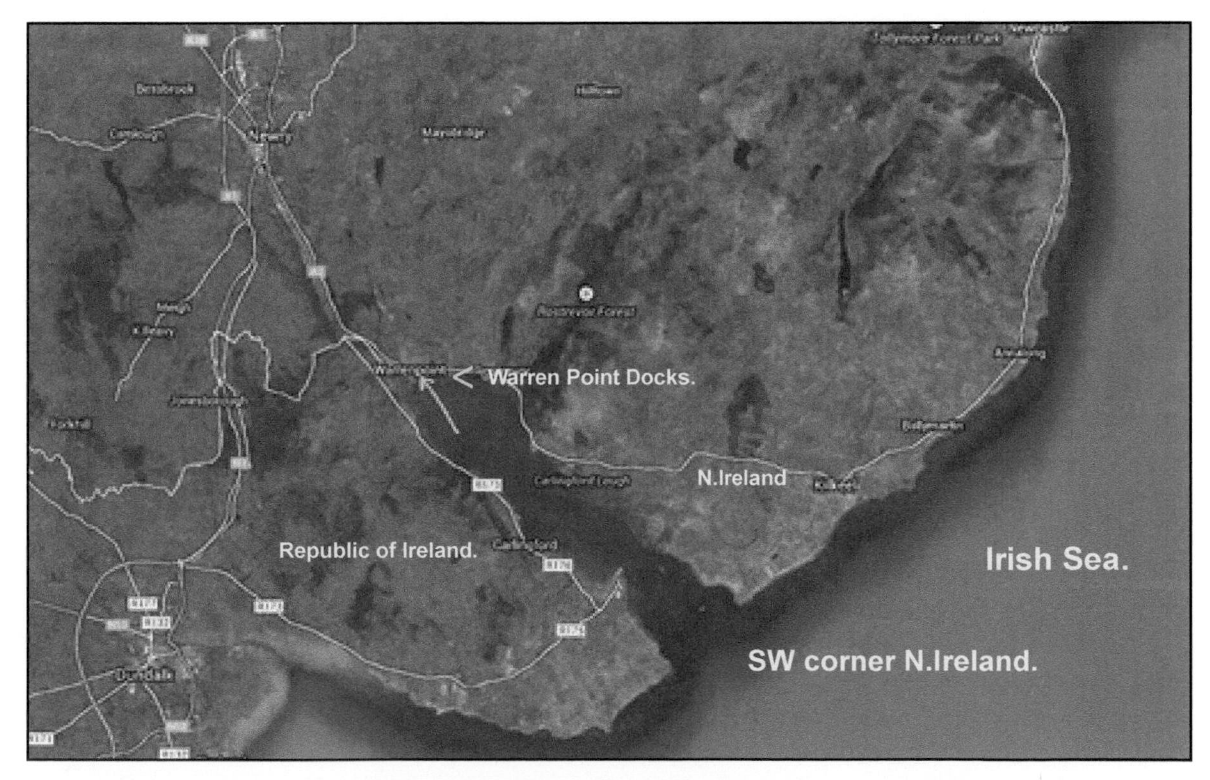

The docks at Warren Point N. Ireland where Narfoss was apparently heading for.

The aircraft descended quite quickly now, making one's ears pop. They were then given the thumbs up by the dispatcher and the rear ramp slowly opened. The noise of operating hydraulics and wind rush was deafening, and then one by one, they all stood up and hooked up their ripcords to the aircraft's jump line, as this was going to be a static jump, not free-fall. They shuffled up to the ramp, one behind the other, their equipment and weapons in a valise, strapped to their right legs and all wearing life-vests.

They were all watching and waiting for the red light above the doorway to go out and the green jump light to come on as this would be the signal to go. One after another, they ran off the ramp and out. The ripcords deploying their chutes would now break away and remain with the aircraft, as they descended one by one and straight into flight beneath the canopy.

TC looked up and saw the aircraft disappearing, with the last two bailing out of the back. He looked all around and saw the rest of the teams in close proximity then down below, he could make out red smoke on the water, which indicated the position of the three RIBS, waiting at the DZ, also the wind direction to guide them onto their target. Less than a thousand feet to go, so a quick pull on a cord to remove the pin, that secured the valise to the harness by a 'D' ring. This now fell away fifteen feet below, giving a sharp tug on the parachute harness.

TC and the teams glided in, close to the three RIBS hovering in the water below. He sat back in the harness, now one hundred feet from touch-down and some thirty feet away from the RIBS. He released the harness and like sitting on a swing now, watched the valise, and the split second it hit the water, his arms reached straight up. He straightened his body and slipped out of the harness a second later into the water. His chute fell away. He trod water for a short while, until one of the RIBS picked him and his equipment up. Most of the teams were already in the water, waiting to be collected.

Once all were out of the water, the submarine submerged about a mile away. This was to prevent any parachutists accidentally landing on or crashing into it. Otus now broke the surface and stopped. The three RIBS made their way to HMS Otus and all boarded her. All their equipment was recovered and loaded on board, then she secured, blew her tanks and dropped below the surface out of sight and made her way to the RV (Rendezvous point), which had been pre-determined.

Once more, they were all packed in like sardines in a can, roughing it in the forward torpedo room. They carried out final equipment and weapons check, as in just a few hours, they would be leaving the sub again to carry out the operation. The boss had left the room for an hour or so then came back with up-to-date orders. The target ship Narfoss, was being shadowed off her stern by HMS Otus, from two miles away and also showed up on the Nimrod's Radar.

Narfoss had switched off her transponders but she still used her radar. This is how the submarine and Nimrod were able to track her movements, course and speed. She travelled North West at approx 11 knots, heading between Malta and a small Island called Lampedusa, which is part of Italy, situated one hundred and eight miles South West of Malta.

Narfoss was an old cargo ship of three thousand six hundred tons, with a single screw, (prop.) The crew was believed to be now seven to nine persons. The plan was to intercept, board and arrest by carrying out a rapid clandestine boarding at 0100hrs. This time was chosen because apart from essential personnel, the captain, engineer and radio operator, the remainder of the crew should be asleep. Once the ship was secured, two Royal Naval Officers would come on board from Otus and the ship taken into Malta, where the crew would be taken into custody, questioned and probably returned to their respective places of origin.

The teams were now given the signal to get kitted-up. The sub had closed in on the Narfoss to about eight hundred yards then she quietly surfaced. The crew quickly had the Geminis out and ready to go but as the three teams of SBS went up onto the sub's casing, they were greeted with heavy wind and driving rain lashing down, causing a mist. Visibility was down to 50 or 60 yards, with seas quite choppy. As the submarine was pitching around quite a lot, launching by float-off was not an option but it was important to get off the sub quickly so she could submerge. The RIBS were put over the side while the boat was still on the move. The teams piled into the RIBS with all their kit and then releasing their bow lines, quickly shoved off under power.

Narfoss was not visible in the distance without night bins, (binoculars) as the rain had caused this curtain of heavy mist, which would be to their advantage on the final approach to her stern. They were being guided by the boss in the lead boat, as he had one of the night bins and a compass bearing.

They travelled together in close formation, the lead boat No.1 out in front, with No. 2 and 3 tailing close behind but to port and starboard (left and right) of No.1 so as not to travel in each others wake although with the bad weather and choppy seas, it was hard going and they were having a very rough and bouncy ride hanging on tightly, so much so, that there could be a possibility of an abort, for safety reasons.

They kept going, travelling at about 15 to 20 knots, albeit the crafts were capable of double this speed but in this swell it would be suicide, as the crafts could easily get flipped over, tipping all the guys and contents into the sea. The teams hung on to their kit and to quote TC, "We were hanging on to our stomachs too", when suddenly they picked up the white wake of Narfoss. They closed in fast and within a couple of minutes, the black shadowy shape of her stern came into view. The boss then gave the signal to close right up to Narfoss, as he couldn't see any lookouts on her decks, especially at the stern, where the boarding would take place, which was very good news.

This ship is not the actual Narfoss but almost identical.

HMS Otus underway in the med.

RAF Nimrod, very high altitude AWAC (Airborne Warning & Control System) re designed from former Comet aircraft.

The three Ribs had settled down now, as Narfoss was displacing water and leaving fairly flat water behind her. The boss and team of boat 1 deployed the caving ladders onto the stern rails of Narfoss. The team went up very quickly and held their position at the top. Teams from 2 and 3 went up and joined them, so far so good, they had not been noticed. TC had joined the boss with two others from the first boat. Their task was to seize control of the bridge. Team 2 had to take care of the crew on their mess decks, with team 3 to the cargo hold to search for the contraband and photograph it.

Once the crew were safely under guard in the crew room, two members of the team went down to the engine room to collect the engineer and search the rest of the ship for any stragglers. At this point, two Naval Officers would have been ferried from Otus to take control of Narfoss but these operations hardly ever go to exact plans and this one was no exception. Narfoss fell quiet, as her engines had now stopped. The ship slowed and came to a halt. She was now officially adrift in open seas. Apparently the engineer had been secretly signalled to by the Skipper to carry out a procedure that they had arranged between themselves prior to sailing. The engineer had not only shut down the engines but had cut and damaged the fuel lines, plus opening the sea cocks. Sea water was now rushing into the engine room. It mixed with the leaking fuel oil and was quickly flooding the compartment.

The engineer was caught running from the engine room and straight into Mac, from team 2. The engineer had decided he was not going quietly. Coming face to face with Mac, who was all dressed in black, with a ski mask and carrying M16. The engineer had pulled a fire hatchet from the bulkhead (wall) and went in for an attack on Mac with it. TC thought, that it was a bloody stupid thing to do. Mac could have quite easily given the engineer a 'double tap' (two quick shots), and the engineer would have been immediately despatched but again as TC mentioned before unlike many other special forces, the SBS are not trigger happy. Firing two shots would have been the very last resort. Mac parried the hatchet to one side with the barrel of his M16 and in a single follow-through movement, smashed the engineer full in the face with the butt of the weapon.

The engineer fell to the floor screaming, holding his face, with claret (blood) pouring profusely from his mouth and nose. Mac had broken the engineer's jaw, nose, eye orbit and removed a couple of teeth. The engineer was dragged still screaming to the crew room, where one of the crew attended to him with first aid. The rest of them, whatever they were thinking of doing, seeing their shipmate, decided to behave and did not cause any more trouble.

Team three who were down in the hold had broken open several boxes, some of which had assault rifles, hand guns, grenades and an assortment of ammunition hidden in amongst equipment and spare parts. In one of the crates, they uncovered two hundred blocks of Semtex, (plastic explosive). The team took photographs as they went, carrying on breaking open boxes, unaware that the ship had taken on so much water, that she was now listing to port (left) by about 5 degrees.

Over their head comms, they were told to get out and up on deck as water was now flooding into the hold. Barry from team three, decided to try and get into the engine room, dive down and try to shut off the sea cocks but as the teams had no diving gear with them at this point, he would have to do it blind without goggles and just by holding his breath and groping around in the black soup and in complete darkness. Unfortunately as he was making his way along the corridor toward the ladder, leading down into the engine room, not only was the engine room under water but the corridor was also under a foot of water mixed with fuel oil. Not knowing where to find the sea cock and whether there was one or two, he realised this would be an impossible task so quite rightly he decided to abort. He turned and made his way back to join the rest up on top, along with the now arrested crew and the other teams.

The submarine had been informed of this situation, surfaced and came up close to Narfoss about sixty yards off her port bow. Otus put all her floodlights on, lighting up the sea and the port side of Narfoss. This operation had now changed to a rescue situation.

TC, the boss and Jim escorted the captain to his cabin in order to seize all the papers, ship's log, and the ship's manifests/instruments. One of the team tried to remove a brass porthole as a souvenir, this was tradition with a captured vessel, unfortunately they had ran out of time. The boss then instructed everyone to muster on the port side upper deck for a head count, not only for the SBS teams but also for the Narfoss captain to identify his crew in case any were missing or hiding bearing in mind that the ship was now sinking. The three RIBS came up tight alongside. The crew of the Narfoss were put in first and ferried across to Otus. The three SBS teams waited on Narfoss for the RIBS to return for them. The boss asked TC to go with him to the cargo hold as he had something to do. They collected three satchels from the rest of the teams. These satchels contained made-up demolition charges with timers.

Narfoss was now in a bad way. The two of them made their way below to the forward hold, where the illegal arms cache had been hidden. They waded waist deep in fuel oil contaminated water. Things were floating about. As they reached the cache, they took out several charges, setting the timers for thirty minutes and placed them under the water, in among the ammunition and grenades. The boss put one in the box of Semtex but decided to keep one of the blocks, which he put in his satchel, not just for evidence, (as they had photographs), but because it is possible to trace where it was manufactured and supplied.

Job done, as the boss said calmly, "Well done, now let's get the fuck out of here, double quick". On the way back to join the others, the boss slipped on a steel ladder going up, as they were both covered in stinking slippery fuel oil. TC grabbed the boss, who had fallen under three feet of water and had twisted his left knee badly. He could just about walk, although he was in severe pain, cursing and swearing. TC helped him up and they managed to get back up on deck. Two of the RIBS had already ferried the rest of the teams back to Otus and they were safely on board, while two of the team had waited for TC and the boss to return. They went over the side and into the waiting RIB. The boss turned to the marine coxswain and said, "Don't spare the horses lad, that fucking lot is about to go up with a big bang". The look on the marine's face said it all. The outboard motor screamed on full throttle, the bow of the craft rose up out of the water and they were away at high speed toward Otus.

In less than two minutes, they were back alongside HMS Otus. Once out of the water and onto the casing, the boss informed the Otus Skipper of what had taken place and what was about to happen. The submarine stayed on the surface and sailed well away, not only monitoring the slowly sinking Narfoss but keeping a check on any other shipping that may be nearby. Fortunately, he was informed that there were none within at least a seventy mile radius. They all stood around on the sub's casing, as the Narfoss sunk lower and lower into the sea.

Twenty minutes later, she rolled over and disappeared from sight. Just a ripple of white foam breaking the surface from trapped air blowing from her. This was all being recorded by Otus. Still they waited on deck, one minute to go. The boss and TC were both checking their watches now and by this time, the boss's face showed signs of being in real pain from his knee injury.

Then he started his countdown, 5, 4, 3, 2, 1, then nothing, a long pause. TC muttered, "Oh shit" but suddenly there was a huge muffled rumble followed by a massive white water spout erupting from the surface and up into the air. TC said that he thought it looked like an enormous white oak tree and that it must have been about a hundred feet high. They were about half a mile away at this point but within a couple of minutes, the submarine was suddenly hit and buffeted by a few large waves, one of which broke over the casing. All kit had been recovered, stowed away and the casing cleared. Otus blew her tanks and dropped below the surface and out of sight once more.

As the ship Narfoss no longer existed, it was decided not to go into Malta with the prisoners but to sail strait back to Gibraltar instead. TC was disappointed, as he had hoped to have a day ashore in Malta and although the marines and other British forces had left he still had some local friends he would have liked to have called upon but it was not to be.

By the following evening, they had reached Gibraltar once again, TC commented, "What a relief to get off the submarine and seriously stretch my legs". Once the submarine had docked, the prisoners on board were met by Royal Naval Police and taken away.

The SBS teams unloaded all their gear and went straight for a full de-brief and to prepare individual statements as to what had happened.

TC thought that they would all probably be called or summoned to a board of enquiry but this never took place. It was a well-known fact at the time that Libya and Gaddafi were supplying arms, money and ammo to the PIRA. TC said, "That was one huge arsenal that never found

Boarding team assaulting a ship on the move from a Zodiac craft.

Underwater explosion similar to Narfoss when she met her end.

Port window similar to the one in Captains cabin of Narfoss, not enough time to remove it unfortunately.

Assault team making their way to captains cabin along port side, forward to aft.

its way onto the streets of Northern Ireland". He also remarked that Libya was not alone in supplying the PIRA with the means of indiscriminate death and destruction.

No time to sit around and ponder. The very next day, TC and the teams were on board a C130 whizzing across the Channel back to Brize Norton and were bussed down to Poole in Dorset and SBS company lines. As there was no work for them at this time, TC took some leave and went home to Deal, where he had previously bought a house and met up with a lot of old mates. His drinking hole was 'The Lifeboat' pub on the sea front. This was full of 'bootnecks' in the evenings. When this closed, there was a private drinking club, just a hundred yards from the pub. This was called the 53 Club. It was a normal property, a dwelling with the upstairs turned into a private bar, run by Olive, who owned the property. If you were a regular you had a front door key or you knocked on the door and a chap would let you in. Again, this would be packed to the gunwales with bootnecks and Wrens until it closed when about 0200hrs.

There was very little trouble from drunkenness. If anyone did get out of line, they would be swiftly taken care of by the other patrons, as they did not want any trouble from the local police, (most of which were former Royal Marines and had used the place for after hours drinking, themselves).

Just a few yards away from No 53, was the Royal Marines Association. Not many serving members used this, unless it was with their families, the rest were mainly retired members of Royal Marines and some WWII veterans. TC felt very much at home in Deal, more so than his home town where he was born and grew up.

He was not aware at the time that his leave would be short-lived, as he was about to receive a signal from Poole, that he would be required to report to CTCRM at Lympstone in three days time, with all of his kit and uniforms. He had been selected to attend a Senior Command Course (SCC). TC was surprised yet delighted with this because upon a successful completion, he would gain his third stripe and be promoted to Sergeant.

SCC (Senior Command Course)

The course lasted eight weeks and had to be passed in order to be promoted to the next rank of sergeant, which TC wanted very much. He returned to Poole straight away to collect his kit and clothing. Then it was off to CTCRM Lympstone.

When he arrived to start the course, TC discovered that a few of the mates with whom he'd had the pleasure of serving in Singapore and Malta, were also on the course. There were eighteen corporals on this course, all of whom were senior corporals in the Corps. It normally takes eight or nine years to get on a SCC after having been a corporal for five to six years.

TC knew that this course was going to be extremely hard but nowhere near as hard as the selection for SBS and pretty soon they would all find themselves back on Woodbury Common, going back over the endurance course but this time carrying telegraph poles. They had six men to a pole, which must go over and under all the obstacles without touching the ground. Once round the circuit, the pole would have to be carried all the way back to the camp, four miles of narrow, twisting lanes and of course, Heartbreak Lane. Needless to say, it was very exhausting at the finish. Physical training was paramount, as a troop sergeant has to lead from the front, and would be in charge of extremely fit men.

In the evenings it was either a few bevies in the JNCO's Club, or go into Exmouth, seven miles away and do the pub rounds. Of course, like anywhere else, there were always the popular pubs for Bootnecks and Exmouth was no exception. The favourite was The Ship, run by a little old Portuguese man. He'd had the pub for many years and was quite used to marines of all ranks packing into the pub in the evenings. This also brought in many of the local girls. It became a busy meeting place, where they could expect to get invited to the dances back at the camp because there was very little else to do in the town.

TC and his mates could not help making fun of everything, even when the going got really tough. One night six of them decided to go ashore into Exmouth and have too much to drink. They started in the JNCO's Club and having a quick one, before piling into TC's car. (He was the only one with a car at this time), when a matelot came and sat with them. He said that he had noticed over a few days, that TC and his friends were always joking and messing about and that he was at Lympstone on a course but did not know anyone. He asked if he could join them when they went into town. They agreed that this would be fine, so all seven squeezed into TC's Ford Consul 315 and off they went, whizzed out past the sentries on the Main Gate, who shook their heads in total disbelief at their antics as they drove past. They had a certain reputation by now.

First port of call was The Ship and they decided to play 'The Seven Dwarfs'. The matelot did not know what they were talking about, so TC explained that when they get there, they stay outside, give you the money and you go in and order seven pints of lager. When they start to come up on the bar, make a big fuss by lining them up at equal distances apart and make a point of looking down the row of pints. Move one or two slightly to make sure they are perfectly in line. By this time, you will have everyone's attention and they will find this really weird. They will wonder what the hell you are doing. TC continued to explain, that they will stay outside but watching through the window and when you are ready, shout as loud as you can, Hi Ho, then they will all come in, one behind the other on their knees with their left hands on each others' shoulders and singing, Hi Ho, Hi Ho, it's off to work we go.

The matelot burst out laughing and said, "That's great, brilliant". TC gave him the money and he went into the busy pub. They watched Jolly Jack through the window, as he ordered the seven pints and began lining them up. The bar owner looked towards the window with a grin on his face, he had seen this many times and so had most of the patrons, who were chuckling to themselves.

Once all the pints were lined up, Jack turned to the door and shouted,"Hi Ho." At that point, TC and the rest all buggered off and left him in there on his own feeling a complete pratt. They never saw him again that evening. The next day, he came looking for them at lunch time and called them all the bastards under the sun. Albeit, he thought it was very good, that he would be trying it out on some of his own guys when he got back. Great!

On another occasion, the lads went ashore on an alarm clock run. They bought big alarm clocks, the ones with a handle and two bells on top. They tied them around their necks and just before going into the pub set their alarms for ten minutes. They were all drinking, when the alarms suddenly went off together. They quickly downed their pints, (this is known as sandy bottoms), then rushed out of the pub leaving the patrons in hysterics and many completely bewildered. They repeated this at several other pubs too.

Another time, six of them jumped into TC's car, during one lunch time and went to The Ship in Exmouth, instead of using the JNCO's Club on camp. After a few quick pints and forgetting to keep check on the time, they hurriedly piled back into TC's car and sped back to the camp, as they were resuming at 1400hrs. They had to attend a lecture in one of the many wooden huts that were there and did not want to be late and risk getting a Yellow card.

They sped through the gates without stopping, ignored the Provost Sentries who jumped out of the way. Without stopping, the car careered down the main drive toward the JNCO's club car park. On this course, there was a coloured card system in operation for any misdemeanour's similar to the yellow and red cards used by referees at football matches. One yellow card meant a warning; these could be for untidiness, or late on parade. Get three of these and one would get an RTU (Returned to Unit). If the offence was of a more serious nature, one would receive a Red card. This would be an immediate RTU.

TC sped down the main drive, turned left half way down, into a cul-de-sac, tyres squealing and parked his car outside the JNCO's Club, which was also next door to the wren's accommodation. TC was driving very fast and as he got down to the JNCO's Club he slammed on the brakes, then all four doors flew open and they fell out, (including TC) onto the road, to the complete astonishment of the wrens and the corporals, who were coming out of the club, (TC had pre-arranged this little episode as another one of his pranks), one or two of the wrens gave a startled scream, then one of the corporals said, "Don't worry, it's only the SCC playing around again". Everybody thought that it was hilarious seeing TC and his mates lying on their backs in the road with their feet still inside the car.

Their joviality quickly wore off, as they had to run like hell up to the hut because they only had a couple of minutes to go and no one wanted to be the first receiver of a yellow card. Up until then, no cards had been issued. They rounded the corner and saw the rest of the course who were mustered in three ranks outside the hut and the colour sergeant instructor was chatting to them while waiting for the sergeant major to arrive with keys to the hut.

They just got in the ranks when the sergeant major arrived and opened the doors. The course started to make their way in, when suddenly the sergeant major told them to fall back into three ranks outside, which they did. This was unusual but they were then told that the course officer, Lt. Palmer, would be arriving. The sergeant major called them to attention, as Lt. Palmer arrived and halted behind him. They saluted each other. The officer then told the sergeant major to bring the course to open order. This means that the centre rank stands fast and the front rank takes one step forward, the rear rank one step back.

This is for inspection purposes. All TC heard were very low whisperings, like, "oh shit, oh bollocks", as they were not expecting an inspection. TC was in the centre rank, about half way along when the sergeant major bellowed, "Shut up" because of mumblings going on in the ranks. The officer walked along the front rank slowly with the sergeant major. The officer looked as though he was in a bad mood because he found fault with nearly everyone and ordered the sergeant major to take the names of offenders.

Mostly, it was about boots not being cleaned during the lunch-time period and some needed haircuts. The officer was in a really bad mood now and had insulted one or two. TC remarked, "He was just being a real pratt". Eventually, he came to TC and stood in front of him looking him straight in the eyes then stared down at TC's boots but even though TC had not cleaned them since the morning first parade, he made no remarks at this stage. Slowly, the officer's eyes moved up from TC's boots to his combat trousers, belt and shirt, then, looking at TC's beret, he said, "Place your index finger on your beret badge now".

TC raised his left hand and placed his finger on the badge without hesitation. All very good but the badge should have been directly over his left eye and TC's badge was between his left eye and his left ear, about two inches adrift. The officer raised his voice and said, "Stand at ease and correct your beret now." TC did this but as the officer went to move on to the next person, he turned back at TC and said, "Do you now know how to wear your beret properly corporal?" TC replied, "Yes Sir." The officer said, "Good," then he paused and said, "How long have you been in the marines, corporal?" Without a second thought, TC said, "Five years Sir." TC surprised himself and thought, "Why the fuck did I say that, when I have been in for almost nine years?"

At this statement, the officer frowned and did a double take. He must have thought to himself, five years, why is this corporal on a SCC after only five years in service? He then said, "Five years?" Quick as a flash, TC was now very pissed off at this. He made things worse by replying, "Yes Sir, five years longer than you." TC thought that this would be taken as a light-hearted remark but it went totally wrong because now the rest of the course fell about laughing but the course officer was not. He turned to the sergeant major and scowling said, "Give him a red card and get the rest in the class room." Immediately, the laughter stopped abruptly. TC's heart sank and he thought, oh shit I can't believe I just said that.

The sergeant major walked up to TC and right in his face said, "You fucking twat". He then ordered TC to report to his office and wait for him. After about half an hour, the sergeant major came in and said angrily, "That was a pretty fucking stupid thing to say to the boss, very funny but fucking stupid. You could have been done for insubordination," he continued, "I have just had a meeting with Lt. Palmer and pleaded your case. He did find your remark quite funny but your saving grace was your immaculate and impressive service record, therefore on this occasion, he will accept an apology and waive the red card but from now on TC, keep it zipped." The course officer did agree, that having people like TC making light of all bad situations, was very good for morale, especially when everyone is under extreme pressure and suffering from exhaustion.

Two weeks went by, working hard, mostly out in the field with TEWTS (Tactical Exercise without Troops). They were given an area up on Woodbury Common again and had to make a plan of where they would sight the trenches, the troop HQ, the gun groups, covering left

Main Gate at CTCRM Lympstone Devon.

Relatively new to TC, monument at CTCRM.

TC's regular watering hole along with many marines.

Ford Consul 315, similar to TC's. Unfortunately, TC blew his up.

and right of arcs, which should overlap with the adjacent troops on the left and right. It was a full day out. This area was regularly used by the recruits to do various field craft day and night exercises, as TC had done years earlier, when he was a recruit. It is usual practise that when you leave a designated area, which you have been occupying, you are told to make sure that you fill in all the trenches that have been dug before you go, as members of the public use this area as well, however this didn't always happen.

On this particular day, after stopping to eat a packed lunch, they all sat around chatting laughing and joking as usual, when suddenly TC spotted Lt. Palmer approaching from below a small hill, about one hundred yards away. The first time TC noticed him it was only the officer's beret which was all that was visible but as he got nearer, his body gradually came into view and he was walking through tall ferns which were about three feet high.

TC drew his group's attention as he said, "Pig off the Port Bow." This was a commonly used derogatory term in reference to an officer, although sometimes they were referred to as Grunts or Ruperts. They watched, as Lt. Palmer got closer. He was up to his waist by now in fern and wading through it, when all of a sudden, he completely vanished, all except for his beret, which was on top of a fern stalk and swaying back and forth in the breeze. The whole group burst out laughing, as it became apparent that he had fallen down into a trench that had not been filled in and by now was covered by a layer of thick undergrowth.

Suddenly Lt. Palmer emerged on all fours. He stood up, well aware that the group was in complete hysterics. He snatched his beret from the top of the ferns and stormed towards them shouting, "I suppose you fucking lot found that very funny. That's why we back-fill the trenches when we leave. It could have been an unsuspecting rambler, who could easily have broken his fucking neck and all you bastards can do is laugh." As he stormed off, the colour sergeant instructor called to him, "Sir, your beret is not on straight," to which came a very posh reply from the officer and gentleman, "Fuck off".

The final part of the course came, which was a four day exercise in Sennybridge, in the Brecon Beacons, Mid Wales. This is one of the biggest military training areas in the UK. It not only caters for live artillery firing but ground troops as well. This is the playground for SAS and SBS training. TC was well acquainted with this very unforgiving and hostile landscape, especially in winter. Always wet, cold, windy, it takes no prisoners if you're not prepared or ill equipped, as it's full of bloody big hills, waterfalls, bogs and mountains. The ogre of them all is the Black Mountains.

Once again, TC found himself yomping with a massive backpack of about one hundred pounds plus. When they did stop, they were told to dig in but before they had dug less than halfway, they would be attacked by members of the training team acting as the enemy, then they would have to up sticks to give chase, (seek and destroy). At night, they went out on various patrols and returned just before first light. By the time they had arranged to make a brew, they had to break camp and move on. All day spent yomping, although now and again, a lone sniper would open up on them, whereby he would be located. Then a carefully orchestrated assault on his position would be carried out, his position or hide over run and he would be destroyed.

Each member on the course over the four days would be selected to take on the various duties of a Troop Sergeant and Troop Officer respectively. They also carried out vehicle ambush drills using four ton Bedford lorries with the canvas canopy removed, just leaving the metal hoops in place. The course were driven along dirt tracks and at some point along the way, members of the training team laid in wait and ambushed the vehicles. They all bailed out, returned fire and counter-attacked the insurgents. This took a couple of hours.

During the night, they marched to a given location and laid an ambush to catch and destroy the enemy, this could be all night. By now, it was very difficult to stay awake and alert. Needless to say, for some reason the ambush was never sprung, so just before first light, they abandoned the position and did even more yomping, about 60km by the following evening, when they were told once again to make camp in the woods and dig in for long term occupation.

As this was a tactical exercise there would be no cooking or naked lights allowed but TC and two of his mates dug a large hole, put a waterproof poncho over the top and lit up a small gas cooker, making tea and soup. Everyone had to do a stint on guard duty during the night.

By first light, on the last day, they packed up and moved off. They were given a grid reference, which would be the final RV End Ex (end of exercise). The only real downside was that they still had to yomp another 25km and by now, no one had any sleep over the past four days and the silence and lack of morale spoke volumes. They yomped along now like a bunch of Zombies.

About a mile away from the RV, some lads put it around that when they arrived, they would be given another grid reference and another RV to get to before last light. This was common practice to see how many could take the pace and who would crack up. This now took effect and everyone was really down. In spite of this the instructor who was with them, stayed silent, not making any comments.

The previous day, one of the lads had wrapped his hand in (given up). He wanted to come off the course. He stated that he was only a cook and did not see the need to go through all this misery but he was told by the training team that he just had to carry on, as they had no means of getting him back to Lympstone. This was very unfair on the rest of the course, as this chap was allowed to walk along smoking. The previous evening, when everyone had to be tactical, he was allowed to smoke and cook his food, also he quickly got his head down as soon as it was dark and did not have to do any guard duty. TC said, "It was a bloody unfair situation." To add insult to injury, at

The correct way to wear the green beret, badge over left eye.

The wrong way or when you are an old sweat, long service.

The disappearance of Lt Palmer, leaving behind his Green Beret...

Woodbury Common landscape, covered in gorse bushes.

Pen-y-Fan, the highest point in the Brecon Beacons Wales.

TC and Peter on top of Corn Du early February.

Troops on top of Pen-y-Fan being lit up by helicopter night sun search light.

the end of the course, he was given a pass. Unfairly a few more deserving guys were failed.

Nearing the RV now, they could all smell bacon frying as it drifted on the breeze from miles away, their stomachs began to make funny noises. The mouth-watering aroma of this bacon tantalised them. The pace now picked up. Instead of a stroll, some of the lads called out, "Break into double time." Morale lifted immediately. They jogged in time to their singing. Three hundred yards up the road ahead, they saw the vehicles parked in a field and blue smoke rising up. This was not only the RV but it had been the instructor's base camp for the duration of the four days and also the final RV.

They were told to get washed, shaved and get into clean gear. The food was waiting for them. Big mugs of hot tea or coffee and a plate full of eggs bacon, fried bread, mushrooms and baked beans. Brilliant. They sat around on the grass, eating and chatting about the last four horrendous days and before long they were on board the lorries making their way back to CTCRM Lympstone.

As the lorry left the area, TC looked out and said goodbye to the massive hills, mountains and the whole treacherous area. Less than half an hour on the road, everyone was lying on their kit on the floor of the lorry and crashed out, asleep, all the way back. TC thought, thank God that's over. Back at camp, all kit was cleaned and packed away, weapons and ammo returned to the armoury.

The next morning, they all paraded at the hut again at 0800hrs. This time there was no inspection. One by one, they were called in to the course office, in front of all the training team and given the good or bad news as to whether they had passed or not. Happily, TC had passed but two of his mates had failed on this occasion but would be allowed to return to go through everything again. Poor sods, thought TC.

The course now dispersed and they made their way back to their respective units. TC decided to stay for the weekend, finish off his leave and at the same time put all his uniforms into the tailor's shop to have his stripes sewn on. He was chuffed to bits now having his third stripe up and welcomed into the sergeant's mess.

Hopefully, it might not be too long before he would get promoted from SC3 to SC2. This would really be something special.

Back at SBS HQ Poole, he showed off his new stripes and was congratulated. Later he was informed that he was about to be deployed on another mission very shortly. But where?

SBS Northern Ireland

A week went by. It seemed to drag on forever then he eventually received a movement order. He was heading back to N.Ireland, this time to join his old Unit, 41 Cdo. They had been disbanded upon leaving Malta but had now been re-formed at Depot Deal in Kent. They were in training and rehearsing many various drills for their forthcoming deployment. At this point, 42 Cdo were already on the ground patrolling the southern border of Crossmaglen and operating mainly from Bessbrook Mill.

TC was shuttled to RAF Lynham, where he met up with two more SBS operatives, Sid and Patrick. Sid and TC had met before but not Patrick, who was an SC2 and while they were waiting to board a C130A Hercules, they were approached by another sergeant. This man was known as Skull. TC thought this was because he was bald but he found out later that it was because his voice was so loud he was referred to as 'Screaming Skull'. He was a member of the SAS and an instructor for 14 Det.

Three hours later, they landed at Aldergrove RAF base, which TC had left several months previously. They were met by two more SAS operatives, Tony and Spike. Tony was their driver and Spike turned out to be Lt. Milligan, (hence Spike).

They all piled into a VW people-carrier and set off for Belfast, taking the Antrim Road. On arrival at King's Hall, Balmoral, Belfast, the first item on the agenda was scran. Having not eaten for some time, TC's crude remark was that he could dip his bread in a leper's neck. This always raised a laugh and a cringe, especially at the dinner table. The six of them sat down to eat and get to know each other, as they would be working together for the duration.

They spent the night at Balmoral and after breakfast next morning, Tony drove them to Palace Barracks, North Down, just outside Belfast Docks, where they were led to a large room upstairs. There were other men in the room, some in uniform, a Captain, a Major and a Lt. Colonel, also two men in plain clothes with long hair, (obviously undercover). One of these last two was an I.O. (Intel Officer) from 14 Det.

Once everyone was seated, a briefing began but due to reasons of security, TC was not able to divulge the content of the briefing. They were going to different locations to search for several bad boys and were split into small groups. They were also joined by some personnel from 41 and 42 Cdo. By now, 41 had arrived and were billeted in three different locations around Belfast. TC, Pat and Tony were tasked to work together, along with a 7-man patrol from 41 Cdo.

These three were based at the old Flax Street Mill on the Ardoyne Estate. Just brilliant, thought TC, what a charming area to work in. It was full of tightly packed terraced dwellings, most of which were back to back with a multitude of dead-end roads and a labyrinth of small alleyways, mainly, inter-connected.

The estate was notorious for IRA hit-and-run tactics, as many of the residents were supporters but in addition, the Crumlin Road ran right past the western edge. The sound of gunfire was almost an everyday occurrence in this area. Their task was to assist patrols on the estate, being close by in an unmarked Ford Cortina and trying to identify wanted suspects.

They monitored the exchange of radio messages and if the patrol came upon any suspects, whether they could be identified or not, TC and the crew did a drive-by to make a positive I.D., so the patrol could sweep in and effect an arrest. The patrol would have an RUC officer (Royal Ulster Constabulary) with them as the British forces were there in theory to assist the Police.

Additionally, if a property was raided, TC and his lads would be parked round the corner as cut-offs, in case anyone decided to leg it. On one occasion, just as a property was surrounded and entry made, Pat caught sight of a lone gunman skulking in one of the alleyways, about 50 – 60 yards away, on the opposite side of the road. The man was holding a hand gun and took up a position to aim a shot at one of the lads in the patrol outside the premises.

There was no time to call up on the radio and warn them, so against one of the golden rules, (don't show out), TC and Pat leapt out of the car, while Tony immediately took off down the road to get away from the area and avoid becoming a sitting target.

TC and Pat, handguns drawn, sprinted across the road towards the gunman, ready to take him out. The first thing that crossed TC's mind was that if any of the patrol saw them running up the road towards them carrying handguns, they would more than likely open fire on them, (blue on blue, as it is called). The next thought was that if TC took a shot at the gunman now, this would more or less have the same effect. If he wasn't hit with the first shot, he would probably make a run for it but then again, the patrol would likely fire on TC and Pat, not realising what was happening.

At this stage, the pair of them were less than 20 yards away. As TC levelled his pistol and about to fire the gunman turned his head and saw them. He turned and ran off down the alleyway. Pat managed to call up the patrol on his headset and informed them of what was happening.

TC gave chase into the alleyway and saw the gunman disappearing round the corner. He fired two shots at the gunman while still running and Pat gave a commentary over the radio. TC was furious that he missed but the shots caused the gunman to drop his weapon in his panic to escape and not to be caught in possession of a firearm, knowing also that he would not be shot while unarmed. By the time TC arrived at the corner where the gunman had dropped his weapon, there was no sign of him, he had just vanished.

He knew this area very well and had now disappeared, although he could have gone in any one of three different directions. TC and Pat decided not to pursue him any further, in case he had back-up and they did not wish to run into an ambush, plus by now there would probably be a cordon put in around the area. It is normal practice by the IRA to have a waiting getaway car standing by, with three or four IRA members in it.

By now, there was plenty of back up for TC and Pat, who had given a very good description of the gunman over the net. As they both emerged from the alleyway into the road, neighbours were out in their droves to see what was going on and curtains twitched at every window. TC thought, this is not a good place to be at the moment so he called up Tony, who told him where he was parked. They quickly made their way to the car and left the area.

TC had the pistol that he retrieved from the alleyway in his pocket. It was an old 38 Webley, WWI Officer's Issue and very effective. This weapon was handed in, along with their reports. It later transpired after forensic tests that this weapon had been used in the murder of a Police Officer in Belfast the previous year and fingerprints on it were also on file. The owner of the prints was caught and arrested two weeks later. He was the same gunman, who TC and Pat had chased in the alleyway, good job done.

TC took a lot of stick because he had missed the gunman but he countered with this statement, "I had no wish to shoot an unarmed man in the back under any circumstances, and in an alleyway, where there may have been many witnesses". Yeah right, he thought.

Four days went by without incident. Two of their targets had been picked up and were in custody. The job was going well so far. They still had four on their list, one of who would later became a Member of Parliament. He was wanted for questioning regarding being an active bomb maker.

TC, Pat and Tony were touring in the late afternoon on the outskirts of the estate, when they stopped at a junction in Cavehill Road, deciding whether to go left or right. It was then that they noticed four lads on the corner who were eyeballing them. One of the lads quickly put his

RAF Aldergrove, Belfast, also known as Belfast airport, N.Ireland.

The famous Kings Hall, Balmoral Belfast, used as one of the barrack accommodation during the troubles.

hand inside his jacket, as if to reach for something. This was a very stupid thing to do, as TC and Pat were both sitting with their guns in their laps.

Tony decided to turn left and put his foot down. The lads waved at them, as they drove away. The one with his hand inside his jacket pulled his hand out and made a hand gesture, by pointing his fingers at them like a gun. They had now been 'sussed'. It was time to get rid of the Ford Cortina for another vehicle.

They quickly turned into Old Park Road and at the bottom it joined the Crumlin Road. They noticed that a blue Vauxhall had followed them when they turned out of Cavehill Road. As they stopped at the junction with Crumlin Road, the Vauxhall ran into the back of them quite hard. A quick glance in the rear-view mirror told them that there were four in the car behind but they made no effort to get out. Were these Special Forces or baddies? There was no way to identify these at this time.

Like a flash of lightning, Tony took off into the Crumlin Road. The Vauxhall gave chase and was close behind. TC was wondering if it might be friendly forces. If that was the case, they might think they were chasing baddies and engage them in a shoot-out. This had happened on a couple of occasions but there was no time to establish facts. Tony drove at speed and turned into Clifton Park Avenue, then carried out the normal evasive techniques through the streets, turning left, then right, then right again. By now the Vauxhall had fallen behind and was out of sight.

They had decided now that if these were friendly forces they would know the routine and would have still been behind them but as they lost the Vauxhall so easily, it became obvious that they were not UKSF.

They drove slowly down one of the many narrow streets, then came to cross-roads and drove slowly over into the next street. Suddenly there were several loud bangs and a couple of bullets slammed into the side of the Cortina. The door glass in the passenger's side shattered, spraying everyone with shards of glass oddly there was no sign of the blue Vauxhall. Tony shouted, "Where the fuck did they come from?" He took off again like wild fire, carrying out the immediate action. They could not see where the shots had come from but turned left and right as quickly as possible, to break the line of sight, hoping that they had not turned into a dead-end road.

Tony had his pistol on his lap. TC and Pat were holding theirs, ready for instant action but still they did not know where the shots had come from. TC shouted out, "Anybody hit?" "No" came the replies. Pat reported over the headset, that they had contact and a fast response team was being deployed.

As Tony reached the T-junction at the end of the narrow road, he was about to turn left, when the blue Vauxhall suddenly appeared 200 yards away. It started to come towards them. Tony swiftly turned right and took off again at speed. He called out that another car was right behind them. This one was a maroon Ford Escort, with four up.

Tony began his evasive driving again. TC remarked that he was a bloody good river. Pat gave a running commentary over the radio as to their position and direction out of the estate. Once back on the Crumlin Road, they headed south. The traffic lights ahead were red and the traffic had stopped. Tony put the car up on the pavement and drove through the junction, turning right. He had near misses with three vehicles or it was precise manoeuvring at speed but he never faltered once, he stayed cool and in control.

He turned hard right, straight into a large private car park, where he drove in between several parked cars. They all bailed out and took up a firing position behind a small brick wall, where they were prepared to take on the suspected bandits. Pat gave an update over the radio but because there was no feed-back about any other covert operatives working in the area, it was assumed that these two vehicles would be treated as hostile and dealt with as bandits.

They waited and watched, leaving the car where it was, for about fifteen minutes. Pat volunteered to have a walk round, so TC and Tony split up and moved position so they could keep eyeball and cover Pat. After a few minutes, a mobile patrol arrived. Pat made himself known to the patrol. Thank God for that thought TC, the cavalry to the rescue.

They gave a brief outline of what had happened and a description of the two vehicles in question to the patrol officer then all three got back into their car and were escorted out of the area back to base, where the car was taken out of service and underwent a thorough forensic examination, due to the damage.

After two days at base they were sent to Thiepval Barracks in Lisburn, about six miles SW of Belfast. This was the main UK army barracks. Upon arrival, the first stop was the galley. Whoops, they were now on pongo territory, so it was the cookhouse.

After a mega meal, they collected another 'Q' car. This time it was a green Ford Orion belonging to 14 Det. It had all the bells and whistles on it. Tony nearly had an orgasm when he was shown what was fitted on the car. There was a hidden switch to cancel stop lights as usual but also a hidden radio and microphones. The doors had Kevlar bullet-proof panels fitted, also a hidden shotgun and places to hide automatic weapons, like the Heckler Koch MP5 K, a short-barrelled weapon, capable of being discreetly secured under clothing and many more which TC did not wish to reveal.

This vehicle had more goodies and it went really fast. Exactly what is needed to get out of sticky

Palace Barracks, Holywood East, Belfast near Belfast docks.

Palace Barracks, failed attempt at blowing the wall by the IRA.

The old Flax Street mill Ardoyne Belfast. Another temp Barracks for British forces.

Ardoyne estate viewed from the OP on top of Flax Street mill Belfast.

Aerial view of the Ardoyne estate, note the compact design and maize of alleyways.

situations quickly. With a tank full of gas and all their kit on board, they left Lisburn and made their way south to Bessbrook once again, TC's old base.

Once there, they reported to the Intel Centre, where they met up with Sid and Skull again and after the briefing, they stayed the night. The following morning, they left in two separate cars and drove down to Warren Point, where they liaised with a section of Royal Marines, who were based at the harbour on security duties.

Intel informed them that there were three people working at the docks who had been waiting for the ship Narfoss but when it failed to arrive, they disappeared, returning two months later, after the dust had settled. The two teams were given a room within the Harbour Authority office, which would be their base. They set up cameras in the top office for surveillance in order to observe these three suspects and they moved around as normal, so as not to attract any attention to themselves.

Now and again, they used the pub just outside the harbour. It was called The Victoria in Dock Street. This was fairly safe, used by many foreign nationals from the various ships. TC and Skull both had a very good Irish accent, so they were able to blend in quite well.

After a couple of weeks without any sightings of the suspects, they were told to pack up and withdraw because the suspects were arrested by the RUC and in custody, charged with other offences. They returned to Bessbrook and were debriefed. It had taken a while for the intelligence to filter through from the RUC, as to the arrests of the three suspects, whose names have been omitted, for security reasons.

TC and Skull were teamed up with a section of Royal Green Jackets, to act as advisors and were flown down to Crossmaglen by helicopter. The area was very dangerous for troop transport movement when using certain roads, due to many ambushes, PIRA illegal road blocks and the infamous roadside bombs, that had previously claimed many lives. Not just military personnel but civilians, as well as RUC officers.

They were dropped on the outskirts of Crossmaglen, just off the Newry Road, into a field. The officer in charge was very young. His name was LT. Carlton-Smith and this was his first time in the province. The rest of the patrol were mainly mature soldiers, a couple of whom had seen action in N.Ireland before and this was their second or third tour of duty.

Their objective was to patrol across open country, skirting round the North West side of Crossmaglen, just south of Lough Ross and hole up in two separate areas to observe the border with the Republic where insurgents or PIRA were crossing over to carry out hit-and-run tactics. This had been done many times in the past.

The problems facing British forces were that many of the locals, in this particular area, were supporters of the PIRA. The Provisional IRA was also known as the South Armagh Republican Action Force.

This group was involved in the Drummuckaval Ambush in 1975, on a part-time observation post. This was situated south of Crossmaglen. Fusiliers were manning the post at the time, when twelve PIRA crossed the border from the south, attacked the post, killing three fusiliers and wounding one. There were no casualties on the PIRA but they left behind one of their assault rifles, a Colt AR15. This was the early model of the M16, used for the first time in Vietnam, which TC had mentioned in earlier chapters. Ballistics proved that this weapon was also used in the killing of five civilians earlier, also for the deaths of two Royal Marines in 1974, at the same location.

As a result of the Drummuckaval Ambush, the Secretary of State for Northern Ireland, Merlyn Rees, dubbed South Armagh as Bandit Country and this brought in the SAS and SBS, UK Special Forces to seek out and deal with these insurgents. This is where TC and the patrol, were heading.

TC had advised the patrol officer to keep off roads, stick close to hedgerows and not to walk across open fields. Do not pass between gaps in walls, nor use gateways, as these are prominent places where IEDS (Improvised Explosive Devices) are likely to be placed by the IRA. This made the going very difficult and slow progress but it had to be done like that for safety's sake and to keep a low profile.

This started off well but about halfway, time was getting on and the Lt. decided to increase progress by ignoring some of TC's advice. TC was unhappy and angry about this, especially when they reached Loughross Road, the officer ordered them to follow the road at a jog, (known to marines as a speed march).

This road was actually a narrow country lane with high banks and bushes on either side. If they were ambushed here, there would be virtually no escape, fish in a barrel, as TC called it. He then got into a furious argument with Lt. Carlton-Smith, who arrogantly pulled rank on TC. Quite a lot of the men in the patrol were unhappy about being in such an exposed position and Skull stepped forward to back up TC's advice but to no avail, it was ignored.

Following on, TC and Skull decided to get off the road and travel one either side of the hedgerows to give good observation and maybe an early warning. Two cars passed by with the occupants inside taking a good look at the patrol jogging along the road. This really annoyed TC and Skull now, as this was in his opinion, bloody stupid. At this point, TC jumped over the hedgerow into the road and ran to the front of the patrol shouting, "Follow me and get off this fucking road now". The men did this immediately and without hesitation. They had no desire to get caught out.

Main entrance to Thiepval barracks, British army HQ Lisburn N.Ireland.

The Heckler & Koch MP5K a favourite with special forces. Hard hitting, easy to conceal, massive fire-power.

The .38 Webley revolver dropped in the alleyway and recovered by TC.

MP5K small but deadly, light and easy to use, note the folding stock.

Ford Orion, similar to the one TC and the team used.

TC and Skull took over, leading the patrol off the road and into a nearby wooded copse, out of sight. They had less than one mile to go now. They took up all round defence positions in the woods for a short while, observing, waiting and listening to make sure they had not been compromised. TC was watching the road they had just come from, to see if either of the two cars had returned but nothing transpired and it seemed that they had got away with that stupid performance.

Thirty minutes went by, when Lt. Carlton-Smith came over to TC and Skull and informed TC that on his return to base, he would be reported for insubordination and disobeying orders, which could amount to a court martial. TC then had a brief altercation with the LT. telling him that he was very inexperienced, bloody dangerous and that his basic field-craft was absolute shite. Voices were raised and TC was furious. He turned to walk away, calling the officer an idiot. The officer was livid and shouted at TC, "How dare you walk away from me?" He reached forward and grabbed TC's left arm to pull him round.

TC's lightning reaction as he turned round, knocked the Lt.'s hand to one side and with the heel of his right palm, struck the officer in the centre of his chest, pushing him away. This sent the officer of balance, reeling backwards and stumbling to the ground. TC's comment was, "Heels, arse and head."

There were a couple of murmurs from the patrol, seeing what had just occurred, one saying, "Oh fuck". The officer jumped to his feet, a little dazed and wobbly. At this point, Skull seeing the look on TC's face and realising that he hadn't finished with the officer just yet, stepped between them and said to TC, "That's enough". TC replied, "Ok, no problem".

The officer said very loudly to TC, "You have just got yourself one big court martial". He turned to Skull and said, "You saw that, didn't you?" Skull replied, "I saw you manhandling TC Sir, then you fell back over a log". The Lt. said, "OK, very funny but my lads saw what happened, I have plenty of witnesses". He then went to his lads one by one but none of them owned up to seeing anything. They were too busy scouring the fields and hedgerows for bandits.

They moved off now for the final RV. TC thought to himself, Christ, I've only just had my stripes sewn on, they could be coming off soon PDQ (Pretty Damn Quick), then he thought, well, without any witnesses, he does not have a leg to stand on. Oh yes, that's why he fell over.

They arrived at their RV and imbedded themselves in amongst the undergrowth and covering two separate positions, lasting all night. It was still just light when they reached their RV and after a little while, TC noticed a much better position, about two hundred yards away. After the light faded, TC approached the Lt. and suggested that they quietly move out to the new position in case they had been sighted. That way, there would be no nasty surprises.

On this occasion, the officer agreed, so he took one group and TC and Skull took the other. Very quietly, they withdrew back fifty yards, then moved two hundred yards to their left and repositioned themselves into the much better location. They watched, listened and waited.

The night went by very slowly and TC heard a couple of the lads getting restless and moving slightly. They may have not been used to laying up for long periods without moving, so he crawled to them and told them how to relieve muscle spasms without actually moving and possibly give away their position. This is by using 'Dynamic Tension'.

Squeezing and relaxing leg, feet and arm muscles, screwing the toes around inside the boots and opening and closing fingers tightly. This helps to increase blood flow and prevent cramps, plus it helps to keep one warm.

The night was almost over and the shadows of dawn became clearer. Vision now increased. This would be the best time for an attack, if it were to come. They waited and waited but nothing happened.

At 0930 hrs they broke camp, slid away into the undergrowth and made off towards the pickup RV, two miles away. The RV was a large piece of scrubland on the southern edge of Lough Ross and right on the border with the Republic. At midday, they received word that they were being picked up by helicopter in thirty five minutes.

When it arrived, they boarded the chopper very quickly, while keeping watch to protect the aircraft from any attack. Soon they were off, skimming across the leafy treetops and swerving around hedgerows at very low level. The machine soared higher and headed back to Bessbrook, passing over Crossmaglen.

Upon their return, shattered and in need of hot showers and food, one by one, the men on the patrol came to TC, shook his hand and thanked him, saying that they had learned a lot in those few hours. They wished him good luck and went away to their respective accommodation areas. Lt. Carlton-Smith came over and said to TC and Skull, "Very well done chaps and thank you but a great pity we didn't have contact with the bandits". He turned to TC and said, "Don't worry sarge, I won't be pursuing any disciplinary, like the rest of my guys, we've all been taught a lot on this trip. I look forward to working with you lads again. Thank you".

TC was very relieved, as he did not wish to argue with the Lt. in a court room, in front of high ranking officers and a judge advocate, mainly because they are deemed to be in the right, even if they are blatantly wrong. They would have supported the officer and TC wouldn't stand a chance. Three days later, TC was back in Belfast, Aldergrove Airport and on his way back home to Lynham. Another mission over until next time.

Harbour front Warren Point N.Ireland.

Foot patrol bandit country Crossmaglen.

Search for arms cache or IEDs.

RUC officer accompanying a patrol.

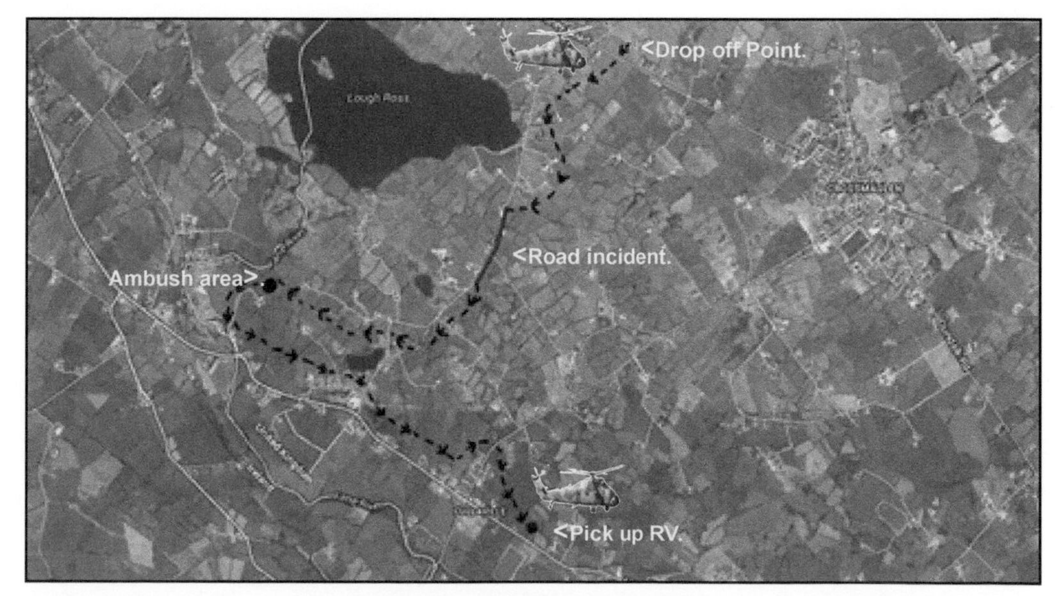

Map of TC's patrol into Crossmaglen, close to the border with the Republic of Ireland.

Back on base at Poole, TC spent a few days playing with boats, in and out of Poole Harbour, trying out different techniques, recovering swimmers and divers from the water, also canoeing out and about into the rough of the open sea beyond the harbour. To TC, this was all good fun, although sometimes it could be dodgy, when large waves threatened to capsize the canoes. (This is not what you want).

A week or so went by. TC and his squadron practised night jumps into Poole Harbour. This sight was probably quite common for the locals. Once in the water, the jumpers were picked up by the Zodiac boats and taken to the jetty. This was done at every opportunity, as this is basic every day training for the SBS.

One morning TC was informed to report to the office on the company lines. He knocked on the door and was called in by Captain McClelland and Sgt. Major Furness. TC's first thoughts were that Lt. Carlton-Smith had changed his mind behind TC's back and made a formal complaint against him. What a bastard, he thought.

When TC entered the room, he saw that there were several SBS members of various ranks. Without hesitation, Captain McClelland spoke out, "Regarding your recent visit to N.Ireland, in particular with a patrol led by Lt. Carlton-Smith". TC thought, Here it comes, court martial, loss of rank, possibly kicked out. What a total bastard.

Captain McClelland then read out a short statement from Lt. Carlton-Smith. TC could not believe what he was hearing. The statement was full of praise for TC, his professionalism, skills, field-craft tactics and leadership. All these phrases threw TC into turmoil, as he was ready with his own explanation about what had happened but unexpectedly, it was totally the opposite.

As he finished reading, TC's feet were back on the ground. The Captain handed over to the Sgt. Major, who stood up and informed TC that he was now going to be upgraded to SC2. TC was stunned but elated at this. The Sgt. Major handed him his SC2 badge, which he would wear with pride, then shook his hand, as did the Captain saying, "Bloody well done". The rest stood up, clapped TC and one by one shook his hand too.

The Sgt. Major piped up loudly, "Right the lunchtime drinks are on you TC, mine's a very large one". It took a couple of days for TC to adjust, as he reflected just how far he had come and what he had to do in order to get there. Superman? No, just well-trained, with plenty of guile.

TC mentioned that it was not down to him alone for his success but for the way he had been well trained and closely supported by his new family of The Royal Marines and the SBS in particular, without these bodies he could not imagine where or what he may have been doing up to now.

Author's Note: A lot more than that – Courage, Determination, Heroism and PMA (Positive Mental Attitude) in abundance.

SBS Out In The Cold Norway

TC's Sergeant Major called TC into his office and asked him if he liked frozen fish. TC replied, "Yes, absolutely, what kind of fish?" The Sergeant Major's answer was, "All kinds, white and pink." TC said, "Oh yes brilliant," thinking that he was about to be given some which might have fallen off the back of a lorry or come in from the fishing boats in the harbour. TC then asked, "Where do I pick it up from sir?" "Norway," was the reply.

His heart sank a little because if there was one thing that TC hated more than being in the desert with no food or water, it was working in the bloody freezing-ass back of beyond in parts of Norway that nobody ever wants. Not even the Norwegians. There again, the marines do have the responsibility of protecting NATO's Northern flank. TC wondered who the bastard was who decided it should be the responsibility of HM's Royal Marines.

TC was a little pissed off about this but orders are orders and must be carried out regardless of all the whinging and whining. Three days later, after a massive amount of kit and equipment were packed up, TC and his section, led by Lt. Bowman, were on board their air-taxi, a C130A Hercules limousine supplied by HM Dept and winging it's way to Norway, the 'Land of the Midnight Sun'.

They landed at Bodø Airport, a former RAF base. Now it was for The Norwegian AF. Once all the equipment was unloaded and placed in a secure lock-up, they were given accommodation in the officer's quarters on the base. They stayed there for two days, chilling out... 'Literally'. They were then joined by two Royal Marines from the M&AW Cadre (Mountain and Arctic Warfare Cadre), who arrived with more stores, skis and snow shoes. TC thought that they were strange Norwegian tennis racquets. His section was about to enter an exercise, arm in arm with the Norwegian SBS and Marines for two weeks playing in the snow.

How wonderful, thought TC, just what I needed, as he recalled all the wonderful places he had been to. Singapore, Malaya, Borneo, Malta, Cyprus, Sicily, even Aden! One thing he did admire was the beauty of the country. The mixture of rolling hills, high mountain ranges and

On the approach to Bodø airport Norway.

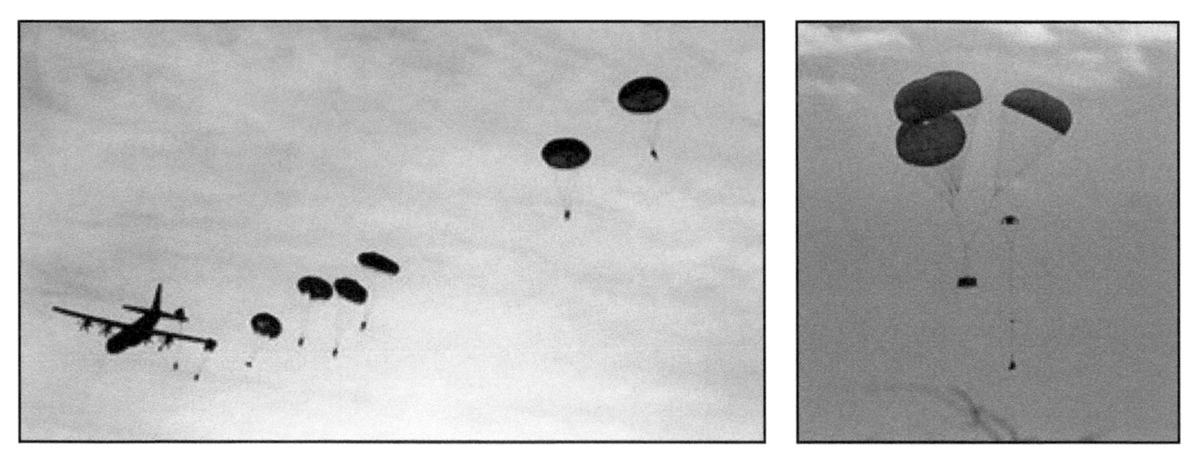

Teams out the rear ramp of a Herc, including the kit, right.

Typical snow patrol Norway with sledge carrying essential equipment.

Land of the midnight sun and Northern light show.

of course the magnificent pine forests, all covered in metres of snow. Snow everywhere.

After a short briefing the following morning, they loaded the equipment onto wooden pallets, which were then packed into the C130A and off they flew to a small location, just about eight miles North of a place called Kaldelva. To TC, this area was the middle of nowhere and resided at the foot of a bloody big mountain, also smothered in the cold white stuff.

On the approach to the DZ (Drop Zone), the rear ramp of the Herc opened. They were going to jump. (Yes of course, what would you expect?). Everyone was standing up now, facing the rear ramp. It was going to be a static jump with P9 parachutes (round ones) at 1000ft. They were watching the red light above the exit and the Jump Master. Red out and green on the pallets were jettisoned first, followed rapidly by the team. The C130A Hercules was empty of its cargo in just 10 seconds. As the aircraft roared away into the clear blue sky, it appeared to be shrinking smaller and smaller as it disappeared, then pop, all the chutes opened up and they were in flight.

TC could see the large chutes now, with the pallet slung underneath. He had to keep eyeball on this when it hit the snowy ground below, as this was the marker, amid all the carpet of snow, because it was difficult to focus on the ground with everything pure white.

Several figures emerged from the undergrowth below, waiting for the team to land. These were members of the Norwegian SBS. Once they were all down on terra firma, the kit was unpacked and they were taken to a complete underground snow complex, where they were all introduced to each other and given some good food and hot chocolate.

Later in the afternoon, they got rigged-up with their packs and weapons, donned white snow suits over their uniforms, clipped on their skis and picked up their ski poles. Off they went with the Norwegians in the lead, as these buggers lived and trained in these conditions all the time.

TC and the team had a little difficulty keeping up with these guys but after about an hour, they all settled down. TC thought that this was just to show off how good they were in the snow. To quote TC, "OK, point taken".

They entered a large forest area and the further they ventured into the pines, the thicker it became. One hour before first light, they stopped and harboured up for the night. Up went the bivies and hot drinks all round. There was no need to dig in, as this was just an overnight stop.

At first light, the camp was struck and then they were back on the move again. It was very hard going. The snow was powdery and with the massive packs they had on their backs, it was very slow and absolutely gruelling. Just before last light, there was no time to set up camp, as there was work to be done. Three canoes had to be erected for the next leg of the exercise.

They had arrived at a place called Hundberget on the North bank of Beisfjord. This fjord was about nine miles long and one mile wide. The team's task was to launch the canoes and paddle three miles to where a small Norwegian ship called Kjeoy was. It was a 250 ton Logistic Support Vessel at anchor off the Eastern end of the fjord. This vessel was acting as enemy for this exercise and was tasked to place limpet mines on her hull, in the middle of the night, then make off without being compromised.

The mines were inert but exactly the same as live ones. Once their task was completed, they would have to make their escape by paddling out to the mouth of the fjord, under Beisfjord Road Bridge then out into Ofotfjord in order to RV with the submarine, HMS Otus. Their paddle would be about seven miles up to the bridge plus a further two to three miles out to meet the sub.

TC found out that during WWII in 1942, the village of Beisfjord was the location of a German concentration camp, commanded by SS Hermann Dolp. The camp mainly housed Bosnian Muslims, when apparently typhus broke out within. What happened next was infamous. Dolp had 288 of the prisoners dig graves, then made them line up in front of them. The guards shot them all. The sick ones, who could not stand or walk, were then locked in their huts including the sick bay. The buildings were then dowsed in petrol and set ablaze. Three hundred and eleven people perished. These evil deeds have gone down in history as the 'Beisfjord Massacre'.

It was just after midnight when they set about putting the canoes together. The Norwegian SBS left to make their way back, while the team loaded up and checked equipment. They then slid quietly into the freezing water, which was now a little choppy. The snow shower covered their approach to the target ship, which was three miles away.

They paddled one behind the other, about twenty feet apart. The high sides of the fjord channelled the wind and snow straight up the fjord, stinging their eyes and faces. TC could make out one or two small lights coming from various houses on the far side and the odd car travelling along the road that followed the contours of the North edge of the fjord, which led from the bridge to Beisfjord Village.

The lead canoe signalled back that the ship was now in sight, less than 500 yards away. At this point they split up. One canoe went right, one went left. The third canoe headed straight for the stern of the ship. They closed up very slowly and quietly onto the target. TC was in the canoe along the port side (left) of the ship. They carried a magnetised handle, which they would use to pull themselves in tight against the ship's hull.

They placed the limpets on the hull without any problem then were about to push away, when TC noticed a small rope dangling over the side of the ship. Naturally, he could not resist scaling this to have a quick peep to ascertain if he could see anyone. He just wanted to see if there were any crew members on watch, which there should have been.

He shimmied up far enough so that his head was just level with the deck line. He peered over and scanned the craft. He could only see one person, who was up on the dimly-lit bridge. No one else could be seen. He stayed put for a short while observing but by then his boat-buddy, down below, got agitated. The other two boats pulled away. He yanked on the rope to get TC's attention. TC looked down and signalled to him, by showing the palm of his hand, which informed him to wait.

He hauled himself slowly onto the deck of the Kjeoy laying flat on his front and crawled like a snake across the deck to the super structure. He managed to stand up and edged sideways, keeping in the shadows, until he came to a hatchway. TC then pulled out a red aerosol paint spray, which he had secreted in his clothing and sprayed a large red cross on the hatchway. Not satisfied with this, he snuck up the steps which led to the bridge and kept down low. He then put a red cross on the door as well. In the event of being discovered at this stage, TC was prepared to launch the canister through the doorway of the bridge, as though it was a grenade and make a rapid escape over the side and into the freezing water. As he went back to the rope TC sprayed a continuous line of red paint across the deck to where he descended the rope, leaving the aerosol can on the deck. He slipped down the rope and back into the canoe, then they paddled away to join the others.

TC caught up after half a mile or so, as the other two boats had stopped and waited for them thinking that they must have been caught. TC's boat partner asked in a very quiet voice, "What did you do up there?" When TC told him what he had done, he remarked, "Oh fucking brilliant."

All three canoes now hugged together side by side, as TC told the others what he had done. They were all in stitches but still very quiet. Now they made off, paddling hard towards the bridge and the RV with the sub.. On the approach to the bridge, they travelled very close to the South side of the Fjord, in case anyone was on the bridge looking out for them.

They slipped one by one under the bridge, which appeared deserted. They paddled full steam ahead towards the RV and out into Ofotfjord, past the mouth of Beisfjord. The time was now 0300hrs and away in the distance and over to the right, TC could just make out the lights of port Narvik.

They approached close to the RV now but there was no sign of the sub.. They stopped, clung together, waited and listened, then after some fifteen minutes, they heard a low humming noise and white water erupted about a hundred yards away when this sinister looking black shape emerged eerily from the icy deep. First, the conning tower, then the nose cone. She came up to rest with her casing just above the surface.

It was still snowing and very windy.

They pulled their way towards the boat, where a few members of the crew were now out on the subs casing and had slung a cargo net over the side. The canoes were taken on board with the teams and put down the forward hatch into the torpedo room. Within five minutes the hatches were closed and locked. Down she went and away.

TC reflected that it was hot and stuffy on board but at this stage, he was happy to get out of the freezing cold and into the warm. They all got out of their kit and went for hot showers, followed by some very welcome hot tea and food, well earned. They spent a day and a half on board, while sailing down to the Naval Base at Mathopen, just near Bergen.

They offloaded all their kit and equipment and stayed the night on the base in reasonable comfort. At 1100hrs next day, they were flown by Chinook across to the airport at Fiesland, where they transferred to a waiting C130A Hercules.

By now, TC and the team were tired of loading and unloading all their kit and equipment. They eventually took off and headed back to the UK and RAF Lynham. They arrived late in the afternoon, once again unloading everything.

After a couple of hours chilling out in the lounge, they were summoned to a small room by a Senior Officer and informed that they would be required to take part in a short three day exercise in the Brecon Beacons in Wales. TC was gutted because he had hoped to have a few days off but this is the job I've trained for, he thought.

They were going to do an exercise with the SAS and members of the Parachute Regiment. TC remarked "This is going to be very interesting". Ten SAS members had been designated to play enemy. They had infiltrated the UK and were supposedly on the run somewhere in the Brecons.

TC and his teams had to liaise with members of the Paras and Royal Marines to search and destroy and they would be jumping again into the area a few miles east of Sennybridge, where they were to meet up with a Royal Marines Officer. He had to give them the information, as to the area where the SAS had been hiding out.

Once they collected their chutes and kit, TC and the teams boarded a Chinook helicopter and took off. The journey, as usual was very noisy. The jump was again on a static line, low altitude. After an hour, they were told that they were approaching the DZ. They gathered up all their kit and hooked up ready to jump. They waited. The tension increased.

The drop was about 1000 ft but now it was dark and as the rear ramp lowered, they could see a few car headlamps in the distances. There was a bit of cloud and the wind was 5 – 7 knots easterly. They lined up on the edge of the ramp. The green light came on and 'thumbs-up' from the Jump Master. One behind the other and in quick succession they literally ran off the ramp and into the blackness.

Ping, ping, ping went the parachute ties as they snapped one by one in quick succession. Then the usual slight jerk on the harness as the chute opened. A small flashlight on the ground shone upwards to mark the DZ. They were all on target. TC was just about to settle down and enjoy his 40 seconds of flight, when his parachute suddenly collapsed, sending him down fast with a rapid snap back on his rigging lines.

He looked up to see what had happened and just about to deploy his emergency chute, when a body slid down his rigging lines and snagged on his harness. One of TC's team mates had suffered a chute malfunction but before he could deploy his emergency chute, he landed at speed on top of TC's chute, partially collapsing it. As he slid off the side, his foot and part of his kit were caught in TC's rigging lines and he hit TC square in the chest.

TC's reaction was to grab hold of a handful of his buddy's harness as neither could deploy their respective emergency chutes and they went down together faster than they should have, although TC's chute was now ok and fully deployed. They had less than ten seconds before touchdown, or in TC's words creaming in, (landing with style).

In the last few seconds before they hit the ground, they both managed to release the kit that was attached to their right legs, as it would have been disastrous to land with it still attached. They prepared for a bad landing and then 'crash', they smashed into the ground, which was hard, rocky and way off course, unable to roll away properly. It was over in a flash.

TC was lying on his back in pain and heard voices shouting, "Fucking hell man. Are you guys ok?" TC looked up dazed and the guy he was holding on to was looking down at him and he was shouting, "You ok mate?" Another voice shouted, "Get a fucking medic out here now, this chap is in bad shape".

TC wondered who it was. The wind was knocked out of him and as he lay there being told not to move, he was aware his left leg was giving him severe pain. Still quite dazed, he went to move but a much stronger pain from his ribs and right shoulder made him yell out. He was shouting now, "Get me up, I'm ok", then he was told to lie still, while they undid his harness and pulled it off him, bit by bit.

Every now and then he gave a little wince and said, "Oh shit, oh fuck, how bad is it?" A voice said, "You may have broken ribs and collarbone. We are not sure about your neck or spine. That's why you must remain perfectly still. The medics are on the way to get you 'casevacked'. (Casualty Evacuation).

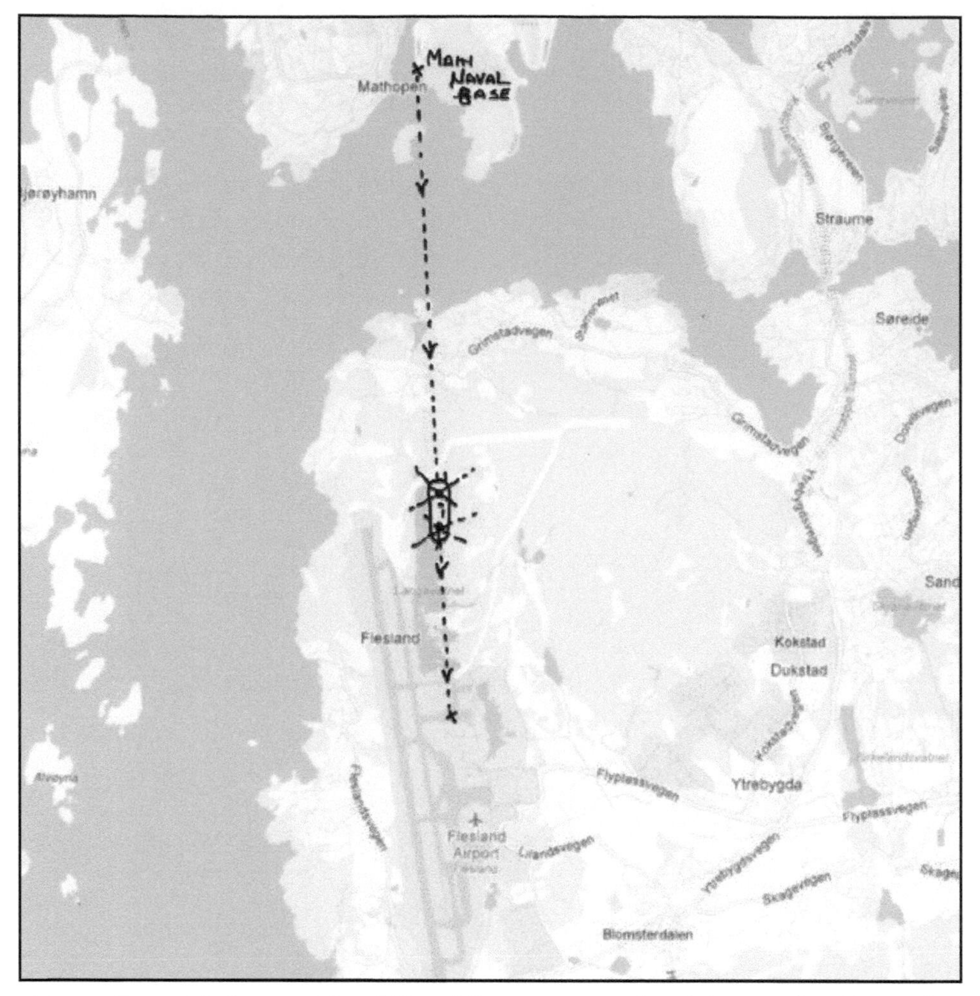

Route from Mathopen Naval Base Norway to Fiesland Airport by Chinook.

Helocasting from Sea King, boats and kit already in the water followed by SBS operatives, very quick deployment.

Two Sea Kings, (known as Junglies) landing in Norway.

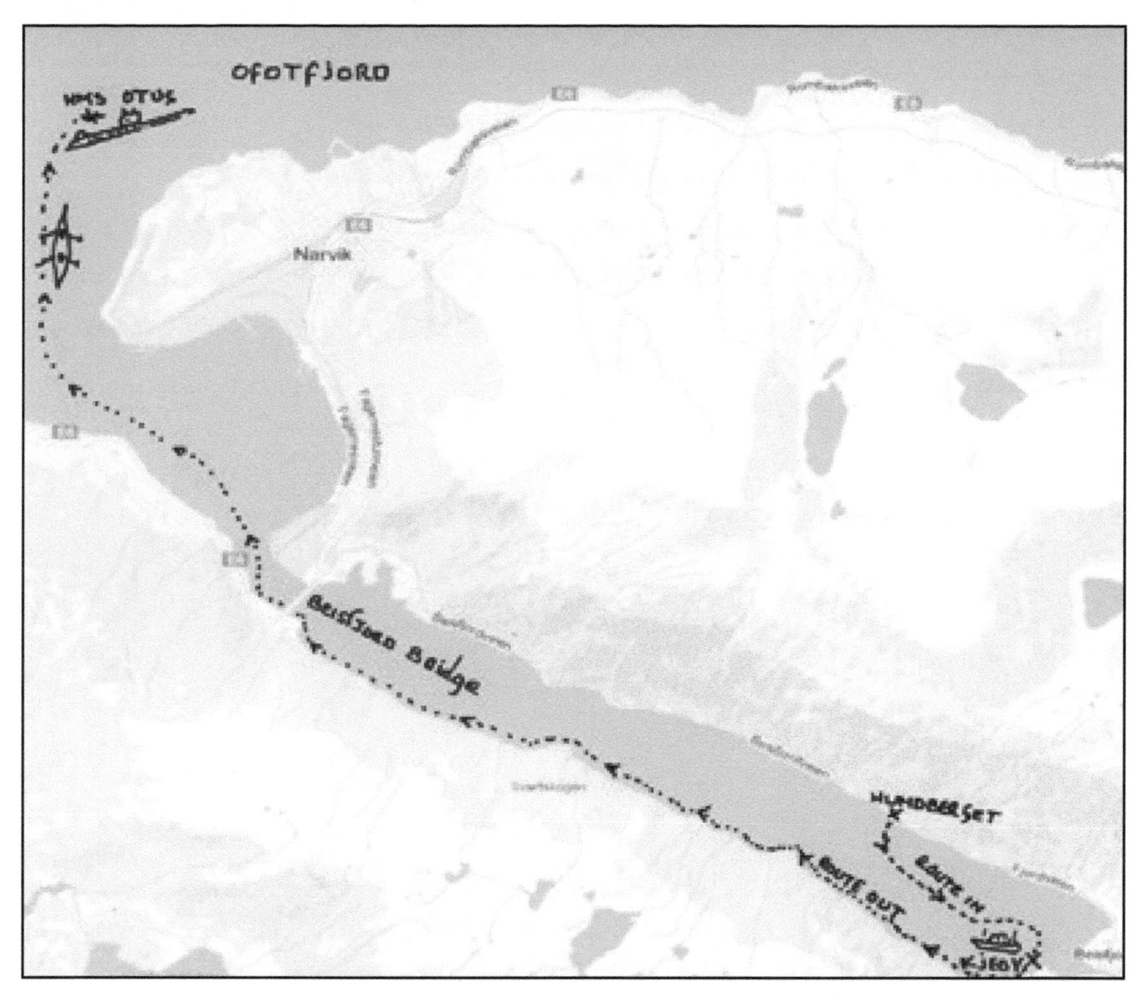

TC's map of Beisfjord operation Norway, route in do the business and route out.

Beautiful landscape of Beisfjord Norway, part of which is covered in thin ice just, sharp enough to cut through the skin of a canoe.

The chap, who got hooked up in TC's harness, knelt down beside him and grabbed his hand. He thanked him for getting him down safely and apologised that TC was injured. He promised him a bottle of whisky, when he recovered. Within a few minutes, a helicopter was arriving and came in for a landing. It was the same Chinook that TC had jumped out of earlier.

One of the crew was a medic and within a few more minutes, TC was strapped to a spine-board, loaded onto the Chinook and off they went. A while later they landed at Hereford County Hospital.

TC was checked over and x-rayed. He had bruised ribs and a bruised reputation, a hairline fracture of the left kneecap and a dislocated right shoulder blade. He spent three days in hospital and with his left knee strapped up, he was allowed to leave but not before the senior consultant could not resist giving TC advice in front of three of his nursing staff, saying, "I am well aware of how tough you SAS are but may I suggest that the next time you jump", at this point TC interrupted him saying, "Beg your pardon Sir, I am not SAS, I am SBS Royal Marines". Then the consultant, frowned and responded with, "Ah that explains it if you had been SAS you would have been given a parachute when jumping out of a perfectly good serviceable aircraft and in the dark".

"Oh very funny", said TC as the nurses were giggling hysterically mainly at the consultant's remark, false laughter though it was.

TC was eventually sent home to his house at Deal in Kent to recover. He had to use a crutch to get about for nearly two weeks and had regular checks at Deal Barracks by the M.O. (Medical Officer). He received a signal that his jump days were probably more or less over, albeit he could remain with the SBS but only on light duties, (non-operational). He said that he felt destroyed.

He was given the choice of any posting he wanted, which was difficult because he enjoyed his deployment in the SBS but non-operational is not an option and by now all the hot sunny places like Singapore, Malta, Aden and Cyprus were closed. The commando units were either in Norway – no thanks, N.Ireland – no thanks or ship's detachment – definitely no thanks.

With this, TC made enquiries at the Depot Deal to see what was going on there and discovered that they needed a boat's NCO to take charge of the Boat Shed and all the equipment that went with the responsibility. The officer in charge was a Naval Lt., who was also known as the 'Schooly', (school teacher).

TC had many good mates at Deal and he felt quite at home and happy there, so he ended up applying for this post. His draft came through two weeks later and he took over from Corporal Lewis, who was leaving the Corps after 12 years. His duties involved having to check and sign for all the boats and equipment, of which there were about three quarters of a million pounds worth. This included several pieces of machinery, sailing boats, a 27 foot whaler rowing-boat and a twin GRP (Glass Reinforced Plastic) hull Dory Motor Boat, powered by a Johnson 40 hp outboard motor. This would be used as the safety boat while the sailing boats are in the water.

In addition to all this, they also had a 38 foot sailing yacht with a 3 hp inboard diesel engine. This was a four-berth yacht, which needed two people or crew to sail it. After a few weeks TC had settled in to his new role and had a civilian working with him, old Stan. Stan was a Royal Navy veteran of WWII and had been working in the boat shed for many years, which was a great asset for TC, as he knew everything about the boats. Now TC was informed by the Schooly, that in his new post he would be required to get properly qualified by the RYA (Royal Yacht Association). He would be needed to run and instruct the sailing courses, held in the boat shed classroom.

He had to go to Chatham on several sailing courses, which he thoroughly enjoyed. After many practical and written exams to include Nautical Navigation, he obtained the correct certification from the RYA. His day-to-day routine was attending to the repair of boats and equipment and organising the running of the sailing courses. In addition to this when any of the marines or junior musicians wanted to take a boat out, TC would have to man the safety boat and on several occasions, he was asked to take out some young children in the speed boat.

He always made sure that they were properly briefed, had their life-jackets fitted correctly and knew the rules when in the boat. No leaning over the side or standing up but mainly to do what they were told and no larking about, as these kids belonged to various ranks of the marines, including officers.

Every so often, TC serviced the 40 hp engine and to give it a test, put it on the Dory and running it across into Ramsgate Harbour, where he tied up and went ashore for breakfast, before he returned back to Deal. This normally took 3 – 4 hours. Another part of his daily routine was to phone the Meteorology Office at RAF Manston to get the daily weather forecast, wind strength and direction. Once he had this information, he posted a board outside the boat shed, as to whether or not sailing was ok or cancelled.

About once a week, he took a trip to Chatham Dockyard to collect stores and to place an order for timber, particularly marine plywood, which had to be cleared by the QM's (Quarter Master) department first.

One day, he received a request from Poole in Dorset, to attend SBS HQ. He was allowed to use a Landrover for this purpose. He was quite happy as he thought that he may be getting reinstated because by now his injuries had long healed up and he was still very fit and active. So after signing out the vehicle from the MT (Motor Transport) Section, off he went for the day. Upon arrival he reported to the Sergeant Major's office, where he was informed that a complaint had been received from the Norwegian Navy, regarding the defacing of one of their ships by someone daubing red paint over it.

TC was the only one who went on board the Kjeoy and he put his hands up to this action. He commented, "This has got to be a joke and quite pathetic". The Sergeant Major agreed and said, "Everyone who had read this report thought it was very funny" and told TC that the complaint was not going to go anywhere officially.

TC was also told that apparently, there were four naval ratings on security duty at the time and that they had expected an attempt at boarding. Apart from the one person seen by TC in the wheel-house, he did not see anyone else on board, which made the complaint even more ridiculous. In addition to this, he was informed that thirty minutes after they left the ship and paddled away, the small team of Norwegian SBS who had accompanied them to Hundberget, fired off several shamoolies, over the ship to signify that it had been struck by the limpet mines.

It was not until next light that it was noticed one of the flares had landed on the deck and picked up by one of the crew. As he picked it up, he spotted the red line across the deck and the tin of paint TC had left behind. Picking this up as well, he suddenly saw the Red Cross painted on the hatch and door to the bridge. The skipper apparently went berserk.

TC went to leave the office when the Sergeant Major called him back saying, "I nearly forgot, this was left for you by Cpl. Redfern". TC said, "Oh that was the guy who got caught up in my chute". "Yes," said the Sergeant Major as he handed TC a bottle of whisky, "Well done mate and don't worry about this stupid complaint, it's definitely going nowhere, take care and good luck".

TC was disappointed as he was expecting to be offered back into the fold but it was not to be, so he walked around to see a couple of his mates and called in at the swimming pool to watch more candidates going through the training mill. He could have been an instructor here but did not wish to do this, if he could no longer be part of any action. He went for a pint and a meal in the Sergeant's Mess then headed back on the road to Deal.

A few months went by with normal routine, when he was asked to sail the big yacht over to Wissant, in France, about eight miles south of Calais. The trip involved taking five Officer's wives, for the day on a 'ban-yan' (picnic) on the beach.

TC contacted RAF Manston for the weather report and off they went. On the way, he let them take turns at the helm. Two of them could already sail, which was an advantage. The main problem was dodging the many oil tankers using the channel.

The general rules of the sea are that power gives way to sail but you cannot expect a massive tanker to give way to you in mid-channel. They had to be very vigilant. A good day was had by all and the next day, TC had to go down and wash out the boat, plus a small quantity of vomit. Every Wednesday afternoon TC had to man the safety boat, as many marines wanted to take out the sail-boats having completed one of TC's sailing courses. Wednesday afternoon in the Navy and Marines is a time honoured tradition known as 'Make and Mend'. Basically an afternoon to play sport, repair any equipment or just disappear for the afternoon which many did.

TC had to fit all this in with his repair work in the boat shed, also on occasions had to do duty as Duty SNCO for 24 hours. He would be on call for this time along with the Duty Officer who between them would have to visit the guard room in full uniform and be present when the Guard Commander (Cpl.) instructed and tested the fire picket normally made up of twelve recruits.

This TC had done a hundred times as a recruit himself and later as the Guard Commander. He detailed who would roll out the fire hoses, who would have the one inch nozzle and who would have the 'T' branch or stand pipe to connect to the hydrant, also who would have the key to turn on the water, this was a drill.

He showed them first how to connect everything up, then put it all away back in the fire cabinet. He lined them up into three ranks and on his word of command, they raced into action. All the kit connected up, two on the nozzle and the water on in one and a half minutes or less. Obviously if it wasn't done quickly enough and properly, they would pack it away and do it again and again until perfect. This duty was carried out every evening, including weekends.

After the conclusion, TC signed the Occurrence Book and logged his visit. If there was any unusual or serious incident, he was contacted by the duty Guard Commander and if the incident was serious, the Duty Officer was also contacted. On any occasion, the Duty SNCO would always keep the Duty Officer in the loop. TC was required to do a duty of this kind at least once a month. The following morning, he reported to the RSM.

This was routine and it kept TC very busy but he was missing something - ACTION! It was a quiet time for the Royal Marines and apart from one of the Commando Units on duty in Northern Ireland and another in Norway, most were exercises, TC had itchy feet and felt rather bored, reflecting on an old tattoo he once saw with two old very skinny buzzards sitting on a dead tree branch in the middle of a desert, when one said to the other, "Patience my arse, I'm going to kill something."

One evening, while having too much to drink in the 53 Club, along Deal seafront, by the Lifeboat Pub, TC met up with an old mate from 40 CDO Singapore. His name was George Gray and he had just landed some interesting private security work in Sierra Leone, on the West coast of Africa. It was very highly paid work and he was looking for a couple of mates to go with him.

TC was very much interested, perhaps the alcohol was helping him. The more he was told about this job, the more TC became intrigued. The discussion went on for quite a few hours and TC started to think of possible options. He told George that he was very interested but would take a couple of days to mull it over.

He thought long and hard the following day, as he was repairing one of the old broken Johnson 40hp outboard engines he found in the boat shed in the corner and in pieces. He had all the bits on the bench, when he received a phone call to go straight away over to see Captain Reid the QM, urgently.

He wiped his hands on a piece of cloth, donned his beret and set off. The QM's office was just a five minute walk away This QM was not well-liked and apart from being very short, he felt he made up for this by being extremely arrogant and rude. It was not surprising that his nickname was Poison Dwarf.

TC knocked on the open door. Captain Reid called out "Enter". TC stepped in, stood in front of his desk and saluted, saying, "You wanted to see me sir?"... "I sent for you sergeant", came the terse reply. TC bit his lip, which was difficult. The QM carried on writing, appearing to ignore TC, who still stood to attention and looking down at Poison Dwarf.

After a while, the QM put down his pen. Looked up at TC and asked. "Why are you wearing No 8 Navy clothing?" To which TC replied, "Well sir, I am part of the Navy". The QM said, "I am aware of that but I asked why you are wearing it?" (No.8 work shirt and trousers are for fatigues and are dark blue). "It's the dress of the day boat shed Sir", "Oh really," replied the QM "Who wrote those orders?" "You did Sir", said TC. By now, TC's internal steam valve was reaching a critical stage but he managed to keep a lid on it.

Unaware of the tension, the QM continued his needling and said, "Why are your hands dirty sergeant?" TC replied, "I am in the middle of stripping down an engine Sir." The QM then said, "Well you could have taken ten minutes to wash your hands before coming into my office". TC had trouble controlling himself and said, "Yes Sir, I could have but the phone message said it was urgent and now, so I came over immediately. However, Sir, I can go back, over to the mess, wash up and change into Royal Marines rig of the day and come back, if that pleases you, Sir".

"Don't be facetious sergeant that won't be necessary, I just wanted to inform you that the

Commanding Officer, Adjutant and myself will be carrying out full inspections of all departments tomorrow morning at 0900hrs therefore I want you in proper Royal Marines' uniform and the boat shed clean and tidy. Is that clear sergeant?" "Crystal as", replied TC. "Carry on then", said the QM.

TC turned and without saluting, left the office and walked back to the boat shed, muttering to himself, "What a wanker, he could have had that message passed to me by phone, what a waste of my bloody time, what an arsehole". TC walked into the boat shed, picked up a large piece of wood and smashed it on the bench, shouting, 'Tosser".

At that moment, a head poked out of TC's office doorway and a gentle female voice said, "Oh, is this a bad time to come and see you sarge?" It was Mary Atkins from the Records Office, a Wren. TC apologised for his outburst, as she had come to book out a sailing boat.

The following evening, TC met George in the Lifeboat Pub and after asking more questions about this job in Sierra Leone, he had practically made up his mind to go but there was still a niggly feeling at the back of his mind about whether he would be doing the right thing.

TC thought, "Would I miss the Royal Marines? Yes, most certainly", they had been part of his life for so long. He still wanted more time to think and make some enquiries of his own. These thoughts left some doubt. To jump or not to jump? This begs the question.

Sierra Leone

A few weeks passed and TC had plied George Gray with many questions about this so called highly-paid, armed security job, patrolling round the diamond mines in Sierra Leone. One evening in the Lifeboat pub when TC met up with George, he was with Sam, another old acquaintance of TC's from Malta and Cyprus. Sam was in 41 Commando heavy weapons which comprised of 3" Mortars, 120mm Wombats (anti-tank) and 50cal. Machine Guns. He had put in nearly fifteen years service and was looking to leave the marines for something more lucrative and active as it was pretty quiet at this time.

As the evening went by, TC made his mind up to take a stab at this job. He reasoned that if it didn't work out, he could always rejoin the marines at a later date. Sam was sold on the idea too. They all thought that it would be a great opportunity, meeting new and interesting people in different countries and not having to kill them.

Two days later, TC put in his papers to resign from the Corps but because he had signed on for twenty two years, he would be required to pay over a thousand pounds back to the MOD. This was called D by P, or Discharge by Purchase. He could have put in his papers to resign without paying any money but he would have had to wait two years for this. He was a bit shocked but because he needed to leave as soon as possible, waiting a further two years was not an option at this point. Once his papers were in and the money paid, TC was out in a few weeks but he felt a little sad. It was like leaving a family behind. Something you never really got used to. TC now had to look forward to the next challenge or adventure.

George, TC and Sam decided to buy a Land Rover between them and travel overland to Sierra Leone. They painted it, kitted it out, and set off. It was February and very cold but unfortunately, they had not realised that the heater in the vehicle was not only primitive but did not work, so until they reached Spain, it was very unpleasant. Still, it was nothing they had not experienced many times before.

They boarded the ferry at Dover and crossed to Calais, deciding not to go near Paris. They travelled down the west coast instead. There did not seem to be very much traffic on the roads and they took turns in driving. One drove, another navigated, while the third slept in the back. They stopped a few times and made camp off the roads and to refuel. Eventually they reached the French/Spanish border, where they were required to produce the weapons and permits to the authorities, which they were carrying with them. These were pump-action shotguns. The French and Spanish Police viewed the permits but did not take any interest in the weapons and just waved them through, without asking to see them.

Having spent the previous night crossing over mountain passes, which at the time were covered in snow and freezing cold, at last, as they entered Jaca, just south of the French/Spanish border, it was becoming a little warmer. They stopped for the night. Their Land Rover attracted quite a lot of attention for the way it was painted. It was done in black and white Zebra camouflage, with a red Springbok head on the sides and the doors. The Springbok being the national animal of South Africa, this was their original destination before deciding to go to Sierra Leone.

They found an all-night café and were having supper and a few drinks, when a couple of local men came over to them. They had been looking around the Land Rover outside and they asked who they were and what they were doing. One of the two got very agitated when TC told him in no uncertain terms to mind his own business. The other man then apologised for his friend's curiosity and explained that the town was home to the Basque Separatists ETA and they were just being cautious.

They left the café around one o'clock in the morning and went to the Land Rover, where TC asked Sam to get in the back, remove the shotguns from their cases and load them. This he did quickly and off they drove out to the edge of the town, keeping a sharp lookout for anything unusual.

They noticed a pickup truck that seemed to be following them at a distance. The roads were very quiet, except for the headlights on this truck. They were now expecting trouble and were waiting to round a corner and run straight into a possible ambush but as TC was driving, he turned sharp right onto an old dirt road, turned off the vehicle's lights, then sped up another track.

There was an old dilapidated barn there, which appeared to be empty. It had no doors. TC parked up on the blind side of the barn, as it may have been too obvious to park inside. They all bailed out. TC went to the rear corner of the barn, where he saw the headlights of this following vehicle now turning up the track towards them. Shit, thought TC and he moved position. He went behind a nearby tree closer to the track, where he watched and waited. Sam had taken up a position behind their Land Rover and George had run across the dirt track and was hiding behind a large pile of old bricks. If they had to get involved in a fire fight, the suspects were now covered on three sides, with no way out.

They watched as the pickup truck stopped short at the bottom of the dirt track. No one got out. It just sat there for five minutes, then slowly, started to move off up the track towards TC, who by now was about a hundred yards from them. TC could just make out three or four people in the truck. He felt sure that they would come up as far as the barn. This was such an obvious place to hide but who were these people? Police, members of ETA or just nosey inquisitive locals looking for a fight? Suddenly the pickup stopped again and one man got out. He walked up the track towards the barn. The truck stayed put about 20 yards from the end of TC's gun barrel with its engine still running.

TC could see that this man was carrying a shotgun or rifle of some sort, or it could have even been an automatic weapon. The thought going through TC's mind was, my shotgun would be no match for an automatic weapon in a full blown shoot out, so it would be essential to get the first volley in and take out the automatic weapon.

TC was ready now and prepared to do this, as he knew George was across the other side of the track. The man walked very cautiously towards the barn. Bringing his weapon up into his shoulder at the ready, TC saw that it was a shotgun after all, "Thank Christ for that," he muttered to himself as the man peered inside the barn and seeing nothing in there, turned and started walking back down the track toward his waiting vehicle. He had not seen their Land Rover, hidden round the other side of the barn, with Sam crouched behind it. He got in the waiting pick up which stayed there for another five minutes, then it turned round and went back down the track, turning left at the bottom and back in the direction of Jaca.

TC spoke up saying, "Bloody hell if they had driven further up the track past the barn, they would have spotted the Land Rover for sure". They decided to stay put for the night and pull out just before first light the following morning. They had very little sleep in the past twenty four hours and now, the adrenaline was pumping through their veins like an express train. They took turns on watch for the remainder of the night. The next morning, they put on a quick brew, while one kept watch, then they headed off towards Madrid.

They arrived in Madrid about one thirty in the afternoon. The sun was shining brightly and it was very warm and welcoming. They parked up and went walkabout for a few hours, getting some food and supplies. Then soon they were on their way again, heading south toward Malaga, where they were to meet a contact, a former Royal Marine and owner of a hotel on the waterfront. This was a contact of George's and here they would be collecting more equipment: hand guns and ammunition.

TC ended up with a Smith and Wesson .357 Magnum and shoulder-holster, his choice. Sam opted for a 9mm Browning, (TC's comment on this was, "Yuk"). George went for the Smith and Wesson 9mm semi -auto pistol. TC was hoping to get his hands on a Sig Saur, which was and still is his all-time favourite but he settled for the .357 revolver instead, as he knew it didn't

TC's old series 1 short wheelbase Land Rover. This model was air portable, meaning the doors just lift off as does the roof section. The windshield folds flat and all this makes it light for a helicopter lift. Paintwork by TC.

TC's stencilled Springbok in red on the side of his vehicle.

An old Stamp of South Africa.

The Springbok of South Africa.

The roundel of the SA Air force.

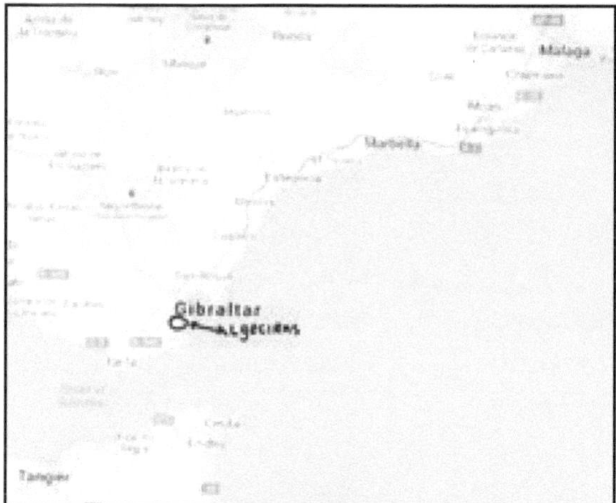

South coast of Spain, Malaga down to Algeciras and ferry across to old Tangiers.

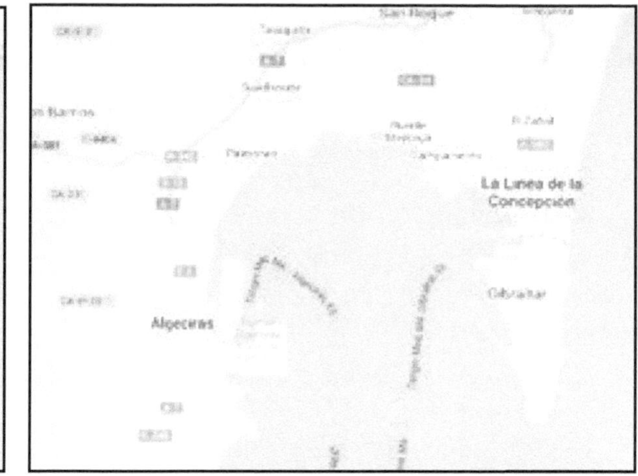

Algeciras ferry port opposite TC's old haunt of Gibraltar.

Old ferry terminal Tangiers late 70's.

A variety of street scenes and narrow alleyways of old Tangiers.

jam and was very hard hitting. After a few hours of drinks, eats and a good chat, they left and followed the coast road down to Algeciras, passing through Fuengirola and Marbella, then onto the ferry across to Tangiers.

Landing in Tangiers at 0130 they were stopped by Police and Customs, who were not pleased, nor very pleasant at being shown the shotguns, when asked for anything to declare. Although they had the permits, these were just ignored and they were questioned as to why they were carrying them. They explained that they would be going across the Sahara dessert into Algeria and the guns were for their protection. The police were still not happy and searched the vehicle. They found nothing else.

Thank God, thought TC thinking that they may have been looking for drugs which they did not have. The police were not aware of the extra storage compartment under the front passenger seat, (on later models of Land Rovers this would have been a second 10 gall fuel tank) where all the different types of ammunition were stored. They did not body search them either.

After two hours of questioning and waiting for the Chief of Police to make a final decision, they were released and sent on their way, part of which was with a Police escort, down towards Fes, then onto Marrakesh.

This took about three days and then out across the Western Sahara Desert and eventually into Mauritania. Although they were getting very funny looks from town to town, the police never stopped them. They crossed over into Mali, then Senegal and Guinea. No one appeared to be surprised or pay any attention to them. Finally, a week later, they arrived at their destination, Freetown, Sierra Leone.

They signed in at the Sofitel Mammy Yoko Hotel in Freetown and later were met by a big guy called Jacob. Jacob was a South African and a former member of SA Special Forces, now head of Security for the company which owned the biggest diamond mines in SL. They had a large room up on the second floor, where three single beds were already laid out. This would be their home for the next couple of days.

Later they were introduced to four other men, two of whom were Danish, one was from SA and the other one was French. These men had arrived the previous day by plane. TC thought with hindsight, that it was probably a much better way to travel.

They spent the next day or two chilling out and sightseeing, after having been well advised not to go into certain areas alone. Of course, they did go into these areas. What a bloody eye opener this place was thought TC. These areas were Madongo and Tengbeh Towns, which had an old disused railway line running through the middle of them. The properties were very old and run down and were known as Ghettos or Shanty Towns.

Basically, these towns were nothing more than old tin sheds, which were smelly, stinking and crammed together. The rivers and streams were full of garbage and rotting, who knows what. TC commented that he could not imagine anyone going in there alone or even in a group and that he felt sorry for the poor sods who had to live there, particularly in a country so rich in minerals, primarily diamonds.

One thing TC noticed within the first few hours was a Heliport right next to the hotel, so a quick wander round (recce) was needed. They were looking for a Wessex Mk5 or possibly a Chinook but all there was on the pad, was an old Russian-built MIL MI 8, which from TC's recollection was not a very reliable aircraft. Many had crashed over the years and had gained the same statistics as Aeroflot, so when Jacob asked TC, "How often do these crash?" TC replied, "Just the once." He told Jacob that these helicopters carry up to twenty two passengers, with a crew of three and that there was a warning panel just inside the doorway, which states, Notice, In the event of a technical malfunction during flight, place all loose items on floor and put your feet on them. Place your hands on your knees and your head between your legs and kiss your arse goodbye.

Jacob met them all in TC's room in the evening for a briefing, bringing with him some large maps. One for each man. He informed them that they would be leaving the next morning and driving to Makeni, where they would be supplied with clothing and equipment. They left at ten in the morning, travelling in a convoy of Toyota 4 x 4 three litre diesels. All fitted with snorkels for deep water crossings. These are four inch pipes attached to the engine air intake and up the side of the front screen, in order to stop water ingress when fording deep water. TC was glad they were not flying in the Mil Mi 8.

They left Freetown and at a place called Waterloo, took the Masiaka – Yonibana Highway to Lunsar, then the Masiaka – Lunsar Highway to Makeni. Upon arrival, they drove into a huge compound, where there were many locals with dark, staring and very inquisitive eyes watching their every move and wondering who and what they were doing there. TC had done his usual research, before setting foot on alien territory. His motto was forewarned is forearmed and it appeared that until April 1961 Sierra Leone was under British rule. It then became a Republic albeit the country is extremely rich in minerals, the majority of its people, mostly Muslims, live in poverty. There were many languages spoken in different provinces, like Krio but the most spoken language is English. (The British are damn good teachers).

Having spent the night in Makeni International, five star Hotel, (joke) they were woken by Jacob at 0630 hours and shown across to breakfast, in the open air. A wooden table had been set up outside, with benches to sit on, no expense spared here and no table cloths either, bloody hell what a bunch of slobs TC thought but they all had a big surprise, when a full English breakfast was served up. TC said that he dared not ask what the meat was in the sausages, he was sure it would not be pork because of their religion but he was completely surprised to discover that it was in fact, pork.

After the meal, they were all taken over to a huge wooden hut, where they were issued with a variety of clothing, which had motifs and badges on. They had to wear these for identification purposes; they were each issued with the real stuff, Kalashnikov AK47 assault rifles and a variety of pistols. They had several makes and models, including TC's most hated one of all, the Browning 9mm. "Stuff them", said TC. He was looking for a Sig Saur again but there wasn't one, however he did zoom in on a big pistol. "Ah," he said, "This looks very menacing." It was in fact a Russian-made Tokarev T33 7.62mm semi-automatic pistol with plenty of ammo. They had not owned up to the fact that they were carrying their own weapons as well. They were informed that they would always be re-supplied at any time. This was music to TC's ears. Unfortunately, there was no PE4 Plastic Explosive available for TC to play with, at least not that he was aware of.

Next morning they loaded up and set off to Koidu, along the Magburaka Road, through to the Kangari Hills and forests. They were told to keep their wits about them, as many small groups of armed bandits were on the prowl, looking for easy pickings, mainly from tourists or buses. It was highly unlikely that they would pick on a convoy of armed personnel but it was safer to be alert nevertheless.

A few times TC had seen five or six people posted by the side of the road with an old 4x4, that looked as though it had seen better days but some of the roads really do punish and destroy most of the vehicles, especially if one goes off the main highway and across country, which they would find out pretty soon.

Every time they passed small groups standing beside the roadside, some of them armed, TC's group would hold up their weapons into the ready stance, in order to let any opportunists see that they were well-armed, after about five hours, they eventually reached Koidu Township. They came to another compound fenced off with large steel gates, which were guarded by a few armed locals. They opened the gates and let them in. TC thought that they must have been expected, as the security appeared to leave a lot to be desired, it was not too good.

They were directed to a large wooden hut standing in a complex, which would be their base for the next few weeks. This was known as No.11 mine Koidu. It was a massive expanse of open-cast mines. They unloaded all their kit. Once again many hostile eyes on them everywhere they went. TC said that it was bloody spooky at times and you went nowhere without your weapons, even for your morning George (shit). There was nothing else to do now, except get some food, chill out and get some serious sleep. TC slept with his pistols under his pillow and his AK47 strapped to his wrist with the other end of the sling. As uncomfortable as it was, this was how he had been trained. All his weapons were loaded and ready to play.

The next day, they were taken around the site and shown how everything worked. They were even shown small samples of excavated diamonds, called 'Rough'. TC's first impressions were that they didn't look like diamonds but he did his research and was soon aware of what they would look like. They were informed that smuggling was rife and that workers would try to smuggle the diamonds out over the border into Liberia and also further down to the River Moa. This ran from Kenema down to the Atlantic Ocean at Kasada Island where there was a small village called Sulima, some seventy miles away.

This had to be patrolled regularly from Koidu, past Kenema and down to Kasada. It was about one hundred and forty miles by road but to follow the river, roughly two hundred miles of mud tracks, rocky terrain and bogs. The main roads were just as bad. If it was dry, there would be dust everywhere and if it was wet, then there was deep mud. Sometimes, if it was too wet, the road was totally impassable, for to get bogged down anywhere was not an option (You can't call out the AA or the RAC to pull you out) and the locals were of little or no use, unless you abandoned the vehicle.

The locals actually seemed to despise them being in their country and carrying loaded weapons. Carrying weapons in a place like this, you certainly wouldn't have them unloaded. The locals referred to them as Mercenaries, who had a reputation for being cutthroats, rapists and various other names and because of this they were shit-scared of them and had no stomach for a fight.

A week went by and they were required to drive down to Kenema and holed up there for a couple of days. The people there were very friendly but TC was not sure if this was just an act or if it was because they were frightened of them and their reputation but when they walked around and had drinks in the bars, even carrying their weapons, no one seemed to mind, not even the local police.

Once back in Koidu, they were told that the next morning they would all be flown down to Kasada Island, following the river route, in order to show them various crossing points and make-shift wooden bridges, which they could use also pointing out some of the hostile villages that they were advised to keep clear of.

The next morning they were up with the larks, in the vehicles and on the short drive to an old airstrip, just outside Koidu. Waiting for them was their aircraft. Their taxi for the day, it was the old shitty-looking Russian helicopter, the Mil Mi 8, that TC had seen back in Freetown. His first thought was, how the fuck did they manage to fly that all the way down here? It was then he realised that the company owned three of them.

TC reckoned that Koidu to Kasada Island and Sulima would be a round trip of some three hundred and fifty to four hundred miles. Oh dear God, he thought, then said to himself, "Why did I have to mention him, he's not coming with us?" They all boarded this rusty old Egg Whisk or Paraffin Pigeon, as he called them then with much shaking, rattling and other weird noises, they lifted off.

The Ghettos of Freetown.

Typical life in Madongo, Freetown.

The Russian built Mil Mi 8 Air Ferry based in Freetown.

TC's Smith and Wesson .357 Magnum Model 686 6" barrel. Collected in Malaga.

Sam's choice, The Browning 9mm Hi Power. TC hated this weapon.

Smith and Wesson 9mm Model 39. George's choice in Malaga.

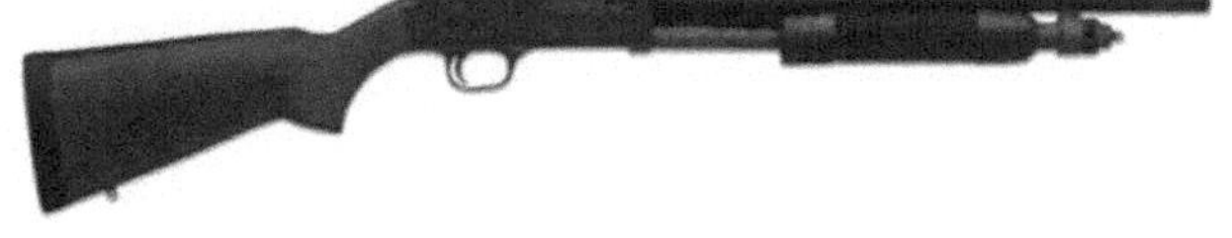

12 Gauge Pump-Action Shotgun they all carried from the UK with permits.

This would have been TC's choice every time, the Sig Sauer Model P226 9mm.

Local mine workers, suspicious eyes everywhere!

Map of Sierra Leone showing Freetown.

TC's Russian made Tokarev TT33 7.62mm Side Arm issued to TC at Makeni.

Toyota 4X4 fitted with snorkel essential equipment in this country for fording deep waters and flooded roads.

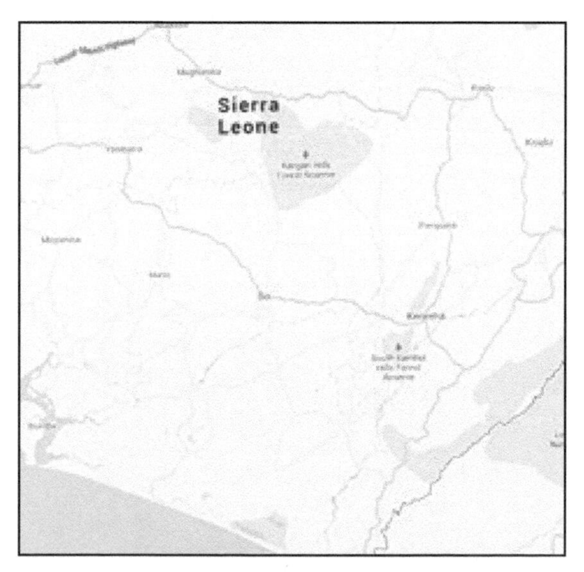

Sierra Leone Map showing Makeni top left, Koidu right, Panguma, Kenema and Bo.

The AK47 7.62mm issued to them all at Makeni.

TC turned to Jacob (at least he was with them, not God) and asked where the life-jackets were. Jacob laughed and told him that they were not needed, as this was an Inland flight. TC remarked that to get to Kasada Island, you had to fly over a great expanse of water in the estuary and if you came down in the Atlantic, that's an even greater amount of water. Jacob just laughed, which made TC a little uneasy, as he was used to taking risks when the time or situation called for it but this was what he classed as an unnecessary risk. He would be ok if they ended up in the drink (TC's playground) but he was not too sure about the others.

The flight was however, quite educational, as TC was following their progress on his map, making notes of the width and flow of various points along the River Moa, crossing places, villages and good and bad tracks that led from the main highway to the villages. After two and a half hours they arrived over Sulima and then flew across to Kasada Island.

TC noticed a very large sand bank which ran across the mouth of the river as it entered the Atlantic Ocean. The sand bank was about two miles long like a peninsula, about half a mile from the estuary of Kasada Island, rather like a breakwater. The Island itself was nothing but jungle.

TC wondered if anyone lived there. The main road down to Sulima just petered out to nothing, as though it was the end of the world. What a weird place, TC thought. The pilot put down on the Southern edge of the Island and they all went walkabout, had a bite to eat, (which was on board the chopper). The Island was sandy and teeming with midges and mosquitoes. There did not appear to be any life at all, although there could have been some fishermen on the other side of the Island. After two hours, they boarded the aircraft and took off.

This time they followed the road back up to Koidu, passing by Kenema. The road was very winding with sharp bends and not a great deal of traffic moving along it. At last, they arrived back at base Camp Koidu. After a shower, a good meal and a few beers, they sat around an open fire chatting and telling jokes and generally relaxing. The following morning, TC and three of his colleagues were given the task of escorting two VIPs from Koidu down to Bo Village, which is west of Kenema. This was an office complex belonging to the Government. The VIPs were travelling in a black 'S' Class Mercedes.

They set off south towards Kenema. TC was leading, with the Mercedes behind him and a third vehicle covering the rear. After half an hour, they were approaching the village of Panguma. The road was empty but TC noticed two vehicles ahead of him tucked back into the bushes, off the side of the road and one on each side.

Terry, who was with TC in his vehicle, immediately called up on the radio to their rear vehicle. They had already seen them too. When they got to within about two hundred yards from them, the vehicle on the right began to emerge from the bushes onto the road and out in front of them, going in the same direction but very slowly, then as they passed by the second vehicle it pulled out behind them and began to follow, about fifty yards behind. Now the vehicle in front of them began to slow down even more and TC was coming up close behind it, this is now a possible ambush.

His gut feeling had kicked in now. He asked Terry to call up to their rear vehicle. Protecting the Mercedes and told them that there were four up and armed in the front vehicle. Now they were calling them bandits. The message came back that there were five, possibly six in the rear vehicle as well. Due to the very poor road conditions, TC knew this was not going to be a high-speed chase and his experience told him that there was likely to be a roadblock further up ahead by more of these bandits.

TC thought to himself, at the moment, there are four of us but not sure about the allegiance of the Mercedes driver, who was a local as well. They could be facing up to ten bandits. He informed his rear vehicle saying that he was going to overtake, as he did not wish to follow the bandits into a possible illegal roadblock. With this, he put his foot down and drove right up tight behind the leading bandit's vehicle expecting him to either speed up to prevent an overtake or stop, in which case TC was prepared to ram it off the road.

At this point TC began to overtake when the bandit pulled out suddenly to prevent TC from passing so at the last minute and levelling his front right hand wheel with the bandit's left hand rear wheel. TC could see one of the rear seat passengers about to aim a shot out of the window when TC suddenly swerved hard right into them, colliding hard and fast with the bandit's vehicle.

Immediately the bandits lost control of their vehicle swerving left and right, almost tipping over. It spun out across the road and disappeared down a steep bank and into the jungle. This manoeuvre is called The Pit Manoeuvre, which TC had been taught many times on his Anti-Highjack and evasive driving techniques before driving in Northern Ireland.

Now the bandit vehicle at the rear decided to have a go and fired two shots, hitting the rear of the convoy vehicle covering the Mercedes. TC told the driver of the Mercedes to keep going and not to stop whatever happens next. TC then swerved his vehicle across the road at right angles and stopped. The black Mercedes containing the two VIPs went straight on and the rear back-up vehicle stopped. TC and Terry jumped out, as did the two from the following back-up vehicle and immediately all four opened up with their automatic AK47s, unleashing a barrage of high velocity bullets into the bandit's vehicle, all weapons blazing away. The bandit's vehicle now came to a slow stop with pieces flying off it and deflated tyres from the hail of bullets slamming into it, there was no returning fire nor did any of the bandits emerge from their vehicle which was now well and truly on fire.

TC and the crews jumped back into their vehicles and took off as fast as they could go in order to catch up with the Mercedes, which was their main priority. The Merc was some five hundred yards ahead of them and well within their line of sight and less than a minute they had caught up. Giving thumbs up to the driver, they resumed their positions within the convoy, as before.

TC still felt that there could be an illegal roadblock further up the road. As they passed by the village of Panguma, Terry quickly topped up the AK47 magazines, as they had practically been expended during the quick shoot out. After about two miles, with no sign of being followed, they still kept a very sharp lookout, just in case. TC was adamant that they could run into a roadblock or another ambush. This kept nagging away at him and twenty minutes later, sure enough they came across four vehicles parked beside the road, in a clearing.

They saw at least eight rough-looking locals hovering in a group by the vehicles. Some were armed with AK47s. They immediately focussed on the convoy as it passed by. TC and Terry were holding their AK47s high up, ready for action but they passed by without any trouble. TC thought that maybe they were going to block them in but had probably received a radio message, possibly from the vehicle that TC had driven off the road. This was a result of their associate's quick despatch and therefore, they did not want to get involved in a fire fight with them.

Eventually they entered Kenema and stopped at a roadhouse/petrol station, The VIPs were in dire need of the toilets and wanted to stretch their legs, also they were a bit shaken up. TC left two of his guys to look after the vehicles, while he and Terry went with the two VIPs. As usual, eyes were on them everywhere they went, particularly because they were carrying weapons as well. Upon their return to the vehicles, TC and Terry stood guard, while the other two went for a pee.

By now, there was a small gathering of kids by the vehicles many of these were eyeballing the black Mercedes in particular. They had probably never seen one before. TC and Terry kept moving around the vehicles and carrying their weapons at the 'High Port'. This is when you hold the pistol grip with the muzzle pointing up and the butt of the weapon resting on your hip. Every now and then, the kids were pushing each other forward, nearer and nearer to the Mercedes. TC and Terry had to stand in front of them, ushering them back. Occasionally a couple of the adults would grab a kid and pull them away. TC was wondering if the jungle telegraph had been sending out messages, as word does travel very fast, in spite of it being a poor country for most of it's inhabitants.

The two VIPs apparently were from Pakistan. They did not speak to TC or any of them but just looked on in some kind of distant awareness and disbelief as to what had taken place on the road. TC thought that if he had told them to take all their clothes off and sing a nursery rhyme, they probably would have done so without any question. Back again, in their vehicles, they drove off toward Bo village, this time no problems.

Upon arrival, they all went into this nice-looking, modern building with air con. The VIPs had a meeting and did not return with TC but were picked up later by chopper and flown up to Freetown. TC and the crew were invited to have a meal before returning back to Koidu. They sat outside in the garden area of this building and were served with lobster and green salad, which was excellent also a nice cold beer or two, then they were ready to leave.

Now they made the big decision as to which route to use on the way back. There was no argument they all agreed to go back the way that they had come. Off they went, from Bo village to Kenema, heading east, the black Mercedes remained back at Bo. They turned north from Kenema and back towards Panguma. They passed the place where they had expected to see the group of guys waiting on the side of the road in the clearing but there was no one there. Further up the road they approached with caution the spot where they had the shoot-out some hours earlier. The vehicle they had shot up was still on the side of the road and completely burned out, just a blackened charred shell and full of bullet holes. They slowed down as they passed by but there was no one about.

Terry asked TC to stop so he could take some photos of the vehicle but as he began to slow to a stop, he spotted a couple of locals yards away, step out of the jungle to take a quick look then duck back in as quick as that. TC drove on and could sense eyes on them but could not see anybody. Two hundred yards further on, they saw the other vehicle, which TC had run off the road. It had been pulled out from the bushes but was in a bad way. Its windscreen was smashed, probably from heads going through it. The front suspension had collapsed, the two front tyres were flat and the whole front end was badly damaged. They must have hit a tree, oops! Once again they could not see anybody around. Terry took a picture as they passed by, this was not a bad idea as it could be used as evidence should there be an enquiry later, because they would definitely be reporting this incident.

Back in camp, TC and the crew were met by Jacob, who took them to see the big boss. TC had never met the boss before. They were all taken to a large office, where they were greeted by a well dressed South African, he was about 50 and had greying hair. He was thick-set and looked quite fit. He stood up and came forward holding out his hand. He shook hands with everyone and introduced himself as Martin.

He asked what had happened on the trip down to Bo as he had received a phone call from the offices at Bo village. The two VIPs and their local driver had told of the incident that occurred and how it was handled. He congratulated them on their quick thinking and evasive techniques saying, “You fellows were bloody lucky to get out of there in one piece”. It appeared that the VIPs were very impressed, albeit quite frightened. Martin told TC, that he had also been a member of South African Special Forces together with Jacob and if he had been in

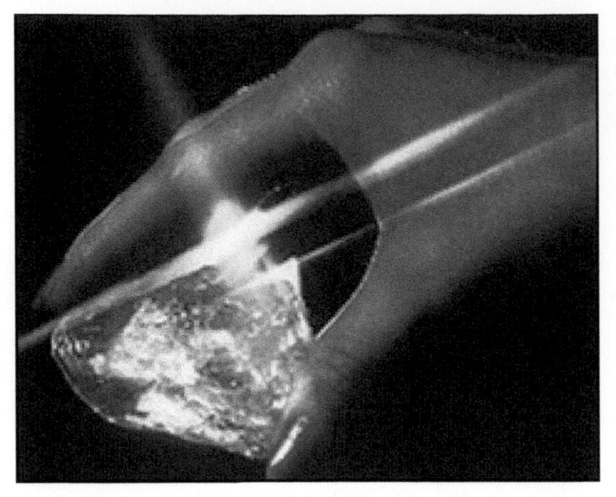

Star of Sierra Leone found at Koidu in 1972. It was bought for $2.5 million and cut into 17 diamonds due to several flaws.

Mine workers panning for diamonds in water holes, there are hundreds like these but they only produce the smaller rough stones.

Township of Koidu back in late 70's.

Typical open cast diamond mining covering several miles, these mines produce the larger rough stones.

Busy main street Koidu district Sierra Leone.

Main town of Panguma, between Koidu and Kenema.

A normal wet main road Koidu to Makeni.

Typical off road track albeit sometimes there is not much difference.

One of the pit falls of going off road for a short cut.

Even tarmac roads suffer these pot holes are deceptively deep, driver beware!

Two good reasons why you have a snorkel fitted to your 4x4. This is a common sight as these vehicles just get abandoned.

Not just a simple pot hole these are dangerous.

charge at the time, he would have gone back straight away and shot every motherfucker in the other vehicle as well.

TC interjected saying, "There was no time for that, Martin they had been put out of action and no longer possessed a threat, plus their main priority was to catch up with the unprotected VIPs, just in case they ran into a roadblock further down the road. With this, Martin said, "Yes of course, fair enough, you're absolutely right on the button, anyway, well done lads."

As the weeks and months whizzed by there was never a mention of the shoot out or any investigations being launched. TC saw members of his crews coming and going without any more incidents. People would leave SL after making a fair bit of money. The average pay was just over three hundred pounds a week. TC was on four hundred as team leader. This was a lot of money back then and equivalent to over six thousand Leone a week. Leone was local currency and most locals don't even earn that kind of money in a year.

TC stayed on for just over a year and was getting very bored with the same old routine plus the steady influx of new bods, mainly from the U.K. and mostly ex-forces. TC saw himself ending up like Jacob, taking them around and showing them all the ropes and procedures. One night, while sitting round the camp fire, TC spoke to his two mates, George and Sam to see if they were interested in going back to the U.K. and to his surprise, George told TC that he and Sam had been discussing this between them for months as all the money they had earned up to now was still in their respective banks and nothing to spend it on.

Now, all three were in total agreement to call it a day. They informed Martin of their decision and although he was very disappointed, he did understand. He offered them a substantial pay rise but this was turned down. Martin told them that if they ever wanted to come back at any time, they would be most welcome and all they had to do was to let him know and he would arrange for a private jet to collect them,

A week later, they were picked up at Koidu Air Strip by TC's favourite helicopter, the old Russian Mil Mi 8. This time they were taken back to Freetown and because they were no longer working for the company, they had to hand in all their weapons and equipment but kept their own for the time being. They had discussed flying back to the UK but this would cause problems trying to board flights carrying weapons.

Landing back in Freetown, they booked into the same hotel, the Sofitel Mammy Yoko, this time they had to pay for it themselves. They went out to the back of the hotel, to where they had left their Land Rover parked but were completely shocked to discover that the Land Rover had been totally cannibalised, it was minus it's wheels. It had not even been put on bricks, plus the engine had been removed along with all the seats.

"Thieving bastards," shouted TC. He stormed into the hotel ranting and raving at the concierge, as they were supposed to be looking after it for them. Although the concierge was very embarrassed and handed TC the keys from the safe. At this TC threw the keys across the foyer and bellowed, "What fucking use are these you stupid bastards, The vehicle's a fucking write off." The staff were staring at TC and a bit frightened at this loony's rantings. The manager and one of the security staff came up to TC and were very apologetic. They had called the police to come and report the theft. A fat lot of use this was, thought TC, the local police here are about as much use as an ashtray on a motorcycle, however as a way of compensation, they agreed to let them stay for a couple of days free of charge. TC eventually agreed to this after he calmed down and eventually when the police did turn up, they took a statement and left. That was the end of that.

The choices left to them now were either, to go and buy another 4x4 and drive back home fully tooled up, or work their passage on a couple of ships, "Fuck that", they all said in unison laughing, "Let's fly back, it would be a lot less hassle," said Terry, so they all agreed on this.

They went out the back of the hotel to where the Land Rover was, unloaded all their weapons, broke up the shotguns and removed all the working parts from the hand guns and distributed them down the various storm drains, along with all the ammunition. A week later, they were all back in the U.K. All the traffic seemed strange after Sierra Leone and TC was missing his AK47 and sidearms. It was weird and felt very strange to him, like being naked. He had been back in Deal less than a week, when he began to regret leaving Her Majesty's jollies. He was not sure whether to rejoin or move on to something else, as times were still quiet with nothing going on. He thought that all the skills he had been taught, along with his vast experiences were now a complete waste of time and energy. It was for sure that an office job 9-5 was not an option, this was just not for him.

One evening back again in the Lifeboat pub with lots of his old mates, TC met another old friend, who had left the marines some 8 months earlier. His name was John and he had left to join Kent Police. He was enjoying the work in the police and suggested to TC, that he might think about it as well. After much thought and several pints of lager he forgot how many Gin and Tonics, TC was prepared to take a look but aimed for the Metropolitan Police, mainly because it would be much busier in the capital than the sleepy hollows of Kent, also the money was much better, which was an added attraction, something that TC has always pursued.

Black Cat Publishing (UK)
black.catuk@talktalk.net
www.blackcatpublishinguk.com